Media, Organizations and Identity

Media, Organizations and Identity

Edited by

Lilie Chouliaraki and Mette Morsing

palgrave
macmillan

First published 2010 by
PALGRAVE MACMILLAN

Palgrave Macmillan in the UK is an imprint of Macmillan Publishers Limited,
registered in England, company number 785998, of Houndmills, Basingstoke,
Hampshire RG21 6XS.

Palgrave Macmillan in the US is a division of St Martin's Press LLC,
175 Fifth Avenue, New York, NY 10010.

Palgrave Macmillan is the global academic imprint of the above companies
and has companies and representatives throughout the world.

Palgrave® and Macmillan® are registered trademarks in the United States,
the United Kingdom, Europe and other countries.

ISBN-13: 978–0–230–51551–2 hardback

This book is printed on paper suitable for recycling and made from fully
managed and sustained forest sources. Logging, pulping and manufacturing
processes are expected to conform to the environmental regulations of the
country of origin.

A catalogue record for this book is available from the British Library.

A catalog record for this book is available from the Library of Congress.

10 9 8 7 6 5 4 3 2 1
19 18 17 16 15 14 13 12 11 10

Printed and bound in Great Britain by
CPI Antony Rowe, Chippenham and Eastbourne

Contents

v

Part III   Business in the Media

Tables, Figures, and Illustrations

Tables

Figures

Illustrations

Acknowledgements

We wish to express our sincere appreciation to all scholars of this volume for engaging with us on the endeavour to explore new ways of relating media and business research. We also express our gratitude to Department of Intercultural Communication and Management at Copenhagen Business School for support during the progress of this book. Finally, we would like to thank our editors at Palgrave MacMillan, Emily Brown and Paul Milner as well as our editorial assistant, Julie Uldam

Contributors

Craig E. Carroll is Assistant Professor at the University of North Carolina at Chapel Hill in the School of Journalism and Mass Communication, and an adjunct faculty member at Empresa Business School in Spain and the University of Lugano in Switzerland. He has published in the *Global Encyclopedia of Communication, Communication Research, Corporate Reputation Review, Management Learning and Public Relations Review*. He serves on the editorial boards of *Corporate Reputation Review, Corporate Communications*, and *Management Communication Quarterly*. He is Chair of the Public Relations division of the International Communication Association. His research examines relationships between corporate reputation and the news media.

Lilie Chouliaraki is Professor of Media and Communications at the Department of Media and Communications, London School of Economics. Her research interests focus on the moral implications of the media in contemporary public life, particularly the relationship between mediation, social action and cosmopolitan citizenship as well as between mediation and corporate communication. Chouliaraki's publications include 'Discourse in Late Modernity' (co-authored with N. Fairclough, Edinburgh University Press 1999), 'The Spectatorship of Suffering' (Sage 2006) and 'The Soft Power of War' (ed, Benjamins 2007), whereas her work has appeared in international books and journals, including Media, Culture and Society, Global Media and Communication, Television and New Media, Discourse and Society, Critical Discourse Studies, Social Semiotics, Journal of Management Studies.

Joep P. Cornelissen is a Professor in Corporate Communication at Leeds University Business School. His research interest spans the domains of organizational theory and corporate communication. He is author of *Corporate Communication: A Guide to Theory and Practice* (Sage (2nd edn) 2008).

Barbara Czarniawska holds a Chair in Management Studies at GRI, School of Business, Economics and Law at the University of Gothenburg, Sweden. Her research takes a constructionist perspective on organizing, most recently exploring the connections between popular culture and the practice of management. She is interested in methodology, especially in field studies and in the application of narratology to organization studies. Recent books in English: *A Tale of Three Cities* (Oxford University Press 2002), *Narratives in Social Science Research* (Sage 2004), *Actor-Network Theory and Organizing* (co-edited with Tor Hernes), (Liber 2005), *Global Ideas* (co-edited with Guje Sevón), (Liber 2005), *Management Education and Humanities* (co-edited with Pasquale Gagliardi), (Edward Elgar 2006), *Shadowing and Other Techniques of Doing Fieldwork in Modern Societies* (Liber 2007).

Wim J.L. Elving is Associate Professor at the Department of Communication, University of Amsterdam, and member of the Amsterdam School of Communications research. Besides numerous articles, he has co-authored two Dutch books on communication management and the communication profession. He is currently editor-in-chief of *Corporate Communications*, an international journal.

Peter van Ham is Director of Global Governance Research at the Netherlands Institute of International Relations 'Clingendael' in The Hague, and Professor at the College of Europe in Bruges (Belgium). He is the author or (co-)editor of several books, including *Global Non-Proliferation and Counter-Terrorism* (Brookings 2007) and *European Integration and the Postmodern Condition* (Routledge 2001). He published in the *National Interest, Foreign Affairs*, the *Washington Quarterly, Security Dialogue, NATO Review* and *Millennium*. Currently he is preparing a book on the role of social power in international politics.

Esben Karmark is Associate Professor at the Department of Intercultural Communication and Management, Copenhagen Business School. He specializes in research related to organizational culture and identity, and corporate branding, as well as corporate communication – particularly the role of organizational culture and sub- cultures in organizational identity formation. Karmark was a member of 'Brandstudies' research network from 2002–05 (a cooperation between academia and international companies, including the

LEGO Group). He has contributed to international publications on corporate branding and cross-cultural management.

Peter Kjær (Ph.D., Stockholm University, 1996) is Associate Professor in the Department of Organization at the Copenhagen Business School. His research interests include: business journalism, management knowledge and institutions, institutional theory and institutional history, public organization and management, and strategic communication. He has published on these and related topics in Journal of Economic Issues, Scandinavian Journal of Management, and Business History. His most recent publication is "Mediating Business. The Expansion of Business Journalism" (CBS Press 2007), which he co-edited with Tore Slaatta.

Annemette Kjærgaard, PhD, is associate professor in IS & Organisation at the Department of Informatics at the Copenhagen Business School, Denmark where she lectures in change management and organisational development. Her research interests are organizational and human implications of implementation and use of information systems with a special focus on organisational identity and organisational change.

Mette Morsing is Professor at Copenhagen Business School and Director of CBS Centre for Corporate Social Responsibility. Morsing's research interests focus on corporate social responsibility within the areas of new social medie, communication, identity, image and reputation management. She a published a number of international books, book chapters and journal articles on these subjects in, for example, Human Relations, Corporate Reputation Review, Journal of Corporate Communication, Business Ethics: A European Review, Corporate Governance, Corporate Communication and Harvard-Deusto Business Review. Her latest books are Corporate Social Responsibility: Reconciling Aspiration with Application (Palgrave 2006), co-edited with Professor Andrew Kakabadse, and Corporate Communication: Convention, Complexity and Critique (Sage 2008) with Professors Lars Thøger Christensen and George Cheney.

Nancy Thumim is LSE Fellow in the Department of Media and Communications at LSE. Her research is concerned with how processes of mediation shape relations between members of the public, media forms and institutions. She has published on questions of representation and self-representation of 'ordinary people' in media and cultural spaces, media literacy and methodologies of audience research.

Joseph Turow is Robert Lewis Shayon Professor of Communication at the University of Pennsylvania's Annenberg School For Communication. He has authored eight books, edited five books, and written more than 100 articles on mass media industries. Among his books is *Media Today: An Introduction to Mass Communication*, the 3rd edition of which Routledge published in 2009. Another recent book is *Niche Envy: Marketing Discrimination in the Digital Age* (MIT Press 2006). A few of his other titles are *Breaking Up America: Advertisers and the New Media World* (University of Chicago Press 1997; paperback, 1999; Chinese edn, 2004), *The Hyperlinked Society: Questioning Connections in the Digital Age* (co- edited with Lokman Tsui, University of Michigan Press, 2008); *The Wired Homestead* (co-edited with Andrea Kavanaugh), (MIT Press 2003); and *Playing Doctor: Television, Storytelling and Medical Power* (Oxford 1989).

Anne Vestergaard is PhD fellow at the Department of Intercultural Communication and Management at Copenhagen Business School. Her research addresses the ways in which humanitarian organizations draw on commercial strategies in the construction of a humanitarian appeal. She has previously worked as a campaign consultant for Amnesty International; her current research on the communication of humanitarian organizations is funded by the Danish Research Council. Vestergaard's publications include 'Branding the Humanitarian. The Case of Amnesty International', (*Journal of Language and Politics*, 7(3), 2008).

Introduction: Towards an Understanding of the Interplay between Media and Organizations

Lilie Chouliaraki and Mette Morsing

The dynamics of the media–organization interplay

The significance of the media for corporate organizations has grown immensely since 2000. Whereas the mass media, press and television, have always been central in the formation of organizational identity, and the promotion of corporate image and reputation (Deephouse 2000; Christensen et al. 2008), the recent spatio-temporal expansion of broadcasting, through global television networks and the rise of business news, has further intensified the debate over the promises and risks of mediated visibility (Henriques 2000). As a consequence, today, more than ever, the media are seen as agendasetters for corporate reputation (Carroll and McCombs 2003), whereby the mediated representation of organizations constitutes a critical influence on the construction and deconstruction of organizational identity.

Some companies might react passively or defensively to media attention, whilst others pro-actively attempt to use, and even create such attention as a tool for self-reflection and identity construction. At the same time, managers increasingly acknowledge that the most influential way of speaking to employees is by means of the media (Christensen and Morsing 2008). In both cases of organizational communication, it is the media, again, that provide the resources for furnishing modern companies with an ongoing self-description.

Whereas the relationship between corporate organizations and the media is often – and rightly – seen as a symbiotic relationship (Davis 2007), recent scandals in the corporate and banking sectors have also shown that the mass media might not unilaterally fall within the realm of corporate control in the same way as public relation

1

agencies, advertising agencies or communication consultants. The mass media and the corporate sector are driven by different logics and, at times, by confrontational agendas, rendering the relationship between the two tenuous and risky.

To further complicate this media–business interplay, new media have increasingly become catalysts in re-structuring the communicative dynamics both within organizations, and between organizations and their social contexts – both internal stakeholder and external stakeholder relationships. For example, the Forrester Research Report documents how Web 2.0. tools such as widgets, wikis and blogs are growing faster than ever and are expected to grow even faster in the immediate future in relation to offline communication.[1] Online forms of communication introduce a new complexity to the media–business interplay, as they allow for viral dynamics, interactivity and co-production of messages, as well as for new spaces of consumer empowerment.

In this way, the new media act as a resource for the production of an autonomous, yet not easily managed source of organizational identity and corporate value creation for companies. The 'mediatization' of businesses (Hjarvard 2004); the digitalization of corporate organizations, including the media sector itself (Bar and Simard 2002); and the rise of 'networked' corporate politics (Bennett 2003) are but a few examples pointing to the growing influence of new media technologies on organizational identities.

What this interplay between organizations and the media – old and new – points to is novel possibilities for the configuration of organizational identity in the networks and practices of social life. In the absence of interdisciplinary scholarly work that focuses on this interplay, our volume aspires to address aspects of this configuration of organizational identity under conditions of mediated visibility. It does so by drawing on an interdisciplinary body of work – ranging from organization theory to the political economy of the media, and from corporate communication and branding to sociology, cultural studies and international relations – in order to bring together significant work that addresses the media–organizations relationship from different perspectives.

After a brief literature review of organization and media studies, showing that both fields lack a conceptual focus on the dynamics of organizational identity from a media perspective, we proceed to theorizing these dynamics in terms of a dialectics of organizational identity. To this end, we draw on recent work on mediation to conceptualize the media as a technologically and institutional-embedded resource for the symbolic production of organizational identity (Silverstone 2004; Chouliaraki 2006; Livingstone 2008; Thumin 2009); we also draw on theories of mediatization in order to provide an account of the current transformations of organizational identity in terms of social-cultural processes that extend, hybridize and adjust organizational communication along the lines of a media logic (Hjarvard 2004; Schulz 2004; Lundby 2008; Couldry 2008).

Our argument is that the relationship between mediation and identity is a relationship of mutual constitution: practices of mediated communication do not simply disseminate a pre-existing identity but, rather, produce this identity in the course of mediation. In so doing, they accelerate the social logic of mediatization that transforms not only the corporate realm (including the media sector itself) by raising new demands for organizational transparency and corporate legitimacy, but also the public realms that lie beyond corporate organizations, by diffusing corporate discourses and practices in other spheres of social life. We conclude with a brief discussion of the challenges that mediatization places, today, on organizational identities, in both asserting and blurring the boundaries between organizations and society, and also a presentation of the tripartite structure of the volume in terms of the thematic units of this co-articulation: *media as business, media in business* and *business in the media.*

Organizational communication and media studies: A selective overview

Despite the general acknowledgement of the media–business interplay, neither organization nor media studies actually thematize the links between the two. In organizational studies, the media are regarded either as a particular industry sector requiring its own management approach (for example, Deephouse, 2000; Pringle and Starr 2006) or, most commonly, as tactical vehicles for corporate communication (Dutton and Dukerich 1991, Fombrun 1996, Fombrun and Rindova 2000). Four aspects of the relationship between media and organizations are in focus here:

- Managing image and reputation, through studies of media *agenda-setting* (Wartick 1992; Carroll and McCombs 2003), or

through media *priming* of powerful corporations (Elsbach and Kramer 1996; Ginzel et al. 2003) and media *iconification* of companies as celebrity firms (Rindova et al. 2006, 2007)
- Facilitating organizational change (Gioia et al. 2000, Gioia and Corley 2002, Ravasi and Schultz 2006)
- Acting as instruments of auto-communication, whereby the addressee of a corporate message is the organization itself either for purposes of organizational cohesion (El-Shinnawy and Markus 1998), or organizational change (Morsing 1999)
- Acting as instruments of pressure on corporate power, as in studies of 'brand communities' where mediated communication is put to the service of consumer empowerment (Muniz and O'Guinn 2001).

These studies have undoubtedly enhanced our understanding of the role of the media in organizational dynamics. Yet, their focus is on the influence of the media on organizational image, change or consumer practice, rather than on organizational communication as specifically mediated communication. What is missing is an account of the complexities of the media as active participants in the construction and legitimization – rather than simply the dissemination – of organizational identity. A perhaps predictable exception refers to studies on corporate scandal and crisis management, which draw attention to the media as particular institutional sites for the negotiation of organizational identity from the perspective of image threats and reputational risks. Taking the symbiotic relationship between the media and the corporation as a starting point, such studies explore the points of tension that lead to the breakdown of institutional symbiosis and the damage of the corporation (Grolin 1998; Jasanoff 2006, Knight 2006). Despite attention to journalistic practices that illustrate how the media set news agendas and frame their stories, this body of work is, again, more interested in the media as an object of stakeholder management than as a constitutive component of corporate communication in contemporary organizations.

From a media perspective, the focus shifts from stakeholder management to cultural or sociological approaches on corporate scandals. Cultural approaches treat corporate scandals as the symbolic terrain for the negotiation of societal norms of morality (Lull and Hinerman 1997), or as the inevitable consequence of the risks embedded in the visual politics of mediated publicness (Jackson and Guthey 2006). Sociological approaches to organizational risks from a media perspective further address scandal in terms of:

- The media exposure of corporate leadership (Hamilton and Zeckhauser 2004)
- The links between a growing PR industry, journalists and corporate elites in today's 'promotional culture' (Tumber 1993; Davis 2002; Cottle 2003)
- Corporate Social Responsibility as a crucial strategic tool of corporate legitimacy, and the management of public opinion in the context of intensified mediation and public visibility (Christensen 2001; Snider et al. 2003; Vallentin 2009).

At the same time, whereas there is a number of sociological or anthropological studies that discuss the media as organizations, exploring the routines of newsroom practices or the formation of news professionalism (Tunstall 1971; Ericson et al. 1987; Underwood 2001; Tumber 2006), their focus is specifically on journalism, rather than on the broad spectrum of media and their multiple communication interfaces with organizations.

If there is a dominant media studies approach on the relationship between media and organizations, this is political economy. This approach theorizes the institutional structures, content and influence of the media in terms of the workings of capitalist markets. Research foci, in this vast literature, include questions of:

- Media ownership and control, demonstrating the dominance of multi-national oligopolistic interests in the political and cultural sphere (Golding and Murdoch 1991; McChesney 2000; Bennett and Entman 2001)
- Market expansion and globalization, exploring the relationship between the dominant Anglo-american paradigm and world media cultures (Herman and McChesney 1997; Golding and Harris 1997; Hassan 2004)
- The link between private interests and commercial media, showing the subordination of media content to advertising sponsors, or economic and political elites (Curran 1978; Tumber 1993; Davis 2002)

- The role of the media industry in the deliberative processes of the public sphere (Bennett and Manheim 2001, Collins 2006), or corporate governance and capitalist markets (Dyck and Zinghales 2002; Graham 2002).

Similarly to the organizational studies literature, this body of work might emphasize corporate aspects of the media industry but is, nonetheless, more concerned with the dangers of the 'complicity' between media and the market in contemporary capitalism than with an understanding of the multiple intersections between the media and corporate organizations at large.

In summary, whereas organizational studies regard the media as a communication 'black box', or an external stakeholder to be managed by PR expert teams, media studies engage with corporate organizations through a basic suspicion, regarding them as disruptive of the democratic function of the media, and erosive of local cultures, public debate and democratic decision-making. At the risk of oversimplifying, we might conclude that organizational studies apply an instrumental or administrative approach to the media, focusing on how to make the relationship work, whilst media studies apply a critical approach to corporate organizations, focusing on patterns of media ownership that reproduce unequal power relations in the spheres of politics and culture (see Lazarsfeld 1941: 4–16 for this classic distinction).

Our argument is not simply that the field of organizational studies needs to take media seriously, or that media studies need to broaden its understanding of the corporate realm in processes of mediation. Our argument is that the intensification of mediated visibility across domains of the social, as well as the proliferation of media uses within organizations today, establishes new mutual dependencies between the two, and requires a dialectical approach to the study of these dependencies. The dialectical approach grasps the interaction between media and corporate organizations across three spheres of articulation:

- The media themselves, as organizational structures in a competitive corporate environment – or, *the media as business*
- The ways in which organizational structures and corporate messages are shaped through media technologies within organizations – or, *media in business*
- The ways in which the media, in representing businesses, disseminate and legitimize a corporate logic across societal domains,

penetrating broader cultural identities and public-political processes – or, *business in the media.*

This volume is organized around these three spheres, each of its three sections providing a discussion of specific case studies within each sphere so as to illustrate aspects of the dialectic.

In the process, we abandon neither an orientation towards 'how things work' (the administrative interest in comprehending the practices and challenges of contemporary organizations under conditions of mediation), nor a deep concern with the political and cultural implications of these practices and challenges for the 'corporatization' of societal spheres of activity beyond the corporate realm. In combining the two interests, we hope to provide a balanced approach of the multiple and complex articulations between media and organizational identities, and more nuanced accounts of their workings and power effects. In order to do so, we now need to clarify the conceptual territory of this articulation in terms of the key terms of our argument: identity, mediation and mediatization.

Organizational identity and mediation

We draw on an understanding of organizational identity as a symbolic process that establishes a common definition in terms of *who we are* and *what we stand for*, both inside and outside the organization (Schultz et al. 2000: 9). We locate our definition in a broader understanding of organizational identity as a conceptual metaphor, which thematizes the multiplicity of organizational identity definitions across traditions of organizational studies, blending distinct but interrelated claims (Cornelissen 2006: 683–709). Specifically, our use of the metaphor brings together:

- The acknowledgment of the linguistic foundation of organizational identity, along the lines of the constructivist tradition
- The view of organizational identity as a socio-cognitive marker of self-description and social differentiation both within the organization (as individual or group identity) and outside (as collective identity), along the lines of a sense-making or cognitive tradition and
- The definition of organizational identity as relatively enduring patterns of meaning, which are contextually constructed through

institutional scripts, narratives and symbols – a discursive psychology view of identity (for a productive discussion of this 'polysemic'
notion of organizational identity, see Cornelissen 2006: 695–98).

This broad definition of organizational identity is appropriate for our
purposes, insofar as the contributions of this volume come from different disciplinary perspectives, often assuming – rather than expli-
cating – their working definitions of identity. The constructivist
understanding of organizational identity as a symbolic process of
producing shared definitions of the self and its representational
value is broad enough to encompass the range of assumptions on
organizational identity informing this volume – from the metaphor
of the nation as endowed with organizational identity, insofar as it is
seen to operate in a competitive market of corporate branding, to the
idea of business press consolidating a particular type of organizational identity within journalistic institutions, through a range of
professionalization practices.

Nevertheless, what remains unexplored in this definition of organizational identity is the role of mediation in the symbolic process of
identity construction within and beyond organizations. This absence
is paradoxical: given that organizational identity consists of multiple
communicative actions that spread their reach to ... *encompass the
interests of all stakeholders, including managers (strategy), customers (marketing), organizational members (organization studies) and all other stakeholder groups* (Schultz et al. 2000:9), then the sheer scale and scope of
such communicative actions inevitably renders the formation of
organizational identity a mediated process, par excellence.

The question that mediation introduces in organization identity is
not simply how media technologies articulate organizational identity, participating in the production of organizational self-descriptions
and the attributes they stand for. Rather, the question is how the
media transform these identities by virtue of mediating them – that
is, how they blur the very boundaries between inside and outside at
the moment of claiming to represent them, thereby rendering organizations 'more like' their broader public contexts (in terms of increasing demands for corporate transparency and accountability), and
these contexts 'more like' corporate organizations (in terms of the
'corporatization' of culture and politics; a move we explore under
the interfaces of *media in business* and *business in the media*. The

question is also how this process of mediation negotiates organizational identity within the media sector itself, reformulating the institutional practices, as well the attributes and values that the media sector stands for – a question we explore in the *media as business*, but also across the three sections of the volume.

Our approach, therefore, theorizes the relationship between mediation and organizational identity as a relationship of reciprocal constitution. The media, in this context, are not purely material or economic entities but, crucially, cultural and symbolic ones. In their dual capacity, the media are thus *doubly articulated* within organizations as both institutionally embedded technologies and as discursive resources for the formation of identity. In so being, they function as *a generalized resource for symbolic definition* (Silverstone 2004) that produces, disseminates and legitimizes organizationally specific meanings about *who we are* and *what we stand for*.

To recapitulate, what the concept of mediation allows us to do is comprehend the relationship between organizations and the media as a dialectical process that does not posit identity as pre-existing communication but, rather, views the two as reflexively arising out of a complex interplay, along the lines of the tripartite structure outlined above:

- How the media, as corporate organizations themselves, are transformed through media technologies
- How corporate organizations negotiate and 'reinvent' identity under the pressure of technology, and
- How the media – mass and new – rearticulate and disseminate corporate forms of identity across spheres of public life.

What the concept of mediation cannot do, however, is situate this process of mutual constitution in a trajectory of broader societal transformations.

From mediation to mediatization

To this end, we introduce the term 'mediatization' to refer to the historical process through which material codifications of information (from print to electronic to digital platforms) have enabled the technological production and circulation of symbolic forms, thereby expanding the reach of communication and shifting patterns of interaction – in unprecedented and irreversible ways.[2] Even though there is consensus regarding the catalytic role that mediatization has played in reconfiguring the spatio-temporal consciousness of modernity (Thompson 1995; Hjarvard 2004; 2008a), the question of how exactly mediatization affects the nature of contemporary public spheres of communication and action remains open – and, even, controversial.

Strong versions of the thesis of mediatization postulate that the authority of major modern institutions, such as government and schooling, has been 'substituted' by the media as privileged forces of moral education in society (Schulz 2004). As central elements of such institutional activities increasingly 'assume media form', Hjarvard (2008a: 12) argues, 'the symbolic content and the structure of social and cultural activities are influenced by media environments and a media logic, upon which they gradually become more dependent'. Even though the mediatization thesis captures significant dimensions of what theorists call a 'late modern' sensibility – including the intensification of mediated visibility in domains such as politics and religion (Bennett and Entman 2001; Hjarvard 2008b), or the 'colonization' of traditionally non-mediated industries by media technologies (Jansson 2002; Hjarvard 2004; Karmark Chapter 5) – we would opt for a more cautious argument.

Rather than assuming that mediatization represents a singular trajectory of expansion for a particular media logic across spheres of social life (see Couldry 2008: 378 for a critique), we use mediatization as an heuristic concept to identify the multiple and complex interfaces between technology and identity, as they come together to reconfigure the relationship between media and organizations within specific contexts of practice (Livingstone 2008). Technology and organizational identity, along the lines of this 'weak' mediatization thesis, are today configured through a series of what Schulz (2004: 89–90) calls 'processes of extension, amalgamation and accommodation'.

Extension refers to the ways in which media technologies perpetually push the frontiers of organizational performance, by radically enhancing the communicative capacities of organizations, and thereby transforming their institutional practices and effects. Extension can be exemplified by looking at the ways in which mediated visibility – from broadcasting to blogging – opens up organizations to new demands of public accountability, and urges them to move reflexively towards new communication strategies and institutional re-structurings in their corporate communications and marketing sectors (Cornelissen et al., Chapter 6). In a different way, the digitalization of media networks also points to processes of technological extension, insofar as it pushes the media industry to shift from the television-box towards cross-platform media uses, thereby modifying the very nature of the sector and changing our experience of television viewing (Turow, Chapter 1).

These cases point, in different ways, to the ambivalent potential of expanded visibility in the process of mediatization as extension. There is a risk for organizations to be caught up in institutional inertia, and fail to manage the risks for mediated transparency (Cornelissen's corporate communicator as a 'technician' (Chapter 6: 162). There is also a danger of, what Turow (Chapter 1: 25) calls a 'new era of consumer surveillance' emerging out of the use of marketing databases as monitors of private choices and lifestyles in the service of media managers – a danger that the surveillance associated with digital media might extend too far into the private sphere.

Amalgamation refers to the increasing fusion of mediated and non-mediated communication within an organization, and between organizations and broader public spheres – thereby also merging media and organizational definitions of reality in powerful articulations of identity and value. The proliferation of mass media messages on Danish corporation 'Oticon' – where the top management strategically advanced its position by speaking to the media but effectively addressed its own employees, providing them with mediated versions on their own everyday experience and 'vision' – is a case in point (Morsing and Kjaergaard Chapter 4). In a different way, digital storytelling, as an organizational initiative that invited users' recordings (usergenerated content) to be broadcast at the BBC, points to a further shift of boundaries between the media, the organization and everyday life, creating new tensions about what the organization is, and what it stands for, among stakeholders (Thumin and Chouliaraki, Chapter 2).

Amalgamation, similarly to extension, is also an ambivalent process, throwing into relief the risks that these interfaces between media and businesses entail for organizations: auto-communication might act as an instrument of internal cohesion, but its strategic use of the media could turn out to be costly if employees put conflict and dissent under public scrutiny. Usergenerated content 'amalgamates' the ordinary with the mediated realm, publicizing audiences' personal media stories online, but the BBC's claim to thus produce 'public value' as a socio-political good, in terms of 'democratizing' the media, might ultimately be compromised by the organization's overriding concern for economic interest: justifying its licence fee.

Finally, *accommodation* refers to the ways in which spheres of social activity, such as politics and culture, adapt their styles and formats of communication to the technological affordances and market requirements of the media – a domain of mediatization much discussed in the critical literature of the social sciences.[3] Instrumental, here, is the emergence of 'branding' as a media-reflexive marketing technique that resituates non-commercial identities and relationships within a commercialized sphere of product competition. Even though it cannot be reduced to its discursive dimension, here, branding interests us as a logic of representation that provides an authoritative source for the formation of cultural meanings about non-commercial realms of social life, and redefines such realms in terms of corporate discourse. It is important, in this sense, to problematize the ways in which branding produces imaginations of the nation-state (van Ham, Chapter 7), or justifications of human rights activism (Vestergaard, Chapter 8), as commodities to be consumed, rather than as historical, cultural or ideological forms of belonging and action. If branding refers to representation as a corporate strategy under conditions of mediatization, then press journalism is a traditional terrain of mediated representation that is nowadays saturated by a commercial logic of entertainment: 'infotainment'. In this context, it is similarly important to reflect critically on the ways in which the 'tabloidization' of the press stereotypes successful businesswomen in terms of a celebrity discourse, and to problematize newspaper representations of professional corporate identity as another aspect of mediatization as accommodation (Czarniawska, Chapter 9).

The ambivalence of mediatization as accommodation points to the intimate links between mediatization and the economic logic of late capitalism, throwing into relief the ways in which traditional spheres of public-political action or cultural identity (such as the nation-state or human rights activism) assume the form of commodities whilst, simultaneously, corporate forms of communication (such as brand-ing) become vehicles for ethico-political values beyond the market. Whereas these trends point to the most significant aspect of media-tization in contemporary culture – namely, the fact that 'while the economy gets culturalized, cultural life gets commercialized' (Jansson 2002) – there are important costs to be considered for this trade-off of value for mediated visibility and promotional success. Which are the implications of subordinating an emphasis on human rights to emphasis on the donor-as-consumer for the organizational identity of NGOs? (Vestergaard, Chapter 8: 200–16). Can the news coverage of successful businesswomen change stereotypical cultural frames for the category of 'women professionals', or does business press con-tinue to nurture the popular imagination of the corporate realm in terms of entertainment-friendly stereotypes of female professional identity? (Czarniawska, Chapter 9: 217–40).

In summary, mediatization does not refer to isolated presences but, rather, to the simultaneous co-existence of all three processes of extension, amalgamation and accommodation in the technological articulations of organizational identity – though, obviously, in vary-ing degrees across this volume's contributions. The value of the con-cept, we have argued, is primarily heuristic rather than diagnostic, in that it enables us to understand the challenges of the media–identity interplay not as causal relations with inevitable outcomes (as a 'strong' mediatization thesis might hold) but, rather, as relatively open processes to be investigated empirically within their specific socio-cultural contexts (a 'weak' mediatization thesis). Drawing on this latter sense, therefore, we use the term mediatization to concep-tualize the contemporary processes by which the media – themselves transformed as an industry by new technologies – not only dissem-inate and legitimize corporate discourses and practices across spheres of public (and private) life but also, in so doing, further transform organizational identities themselves.

Challenges to organizational identity

Central to processes of mediatization is the symbolic function of mediation – that is, the capacity of the media to produce and diffuse meanings about the organization and its values, thereby managing, reflexively, to engage all stakeholders (internal and external) in negotiations of organizational identity. Here, extension, amalgamation and accomodation can be seen both as historical processes of transformation in contemporary organizations, as described above, and as changes in the communicative structures and symbolic resources of organizations – its languages, genres and formats (Chouliaraki and Fairclough 2009).

The professionalization of the corporate sector and the rise of business news, as we shall see in this volume, could be regarded as pointing to a new form of communicative reflexivity in organizations, giving rise to new specialized genres and discourses that are related to the extension dimension of mediatization. Organizational auto-communication practices and the emergence of usergenerated content in digital storytelling similarly point to new forms of hybrid communication, blurring the divides between public and private, or inside and outside, that could be seen as reflecting discursive shifts in amalgamation. Finally, the branding of national identity and political activism, as well as the 'popularization' of professional, female business figures by the press – distinct processes, as they are – provide techno-symbolic platforms for the representation of non-commercial identities as commodities with a market value, within and beyond organizations, that can be associated with processes of mediatization as accommodation.

Whereas the challenges and implications arising from the complex dialectic between media and organizations are many, and often difficult to pinpoint, three specific challenges, cutting across the central themes of the volume, make up our focus:

- Challenges to sense-making and interpretation
- Challenges to legitimacy
- Risks involved in the adoption of new media technologies within organizations.

Challenges to sense-making are explored through a focus on the discursive formations and interpretative practices of/about organizations produced and disseminated through the media – for example, in the proposal for a reflexive understanding of the conflicting sense-making practices between journalists and corporate communication specialists, or in the critique of gendered cognitive schemata the media representations reproduce (for example, Cornelissen et al., Chapter 6; Czarniawska, Chapter 9). Challenges to legitimacy are related to the ways in which mediated transparency creates regimes of surveillance not only for consumers, along the lines of Turow's argument (Chapter 1, but also for corporate organizations themselves – insofar as they now need to justify, renew and sustain their legitimacy with regard to an expanded circle of internal and external stakeholders, including the public (van Ham, Chapter 7; Vestergaard, Chapter 8; Thumim and Chouliaraki, Chapter 2). Finally, mediatization risks refer to clashes within the organization resulting from the unpredictable, and often radical, demands that the media place on traditional perceptions of organizational purpose, value and authority (Turow, Chapter 1; Karmark, Chapter 5; Kjaergaard and Morsing, Chapter 4).

Our volume seeks to address such challenges, but cannot claim to provide final responses. This is not only because an edited book is inevitably a limited and partial contribution to scholarship, particularly an interdisciplinary one, but mainly because there are no hard-and-fast answers to these challenges. As mentioned earlier, we do not approach the mediatization of organizational identity as a series of predictable transformations with given outcomes. Rather, we approach it as an open field of change that blurs the communication boundaries within and between organizations, as well as between organizations and their public environments – extending, amalgamating and accommodating media within (and beyond) business in new configurations of organizational identity.

In this sense, we would reiterate, our volume combines the two epistemic interests that are traditionally kept separate in organizational and media studies literatures: the administrative and the critical. In seeking to understand how organizations adapt and respond to the pressures of an increasingly mediated culture in terms of their uses of media and communication strategies, the volume addresses the administrative interest of research: the interest of identifying 'how things work'. At the same time, in seeking to situate these responses in a broader interpretative framework, whereby the relationship between media and organizations is conceptually understood as a relationship of mutual constitution (mediation), and is historically approached in terms of specific socio-cultural processes of mediatization, the volume draws attention to transformations in the structures of power and influence in, and beyond, organizational contexts: the critical interest.

Three perspectives on *Media, Organizations and Identity*

The volume is organized in three parts:

- *Media as business:* The first part is about the media as a keysector of the information and entertainment economy
- *Media in business:* The second part is about the role of the media in establishing and/or transforming the corporate identity of businesses and organizations
- *Business in the media:* The third part is about the role of the media in construing forms of corporate identity beyond the world of businesses, in other domains of public life.

Each part consists of three contributions. The authors of these contributions were invited to participate in this volume because their work had already addressed, albeit implicitly, the relationship between business and media. They all had, in this sense, begun to shape the contours of this new problematic in important ways. Our invitation prompted these scholars to express their views on the media–business interplay in a more explicit, systematic and empirically grounded manner. Each contribution, therefore, illustrates a particular aspect of this interplay, addressing a specific problematic in a particular corporate context from a discipline-specific theoretical and methodological approach.

The volume thus benefits from its strong interdisciplinarity, ranging from sociological theorizations of the journalistic field by Pierre Bourdieu (Kjaer, Chapter 3), the circuit of culture by Stuart Hall (Czarniawska, Chapter 9), or the humanitarian domain by Luc Boltanski (Vestergaard, Chapter 8) to discussions of the digitalization of television from the perspective of advertising (Turow, Chapter 1), or the professionalization of corporate communication from the perspective of sense-making (Cornelissen et al., Chapter 6). Even though such interdisciplinarity could potentially be seen as disrupting the 'story' of the volume, since there is no single narrative that frames the totality of its contributions, our aim is precisely this: in the absence of a coherent body of work on the interfaces of 'media–organizations–identity', we wish to set the contours of an agenda, offering an overview, however partial, of the first scholarly attempts to grasp how this interplay might be enacted in practice. In this respect, our contributions await their readers to put them in a productive dialogic relationship with one another, rather than providing them with a final narrative about media and organizational identity.

Part I. Media as Business

Part I, *Media as Business*, addresses the media industry as one of the most dynamic, differentiated and powerful business sectors today, looking into both contemporary and historical processes that define the industry: respectively, the digitalization of television and online broadcasting, as well as the autonomization of business press.

In Chapter 1, Turow's contribution examines the implications of the digitalization of the media sector for television. An example of media extension and amalgamation, digital television platforms offer new opportunities for the customization of news, entertainment and advertising so as to target audiences narrowly, and provide full accessibility through both stationary and mobile platforms. Whereas these developments in digitalization render television part of a broader cross-platform activity that effectively addresses marketers' concerns with personalized advertising, Turow argues, it simultaneously raises concerns related to the intensification of 'consumer surveillance' in the name of service delivery.

In Chapter 2, Thumim and Chouliaraki focus on another aspect of digitalization – namely, the emergence of 'digital storytelling' as a strategy of legitimization for the BBC, today forced to compete under conditions of a (quasi-)deregulated media market. The authors identify a basic ambivalence in the BBC's engagement with digital storytelling, which might be originating in the double-edged nature of the BBC's discourse on 'public value' between an ethico-political (serving society) and an instrumental (justifying the licence fee) conception of benefit – an ambivalence reflected in constant struggles over the visibility, as well as the vision, of/for digital storytelling by the stakeholders involved in its execution.

Finally, in Chapter 3, Kjaer turns to a different trajectory within the media sector, offering a historical analysis of the rise of the business press. Drawing on empirical data from the Scandinavian countries, the author suggest that the rise of the modern business press can productively be described as a dual process of expansion (in terms of outlets, readers and total and relative volume of content within national media orders) and autonomization (whereby the emergence of a journalistic sub-field, with its own professional standards, was simultaneously accompanied by a professionalization process within the sub-field of corporate communication – that is, the sources of business journalism). Taken together, Kjaer argues, the professionalization of business journalism and sources constitutes an autonomous field of business news production, giving rise to its specific qualities and paradoxes.

Part II. Media in Business

Part II, *Media in Business*, addresses the mediatization of organizational identity from the perspective of how organizations respond to, and are changed by, relationships of extension and amalgamation with media technologies. Contributions by Kjaergaard and Morsing, in Chapter 4, and Karmark, in Chapter 5 draw explicitly on the concept of mediatization, but differ in their use of the concept. In Chapter 6, Cornelissen, Caroll and Elving, without explicitly referring to the term, similarly address corporate communication and the media as co-extensive domains, and focus on the organizational risks involved in the potentially incompatible frames of interpretation between the two.

Kjærgaard and Morsing, in Chapter 4, use mediatization in an heuristic manner in order to examine the participation of the mass media in catalyzing organizational change through processes of auto-communication. Their case study of a major hearing aid industry, Oticon, illustrates how the media become a discursive amplifier between management and employees, as management strategically uses mass media attention to produce a new form of organizational identity among reluctant employees. In so doing, the case shows how the process of mediatization as amalgamation blurs the boundaries between an organization's inside and outside, constituting new and powerful – albeit risky and fragile – forms of identity.

Drawing on a strong thesis of 'mediatization', in Chapter 5 Karmark explores the corporate branding strategies used by the toy manufacturer Lego, which promoted the 'mediatized brick' as a revolutionary product, and shows how such changes subsume the traditional version of organizational identity when perceived in the light of a new media logic. His analysis of Lego's attempts to 'mediatize the brick' draws on Hjarvard's (2004) concept, but is based on original ethnographic material from the company, demonstrating that such media–business identity articulations might clash with established perceptions of what a company is and what is stands for, resulting in serious internal conflict and loss of profit.

Cornelissen, Carroll and Elving, in Chapter 6, turn from an exploration of mediatization within organizations to the conceptual territory between corporate organizations and the media realm, in order to argue for the establishment of more media-reflexive sectors of corporate communication within organizations. In dialogue with Kjaer's chapter, the authors conclude that, as the journalistic field becomes continuously professionalized, organizations must leave the 'technician' communicator model aside, and become more aware of the different, and often conflicting, 'frames' involved in their interaction with the media.

Part III. Business in the Media

Part III, *Business in the Media*, addresses mediatization as accommodation, looking at the various ways through which traditional public domains (such as public diplomacy, NGO activism and business journalism) acquire corporate and populist spins.

Geographical places, van Ham argues in Chapter 7, follow a commercial logic of branding, as new media dissolve traditional nation-state boundaries and as territorial actors recognize the importance of place branding in their global struggles for investment, tourism and political power. Drawing on cases from the EU and USA, van Ham suggests that the most crucial dimension of place branding is its embeddedness in a hyper-mediated milieu of network-like communications, and emphasizes the need for states to adjust to this milieu in order to remain competitive actors in the contemporary, global mediascapes.

Vestergaard, in her study of humanitarian discourse in Chapter 8, shows how NGOs, in their struggles for mediated visibility, increasingly adopt promotional strategies of the commercial sector. Her analysis points to a tension between the logic of recognition (central to advertising) and the logic of awareness-raising (central to the identity of most NGOs), suggesting that a conflict of organizational identity is at stake when NGOs subordinate the latter to the former.

Finally, in Chapter 9, Czarniawska returns to the domain of the business press, creating a revealing narrative thread between Kjaer's historical account of the rise of business news in Chapter 4 and

Cornelissen, Carroll and Elving's conceptual account of the interface between business journalism and corporate communication in Chapter 6. Focus now falls on the business press as a terrain for the representation of corporate identity, through a critical analysis of the cultural assumptions informing 'infotainment'-style coverage of celebrity businesswomen. This shows that the commercialization of journalism keeps mechanisms of cultural production and consumption intact, legitimizing stereotypical discourses about the corporate realm, and ambivalent interpretative schemata about its women professionals.

Notes

1. 'Forrester: Social networking will be the biggest enterprise 2.0 priority by 2013', posted at BetweenTheLines Blog, 21 April 2008, available at http://blogs.zdnet.com/BTL/?p=8555 (accessed 5 September 2008).
2. This definition draws on Thompson (1995: 46), who uses the term 'mediazation' for the process.
3. The process captures elements of what has been variously defined as the 'refeudalization of the public sphere' (Habermas 1992); the 'commodification of culture' (Wernick, 1991); the 'marketization of public institutions' (Fairclough 1993); the 'commercialization of everyday life' (Slater 1997) or the 'informalization of network society' (Hassan 2004).

References

Bar, F. and Simard, C. (2002) 'New Media Implementation and Industrial Organization', in L. Lievrouw and S. Livingstone (eds), *The Handbook of New Media* (London: Sage).

Bennett, W.L. (2003) 'New Media Power: The Internet and Global Activism', in N. Couldry and J. Curran (eds) *Contesting Media Power: Alternative Media in a Networked World* (London: Rowman & Littlefield).

Bennett, W.L. and Entman, R.M. (eds) (2001) *Mediated Politics: Communication in the Future of Democracy* (Cambridge: Cambridge University Press).

Bennett, W.L. and Manheim, J. (2001) 'The Big Spin: Strategic Communication and the Transformation of Pluralist Democracy', in W.L. Bennett and R.M. Entman (eds), *Mediated Politics: Communication in the Future of Democracy* (Cambridge: Cambridge University Press).

Carroll, C. and McCombs, M. (2003) 'Agenda-setting Effects of Business News on the Public's Images and Opinions about Major Corporations', *Corporate Reputation Review*, 6(1): 36–46.

Chouliaraki, L. (2006) 'Towards an Analytics of Mediation', Critical Discourse Studies, 3(2): 153–78.

Chouliaraki, L. and Fairlough, N. (2010) '"Counter-point", Response to Leitch S. and Palmer I., "Analyzing Texts in Context: Current Practices and New Protocols for Critical Discourse Analysis in Organization Studies"', *Journal of Management Studies*, 47(1).

Christensen, L.T. (1997). 'Marketing as Auto-Communication', *Consumption, Markets and Culture*, 1(3), 197–227.

Christensen, L.T. (2001) 'Corporate Identity and Corporate Image Revisited: A Semiotic Perspective', *European Journal of Marketing*, 35(4), 292–315.

Christensen, L.T. and Cheney, G. (2000). 'Self-Absorption and Self-Seduction in the Corporate Identity Game', in M. Schultz, M.J. Hatch, and M.H. Larsen (eds), *The Expressive Organization: Linking Identity, Reputation, and the Corporate Brand* (Oxford: Oxford University Press, 246–70).

Christensen, L.T. and Morsing, M. (2008) *Bag om Corporate Communication* [Behind Corporate Communication], 2nd revised edn (Copenhagen: Samfundslitteratur).

Christensen, L.T., Morsing, M. and Cheney, G. (2008) *Corporate Communications: Convention, Challenge, Complexity* (London: Sage).

Collins, R. (2006) 'Internet Governance in the UK', *Media, Culture & Society*, 28(3): 337–58.

Cornelissen, J. (2006) 'Metaphor and the Dynamics of Knowledge in Organization Theory: A Case Study of the Organizational Identity Metaphor', *Journal of Management Studies*, 43(4): 683–709.

Cottle, S. (2003) (ed.) *News, Public Relations and Power* (London: Sage).

Coudry, N. (2008) 'Mediation or Mediatisation: Alternative Understandings of the Emerging Space of Digital Storytelling', *New Media and Society*, 10(3): 373–91.

Couldry, N. (2008) 'Mediatization or Mediation? Alternative Understandings of the Emergent Space of Digital Storytelling', New Media & Society, 10(3): 373–91.

Croteau, D. and Hoynes, W. (2006) *The Business of Media: Corporate Media and the Public Interest* (New York: Pine Forge Press).

Czarniawska, Barbara (2004) *Narratives in Social Science Research* (London: Sage).

Davis, A. (2002) *Public Relations Democracy: Public Relations, Politics and the Mass Media in Britain* (Manchester: Manchester University Press).

Davis, A. (2007) *The Mediation of Power* (London: Routledge).

Deephouse, D.L. (2000) 'Media Reputation as a Strategic Resource: An Integration of Mass Communication and Resource-Based Theories', *Journal of Management*, 26(6): 1091–12.

Dutton, J.E. and Dukerich, J.M. (1991) 'Keeping an Eye on the Mirror: Image and Identity in Organizational Adaptation', *Academy of Management Journal*, 34(3): 517–54.

Dyck, A. and Zingales, L. (2002) 'The Corporate Governance Role of the Media', in R. Islam et al., *The Right to Tell: The Role of Mass Media in Economic Development* (Washington, DC: World Bank Publications): 107–40.

Ericson, R.V., Baranek, P.M. and Chan, J.B.L. (1987) *Visualizing Deviance: A Study of News Organization* (Toronto: University of Toronto Press).

El-Sinnawy, M. and Markus, M.L. (1998) 'Acceptance of Communication Media in Organizations: Richness of Features?', *Professional Communication*, 41(4): 242–53.

Elsbach, K.D. and Kramer, R.M. (1996) 'Members' Responses to Organizational Identity Threats: Encountering and Countering the Business Week Rankings', *Administrative Science Quarterly*, 41(3): 442–76.

Fairclough, N. (1993) 'Critical Discourse Analysis and the Marketisation of Public Discourse: The Universities', *Discourse and Society*, 4(2): 133–68.

Fombrun, C. (1996) *Reputation: Realizing Value from the Corporate Image* (New York: Harvard Business School Press).

Fombrun, C. and Rindova, V.P. (2000) 'The Road to Transparency: Reputation Management at Royal Dutch/Shell', in M. Schultz, M.J. Hatch and M.H. Larsen (eds), *The Expressive Organization: Linking Identity, Reputation, and the Corporate Brand* (Oxford: Oxford University Press): 77–96.

Gioia, D. and Corley, K.G. (2002) 'Being Good versus Looking Good: Business School Rankings and the Circean Transformation Form Substance To Image', *Academy of Management Learning and Education*, 1(1): 107–20.

Gioia, D.A., Schultz, M. and Corley, K.G. (2000) 'Organizational Identity, Image, and Adaptive Instability', *Academy of Management Review*, 25(1): 63–81.

Gioia, D.A. and Thomas, J.B. (1996) 'Identity, Image, and Issue Interpretation: Sensemaking During Strategic Change in Academia', *Administrative Science Quarterly*, 41(3): 370–403.

Ginzel, L.E.; Kramer, R.M. and Sutton, R.I. (1993) 'Organizational Impression Management as a Reciprocal Influence Process: The Neglected Role of the Organizational Audience', *Research in Organizational Behavior*, 15: 227–66.

Golding, P. and Harris, P. (1997) *Beyond Cultural Imperialism* (London: Sage).

Graham, P. (2002) 'Hypercapitalism: Language, New Media and Social Perceptions of Value', *Discourse & Society*, 13(2): 227–49.

Grolin J. (1998) 'Corporate Legitimacy in Risk Society: The Case of Brent Spar', *Business Strategy and the Environment*, 7: 213–22.

Hamilton, J. and Zeckhauser, R. (2004) 'Media Coverage of CEOs: Who? What? Where? When? Why?', Paper presented at the Workshop on the Media and Economic Performance, Stanford Institute for International Studies, Center on Development, Democracy, and the Rule of Law, 5–6 March.

Habermas, J. (1992) *The Structural Transformation of the Public Sphere*, first published in German 1989, trans. into English by T. Burger and F. Lawrence (Cambridge: Polity).

Hassan, R. (2004) *Media, Politics and the Network Society* (Buckingham: Open University Press).

Hatch, M.J. and Schultz, M. (2001) 'Are the Strategic Stars Aligned for Your Corporate Brand?', *Harvard Business Review*, February: 128–34.

Henriques, D.B. (2000) 'Learning Curve: The Rise of Business Reporting', *Columbia Journalism Review*, 39(4): 18–21.

Herman, E. and McChesney, R. (1997) *The Global Media: The New Missionaries of Corporate Capitalism* (London: Cassell Academic).

Hjarvard, S. (2004) 'From Bricks to Bytes: The Mediatization of a Global Toy Industry', in I. Bondjeberg and P. Golding (eds), *European Culture and the Media*, (Bristol: Intellect): 43–63.

Hjarvard, S. (2008a) 'The Mediatization of Religion: A Theory of the Media as Agents Of Religious Change', *Northern Lights*, 6(1): 9–26 (Bristol: Intellect).

Hjarvard, S. (2008b) 'The Mediatization of Society', *Nordicom Review*, 2: 105–34.

Jackson, B. and Guthey, E. (2006) 'Putting the Visual into the Social Construction Of Leadership', in B. Shamir, R. Pillai, M.C. Bligh and M. Ulh-Bien (eds), *Follower-centered Perspectives on Leadership* (Greenwich, CT: Information Age Publishing): 167–87.

Jansson, A. (2002) 'The Mediatisation of Consumption: Towards an Analytical Framework of Image Culture', *Journal of Consumer Culture*, 2(1): 5–31.

Jasanoff, S. (2006) 'Restoring Reason: Causal Narratives and Political Culture', in B. Hutter and G. Power (eds), *Organisational Encounters with Risk* (Cambridge: Cambridge University Press).

Lazarsfeld, P. (1941) 'Remarks on Administrative and Critical Communications Research', *Studies in Philosophy and Social Science*, 9: 2–16.

Lievrouw, L. and Livingstone, S. (eds) (2002) *The Handbook of New Media: Social Shaping and Consequences of ICTs* (London: Sage).

Livingstone, S. (2008) 'On the Mediation of Everything', ICA presidential address 2008, Journal of Communication, 59 (1): 1–18.

Lull, J. and Hinerman, S. (1997) *Media Scandals: Morality and Desire in the Popular Culture Marketplace* (New York: Columbia University Press = 1998 [Cambridge: Polity = 1997]).

Lundby, K. (2008) 'Editorial: Mediatized Stories: Mediation Perspectives on Digital Storytelling', New Media & Society, 10(3): 363–71.

McChesney, R. (2000) *Rich Media, Poor Democracy: Communication Politics in Dubious Times* (New York: New Press).

Morsing, M. (1999) 'The Media Boomerang: The Media's Role in Changing Identity by Changing Image', *Corporate Reputation Review*, 2(2): 116–35.

Morsing, M. (2006) 'Corporate Social Responsibility as Strategic Auto-Communication on the Role of External Stakeholders for Member Identification', *Business Ethics: A European Review*, 15(2): 171–82.

Muniz, A.M. and O'Guinn, T.C. (2001) 'Brand community', *Journal of Consumer Research*, 27(4): 412–32.

Pringle, P.K. and Starr, M.F. (2006) *Electronic Media Management*, 5th edn (Boston: Focal Press).

Rindova, V.P.; Pollock, T.G. and Hayward, M.L.A. (2006) 'Celebrity Firms: The Social Construction of Market Popularity', *Academy of Management Review*, 31(1): 50–71.

Rindova, V.P., Petkova, A.P. and Kotha, S. (2007) 'Standing Out: How New Firms in Emerging Markets Build Reputation', *Strategic Organization*, 5(1): 31–70.

Ravasi, D and Schultz, M. (2006) 'Responding to Organizational Identity Threats: Exploring the Role of Organizational Culture', *Academy of Management Journal*, 49(3): 433–58.

Schultz, M.; Hatch M.J. and Larsen, M.H. (2000) 'Introduction: Why the Expressive Organization?', *The Expressive Organization* (Oxford: Oxford University Press).

Schulz, W. (2004) 'Reconsidering Mediatization as an Analytical Concept', *European Journal of Communication*, 19(1): 87–101.

Silverstone, R. (2004) 'Mediation and Communication', in C. Calhoun, C. Rojek and B.S. Turner (eds), *The International Handbook of Sociology* (London: Sage).

Slater, D. (1997) *Consumer Culture* (London: Sage).

Snider, J.; Hill, R.P. and Martin, D. (2003) 'Corporate Social Responsibility in the 21st Century: A View from the World's Most Successful Firms', *Journal of Business Ethics*, 48: 175–87.

Thompson, J. (1995) *Media and Modernity* (Cambridge: Polity).

Thumim, N. (Forthcoming, 2009) '"Everyone Has a Story to Tell": Mediation and Self Representation in Two UK Institutions', International Journal of Cultural Studies.

Tumber, H. (1993) 'Selling Scandal: Business and the Media', *Media Culture and Society*, 15: 345–61.

Tumber, H. (2006) '*Journalists at Work* Revisited', *Javnost – The Public*, 13(3): 57–68.

Tunstall, J. (1971) *Journalists at Work* (London: Constable).

Underwood, D. (2001) 'Reporting and the Push for Market-Oriented Journalism: Media Organizations as Business', in L. Bennett and R. Entman (eds), *Mediated Politics* (Cambridge: Cambridge University Press).

Wartick, S.L. (1992) 'The Relationship between Intense Media Exposure and Change in Corporate Reputation', *Business Society*, 31: 33–49.

Wernick, Andrew (1991) *Promotional Culture Advertising, Ideology and Symbolic Expression* (London: Sage).

Vallentin, S. (2009) 'Private Management and Public Opinion: Corporate Social Responsiveness Revisited', *Business & Society*, 48(1): 60–87.

Part I
Media as Business

1
Rethinking Television in the Digital Age

Joseph Turow

Introduction

This chapter is about the challenges that television faces as it moves towards digital platforms, thereby providing increasingly diverse and multiple options for advertising agencies.[1] However, as advertisers are now using television as one among many media platforms for their marketing purposes, through customizing and personalizing their campaigns, television itself undergoes a process of fundamental change. Part of a broad and convergent media landscape, television today operates ambiguously – not only in both enabling advertising to become more subtle and pervasive than ever before, but also in providing consumers with unprecedented powers of interactivity and choice. This has significant implications in terms of market strategies, consumer practices and media policies – but also, importantly, society at large.

Advertising and the challenge to television

For many US media and marketing executives, the appearance of the digital video recorder marked the beginning of the end of 'television' as they had known it. Essentially a computer with a large hard drive, the DVR acted like a video cassette recorder in enabling its owners to record programmes and to view them at other times. Unlike a VCR, the technology marketed to the public by TiVo and other firms was connected to an updatable guide that made finding programmes across more than one hundred channels easy. Also, unlike a VCR, in some versions made by ReplayTV (and in 'hacked' versions of TiVo) it allowed viewers to skip ahead 30 seconds at a time without viewing what was skipped. That, advertisers knew, would be commercials. In fact, ReplayTV used its PVR's facility for skipping over commercials as a selling point in its early advertisements.

But the concern that marketing and TV executives had concerning DVRs ran deeper than viewers' ability to skip commercials. It reflected a broader worry that digital devices that would remake television to give consumers the kind of control over what and when they watched that was already emerging on the Internet. With the worry that consumers could really push away advertisements better than ever before, and that consumers were increasingly turning to the Internet and other digital media that were often poaching TV materials without their associated commercials, major marketers began to change their own advertising strategies so as to ensure as much as possible that they could follow, and influence, the consumers they wanted to reach wherever they went. As they did that, they were, in effect, helping to bring an end to 'television' as we have known it.

Well into the first decade of the twenty-first century, the domestic box we call 'television' is, in the USA, becoming merely one node in advertisers' attempts to reach desirable individuals as they move across different media. Moreover, the logic of marketer–media concerns points to even greater changes in the decades to come. A variety of overlapping developments suggest a future in which the presentation of news, entertainment and advertising is customized to the individual backgrounds of audience members, and available virtually everywhere through both stationary and mobile media. In addition to a variety of social issues posed by the rise of database marketing, the developments raise the question of what television really means today and whether, not too long from now, it will be a useful label at all.

Coming to terms with digital media

Those who, at the start of the century, said the fear of digital video recorders was exaggerated, pointed out that sales were rather small. One trade article in 2002 called the DVR 'a technology in search of a business model.'(Johnson 2002: 42). Others disagreed strongly. They pointed out that the sales rate of branded DVRs was increasing and that home satellite firms and cable systems were beginning to integrate unbranded versions into set-top boxes. They noted TiVo's admission that 60 per cent to 70 per cent of people watching using its technology were skipping commercials. And they admonished that whatever accommodation advertisers would make with DVR firms, it would undercut the, by then traditional, approach of mounting 15- or 30-second commercials within shows. Of course, marketers have long been irked by the power that intended audience members hold to not pay attention to – and even dismiss the value of – the marketers' advertisements, especially when the advertisements pay for content or activities that the consumers value.

Stories in and out of the trade press have pointed out that people talk, visit the kitchen or used the bathroom during TV commercial breaks. Television executives saw it as their major task to help advertisers draw and keep attractive audiences, as determined by the Nielsen company's ratings. Exactly what 'attractive audiences' meant, and how to draw and keep them, were ideas that changed over the decades in network and local TV. From the early 1950s until the late 1990s, network executives took pains to convince advertisers that, beyond intuition, they were developing systematic survey and programme-analyzing techniques to guide the choice of shows, as well as tactics such as least objectionable programmes, lead-ins, lead-outs and hammocking to array the programmes for optimal audience flow through the prime time schedule.

The arrival of TiVo and other DVRs threatened to upend the routines of predictable scheduling and advertising placement that had become the verities upon which commercial US television was based. Moreover, the explosion of channels to the consumer by means of the web, cable TV, satellite television, and hand-held media, along with their transformation from analogue to digital, led advertisers to question longstanding ways to reach audiences. As an *Advertising Age* columnist noted in 2007, 'Digital media – pretty much on an hourly basis these days – seems to throw out a new way to disrupt the traditional pathways to the consumer' (*Advertising Age* 2007). In this environment of swirling change, advertising executives began to question the verities of media planning and television's central position in them. From the middle of the decade, the consensus began to develop that the way to consumers, particularly young consumers, could not be through traditional television commercials. If TV commercials were to be used at all, they had to be created with the goal of making them so buzz-worthy as to be sparks to discussions among members of the target groups that might even involve sending versions of the commercials on the Internet or cell phone or elsewhere. 'The world is digital', noted the world CEO of the huge Universal McCann media buying division of Interpublic, 'and we must adapt to take full advantage of that as an industry' (Nick Brien, quoted in *Advertising Age* 2007).

One way marketers have come to terms with the digital challenge has been to integrate their products into non-advertising media content, with the hope of getting more attention than traditional advertising would. An early version of this approach was 'product placement', the act of trading or buying an item's position within media content. The practice can be traced back to at least the silent movies, and became a frenzied TV phenomenon in the wake of marketers' first concerns about DVRs. Many marketers have realized, however, that simply mentioning or inserting a product into part of a programme would rarely get them far in demonstrating the item or building its personality.

So, the next step involved integrating the item or service directly into the TV action to bring out its brand character. Yet, advertising executives soon concluded that this approach, too, was self-limiting in an era where their target consumer's attention was fleeting and often far from particular programmes – and even from the traditional TV set. Marketers' current strategy is therefore to create a mix of advertising and product integration that provocatively piques the interest of the target audience so that they visit the marketer's website to see more, share the ideas about it virally via the web and move it across a variety of media platforms, including television.

The Super Bowl provides the optimal service for advertisers looking to use television as one element in a multimedia promotion. In the mid-2000s, the season-ending American football match was still a place on sponsored network TV to find young adult men in huge numbers. Rather than adopting the pre-TiVo goal of aiming 30-second commercials at them, with the hope that the advertisements will enhance brand identities and sales, recent Super Bowl advertisers have seen the game commercial as a way to engage the audience weeks before its airing and far after it. The website naming company Godaddy.com, for example, worked to cultivate a reputation for creating Super Bowl commercials that network executives consider unacceptably sexual. In the months before the event, it whipped up young-adult interest in the commercials it is trying to get past the censors. Then, it used the steamy spot that the network accepted to drive the core audience to its website where they can see those that did not make it through, enjoy racier versions of the accepted one, and learn about the company. 'We can't get across what we do in a 30-second spot,' noted the company's CEO 'so we have to run a spot that is polarizing enough to get people to come to our website to see more.' (Bob Parsons, quoted in Horovitz 2007).

Anheuser-Bush, the largest Super Bowl advertiser, took an even more drastic tack. Apart from encouraging discussion about its spots in the weeks prior to the CBS show, the beer-maker used its in-game commercials to kick off Bud.TV, which can only be described as a clear acknowledgement that the end of traditional TV is at hand for the company's core twenty-something consumers. 'What cable and satellite were to the last generation, digital is to this generation', said the firm's Vice President of global media. Pitching the site as a full-service entertainment network on the web, the company promised to limit product placement drastically and, instead, offer up a place where Bud drinkers could find collegial entertainment that would generate buzz offline and on. 'What they're offering up is bigger than integration', opined an executive from the marketing communication giant Omnicom. Its branded entertainment arm was involved in the project. He explained: 'They're offering up a destination, a community for their audience, and I think that's even a bigger idea than placing products in shows' (Gail Schiller 2007).

Part of marketers' goal of creating a website that is highly trafficked by its target users relates to a second strategy for a post-television world: channelling the audience's involvement in 'user-generated content' into activities that will enhance their identification with company products. User-generated content is a term that characterizes the digital video, blogging, podcasting, mobile phone photography, software and wikis that millions of people are creating as technologies of production and distribution become more accessible and affordable than in previous decades. Wikipedia says the term 'came into the mainstream in 2005', but a Nexis search of *Advertising Age* reveals that it was already on marketers' radar in 2000 as a way to bring people closer to companies (Patricia Riedman 2000: 66). The popular press celebrated Facebook, YouTube, MySpace and similar social media sites as the incarnation of (in Wikipedia's words) 'collaboration, skill-building and discovery' by 'end-users as opposed to traditional media producers, licensed broadcasters, and production companies.' Marketers, for their part, saw the phenomenon as a way to bond consumers to them by giving them the incentive, and sometimes even the tools, to create advertisements about them. While some advertisers sneered – one suggested that user-generated commercials involved the inmates taking over the asylum – many others mounted multimedia ad-making contests with prizes and fame as the rewards.

Television emerged as one node in a multi-channel extravaganza that focused on generating excitement in young male adults around user-generated advertisement messages. The 2007 Super Bowl gave these activities a particularly high profile, as Frito Lay, General Motors and the National Football League announced contests for audience-created commercials, with the winning entries to be shown during the game. The companies' websites accepted thousands of submissions, and blogs and other commentaries around the Internet buzzed with discussions about the commercials. All three firms themselves pumped hoopla around the submissions as well as the final selection in ways that clearly linked the user-generated strategy to the strategy of using TV as only one node – albeit a central node – in a multi-channel strategy.

Early versions of television interactivity

Advertising executives who implement the multiplatform and user-generated strategies are convinced that traditional television – the long-dominant static domestic box – will increasingly have to be used together with other media if it is to be an effective marketing tool in the twenty-first century. The TV industry had worked with analogue versions of interactivity by means of the telephone during the pre-digital era of the 1950s until the 1990s. A few widely promoted cases involved entertainment: the three broadcast networks hyped viewers' interest by encouraging them to phone and vote for plot endings. More common, however, was the use of the phone for direct marketing. With the rise of 800 numbers, advertisers invited viewer contact through individual commercials; in long-form 'infomercials' at odd hours on broadcast or cable channels; at the end of programmes to hawk videos and tie-ins (such as selling a necklace from a soap opera) at the end of network shows; and, beginning in 1982, with entire shopping shows, and even shopping networks.[2]

Attempts to get viewers involved in programming on a more continual basis than through phone or web votes necessitated actual tinkering with TV equipment. In the early 1970s, engineers started sending data through the vertical blanking interval (VBI) of the analogue signal. The VBI is the black stripe at the top and bottom of the TV picture. Broadcasters can use part of it to send data that viewers can receive using a special decoder. In the USA, the most common application was for text captions often used by deaf viewers. But, two VBI technologies that together made inroads into more than a million cable and DBS homes in the late 1990s were Wink and WebTV. Both used the vertical blanking interval to send what Wink called 'enhanced broadcasting': viewers saw commercials during pauses in the shows, at the end of shows, or in their own shows or channels (which, in essence, tried to make the commercials the entertainment). Available by 2003 in over five million cable and direct broadcast satellite homes, Wink and WebTV enabled marketers to go well beyond a 30-second TV spot. Consumers could request more information on a product or service, participate in polls, sweepstakes and promotions.

The first steps cable, satellite and broadcast TV executives took with the rise of digital technology was the direct translation of what had been awkward attempts at interactivity into more fluid, though similar, activities. Now, voting on entertainment could take place easily by means of text messages from cell phones – and entire programs (such as American Idol) could be built around them. Products from TV shows – and even the shows themselves – could be sold on the programmes' websites. And using the Internet or the DVR with a phone line (depending on whether the provider was a cable or satellite system), a content supplier could offer far more interactivity more quickly than the vertical blanking interval would allow. US trade magazines pointed out that, in the UK, News Corp's BSkyB satellite operation pushed set-top-box interactivity to the point that the 'red button' on the remote became part of the national consciousness. It could provide up to eight simultaneous windows on the TV screen, allowing people to watch the news with sound while looking at a weather forecast and viewing a football game (Martha Bennett 2002).

Some marketers, though, wondered whether US viewers wanted that kind of interactivity around products while watching television. Stating that interactive TV commerce had not been terribly successful on BSkyB, a UK analyst opined in late 2002 that '[f]or many, the TV remains a "lean-back" medium, though which people want to be entertained'. In 2005, the Vice President of business development at Visible World, a new-technology advertising company, offered that Americans felt the same way as the Brits about interactive entertainment. Research showed, he said, that capabilities such as the instant replay of football action on digital video recorders get high use when consumers first encounter them. After a short while, they lose interest and simply view what comes at them (Interview with Pat Ruta, VP Business Development, Visible World, 2005).

At the same time, marketing and media executives often added at conferences, in one-on-one conversations and in the trade press, that consumer interest might well change with future generations of viewers. Turn-of-the-century 18- to 55-year-olds were stuck in an old model of TV viewing. Their children, and their children's children, seemed much more comfortable using media in a multitasking, constantly clicking way. 'The issue for us and others [in interactive television],' said a TiVo executive in 2004, 'is getting past the inertia of how people watch TV. It hasn't changed...our whole lives. What we've learned is that all of the advertisers we've worked with have accepted that sometime in the future, the consumer will be in charge. Once you see that, you see there are more opportunities than barriers' (Brodie Keast, quoted in Tobi Elkin 2002: 10).

Encouraging digital interactivity

Among the opportunities marketers tried to exploit were ways to bring audiences to meet up with commercials that they would actively want to watch. Two approaches stand out. The 'targeted pull' approach aims to provide motivated viewers with a place to find commercials they want to watch. The 'customized push' tack sends to viewers commercials that appear to be traditional but are really tailored to their background as a result of database analysis. Both these methods can be combined to yield 'pull' commercials that are customized. Moreover, current technology makes customized and interactive product placement possible. A key question is whether – or more likely, when – marketing and media practitioners will spend the sizeable amount of money needed to roll out some of the more high-tech of these activities.

TiVo – whom advertising people saw initially as the Darth Vader of TV commercials – was actually an important force behind the pull approach. TiVo executives concluded that it needed revenue from advertisers if their company were to survive. The DVR firm's ability to tinker with the TV signals that its million-plus viewers' receive also gave it the ability to point them from regular commercials to its Showcase, a space for watching commercials 'on demand'. So, for example, investment firm Charles Schwab and Co. paid TiVo to link a 30-second network spot starring golfer Phil Mickelson to Showcase by means of a special symbol on TiVo-attached sets. The symbol signalled to viewers that, if they clicked, they could see more; it turned out to be a four-minute video about the company and three segments with the golf pro. Viewers of the Showcase could also order information from Schwab via the TV set. They could then return to the programme they were watching at the exact point they ceased watching it (Anne M. Mack 2004). As the Director of Operations at the agency that oversaw the Schwab presentation noted, this use of the DVR marked a 'TV-plus approach' that 'gave us great response from the hand raisers, as far as a direct-response medium' (Jason Kuperman, quoted in Anne M. Mack 2004).

The idea spread beyond TiVo. Linking its set-top DVR with its satellite delivery system, EchoStar's Dish Network in 2004 started offering advertisers similar packages to around 9 million of its subscribers (Mack 2004). Another version of this targeting of potential hand-raisers involved video-on-demand (VOD) cable services. Video on demand refers to programmes that are stored digitally on huge servers at a cable company and sent to a person's television via the digital cable box when the person presses a button on the remote to receive it. The advertising piece involves placing long-form commercials directly at the end of VOD programmes that seem to resonate with particular advertisers.

On Comcast cable systems, for example, in early 2005 a VOD programme from the Discovery Science Channel was preceded by a message from General Motors Corp. that urged viewers to stay tuned at the end of the programme for a video about a new Corvette. That 15-minute video at the end of the programme was a documentary-style message from GM highlighting the advanced technology in the car, a message that might be interesting to the kind of people who would select a science programme on VOD. Borrowing from the experience of VBI virtual advertising channels and TiVo Showcase, GM also worked with Comcast to develop a VOD channel called the *GM Showcase*, where viewers could select similar programmes about other GM products and ask for more information. 'The thing about selling new cars and trucks is that in any given market, only about 1.5 per cent of the population is looking for a new vehicle,' agreed the General Director of media operations for GM. 'The VOD world's advantage over linear television,' she said, 'is it allows marketers to reach exactly those people' (Gnoffo 2005).

Adding personalization to interactivity

For those consumers who might not be motivated to pull advertisements to them, Comcast and other cable operators were experimenting with variations on the traditional push approach. The aim was to link database marketing capabilities to 30-second commercials during the programmes. In one sense, it was still traditional because it assumed a 'lean back' consumer who did not have to change behaviour in the face of advertisements. At the same time, it marked the drive toward digital marketing discrimination in the TV world.

Comcast, for example, promoted its ability to send different commercials to different areas based upon distinctions that it and its advertisers found between those areas. With a service it called Adtag, the same car dealer could add different voiceovers to an advertisement based on geographic location. From one viewpoint, what Comcast was offering advertisers was nothing more than the ability to target zones based around the distribution equipment – the 'head ends' – of their local systems (conversation with Dana Runnells, Senior Marketing Manager, Comcast Spotlight, 2005). Because the systems covered fewer homes than broadcast signals, advertisers could discriminate between smaller areas based on data from geodemographic research companies such as Claritas that provide information about the wealth, lifestyles and purchasing habits based on postal ZIP codes. Yet, this kind of targeting encouraged greater differentiation among neighbourhoods by television advertisers than was previously possible. The Visible World technology that powered it, though, had far greater capability. Backed by such huge advertising players as WPP Group and Grey Global, the small start-up's Intellispot system could create and deliver TV commercials that changed message and creative elements in real time (Neff 2004: 12). It did this by creating different layers for parts of the commercial that would be changed digitally. At cable system head-ends, the commercial was placed on servers jointly run by the cable firm and Visible World. The layered nature of the commercials allowed the advertisers to change the message for that zone based on anything from the weather, to the time of day, to the day of the week, without delivering multiple tapes.

A Visible World executive said people in homes receiving the commercials would not know (unless told) that they were getting messages targeting their area. He added that the customization could easily be integrated with interactivity. Visible World could work with interactive advertising firms to allow people who receive the customized commercial to click on elements of the commercial to learn more or request information (interview with Pat Ruta, VP Business Development, Visible World, 2005). A little further under the Intellispot hood, the possibility of even greater customization appeared. The software could implement thousands of versions of a commercial in seconds by changing features from music, to voiceover, to characters, to graphics. In the case of a car commercial, for example, one layer might involve the vehicle; another, the driver; a third, the kind of highway; yet another, the song played in the background. Based on database instructions to software in household set-top boxes, Visible World could create commercials customized to different individual homes, not just head-end zones.

Although it was technically quite feasible for cable systems to implement household-customized commercials in 2005, this only happened in scattered tests. One reason was the relatively sparse use of the digital set-top boxes needed to process the commercials. Gerrit Niemeijer, Visible World's Chief Technology Officer, noted in 2005 that cable firms were loathe to spend the dollar or more per box that would be required to give a digital box the ability to process his firm's layered commercial. A dollar seemed a small amount, he pointed out, but for a multiple system operator it added up to substantial money: Comcast, for example, had over twenty million subscribers in 2005 (interview with Gerrit Niemeijer, 2005).

Niemeijer offered an additional hurdle: privacy concerns. He said he has heard cable system executives express worries that the kinds of personal information issues that swirled about the web would hit them. Yet, he firmly expressed the opinion that the Cable Television Act of 1984 does not prohibit cable firms from sending customized commercials to households. No one seems to contest that point, despite the complexity of the Act's privacy section. Using the same kinds of tortured clauses and possible escape hatches common to corporate website privacy policies, the section seems, first, to take away and, then, return to cable firms the right to give marketers ways to discriminate among subscribers. The section also seems to say that cable systems cannot sell personally identifiable information to marketers – except that they can sell basic 'mailing list' information: that means the names and addresses of individual subscribers. The section also gives cable systems the right to collect considerably more data about subscribers for their own use if subscribers give 'prior written or electronic consent' – or if it is 'necessary to render a cable service or other service provided by the cable operator to the subscriber.' One such 'other service' might well be advertising.[3]

Spotlight Managing Director, Hank Oster, stated his belief that privacy laws prevent his Comcast division from selling subscriber names and addresses to advertisers. Spotlight does collect loads of demographic and viewing information about households in head-end zones, and then aggregates the data in order to interest sponsors. Spotlight will also take data from individual advertisers about individual addresses that they want to target and confirm the percentage of the zone's households they represent. So, for example, the cable advertising marketer will confirm to Kraft that 25 per cent of the homes in an area are addresses that Kraft knows buy the company's cheeses. That high percentage might encourage Kraft to advertise in that Comcast zone – or purchase Showcase programming – because it is higher than the national average.

A Visible World executive added that, often, the advertiser is more active than the cable firm in bringing substantial household data to the marketing situation. In the future, he predicted, the advertiser would download personal information to the cable box that would help create the custom layers for the target. The information would disappear after the commercial was created. Because neither the cable firm nor Visible World would share that information, it all would be quite legal and potentially very powerful for sending different commercials offers to households – and possibly, eventually, even people within those households – based on what marketers conclude about them.

Behind such goals is an awareness that much of the digital media world is moving in the direction of database driven approaches to audiences and content. Advertising and television executives see the Internet, now the most interactive of electronic media, as a test bed for gathering and analyzing information about particular members of the audience in the interest of better persuading them. US television executives could hardly stand by and watch the growth of the new forms of database marketing without realizing the importance to the survival of their industry. They also knew, however, that traditional domestic television in the mid-decade had nothing like the interactive capabilities and personalization technologies that were needed to execute comparable approaches to advertising and selling.

'This is the future of TV advertising', contended a venture capitalist with an investment in Navic Networks, a start-up firm competing with Visible World. 'If I were to factor what TV advertising may be like in three to five years, I think today's concept of producing blanket TV ads will be analogous to dropping leaflets out of an airplane' (Dan Nova, quoted in Whitman 2004: 35). Backing up his claim, Forrester Research had found a high percentage of database marketing executives for major financial, telecom, and retail firms very interested in household-level TV advertisement targeting. Their desire to reach the right people was so high that they said they would pay between 50 and 60 cents for each advertisement delivered to a household. It means spending as much as US$600 to reach 1000 viewers at a time when conventional prime time television charged between $30 and $40 per thousand. 'That's off the chart', exclaimed a Forrester analyst (Eric Schmitt of Forrester Research, quoted in Whitman 2004: 35).

The collection of data about viewers, the complex analysis of the data, and the implementation of messages based on them is still in its relative infancy on the web – and even more so in the traditional TV industry. Nevertheless, tailored communication to database driven niches is moving forward according to an industrial logic that marketing and media executives repeat often: To get consumers to pay attention to commercial messages, marketers must know as much as possible about them and interact with them whenever and wherever they can convince consumers to find them relevant. The recipe involves attempting to take charge by attempting to inculcate a strong sense of brand trust, while gathering information with which to decide whether and how a customer is worth engaging in customized digital relationships. Six inter-related activities form the heart of the logic:

- Screening consumers for appropriateness
- Interacting with them electronically Targeted tracking of them
- Data mining
- Mass customization of advertising messages
- The cultivation of relationships based on the knowledge gained.

Visible World was, in fact, working along these lines to make that idea as attractive as possible by making it easy for advertisers to find the households they wanted. They turned to Teradata, a company based in Dayton, Ohio, owned by NCR that sells consumer behaviour data to advertisers such as Travelocity. The advertisers were using it to target consumers with tailor-made advertisements on the Internet. The idea was to do for TV what it does online: to deliver TV advertisements that are not only tailor-made to people who live in certain neighbourhoods, but are also tailored to suit individual interests. 'Our end-game is to mass customize commercials as granular as you can get', a Visible World executive told *Advertising Age* in connection with its Terradata project. 'We envision the day – in three to five years – when consumers will actually request commercials [customized for them], and that is the ultimate relevance.' (Linnett 2004: 36).

The notion that commercials can be tailored – as well as made interactive – for particular households, and even individuals, is such an attractive idea to marketing and new-media practitioners that they often discuss it as the ultimate antidote to advert-skipping. Their expectation is that viewers will pay attention when people see and hear products and claims that speak directly to their interests. An obvious addition to this armamentarium is customized product integration directly into programmes.

Asked about the possibilities of customized product placement, executives from marketing and technology firms say that, while possible today, it would be even harder to implement than customized commercials. Gene Dwyer, Director of Technology for Princeton Video Imaging (PVI), said that his company has the capability to custom insert products into shows during real time. He added, however, that the desire to carry out customized advertising versions of these activities surrenders, at this point, to the demands such household-level customizations make on the set-top box. Database driven product placement requires even more computing power in the digital set-top box than does the Visible-World type of commercial creation. The reason is that, while creating a 30-second commercial requires the combination of layers, the customized product placement requires that together with integration of the material into the flow of ongoing programming.

The rise of many 'televisions'

It is, however, a fairly sure bet that, within the next decade-and-a-half, the customization of all sorts of commercial messages will prove both quite feasible and competitively essential. At this point, the biggest logjam with cable is technical: there are not enough digital set-top boxes in the approximately 70 per cent of US homes that receive their TV via cable, and the boxes that do exist are too primitive to accommodate real-time customization. But the situation is very fluid. Cable firms already see strong reason to pepper their subscribers' homes with digital set-top boxes, as well as add substantial computing power to them. The particular motivation is strong competition from satellite and phone companies (telcos) that aim to compete with cable firms to provide a 'triple play' of voice, video and data. Consumer electronics companies such as Apple, HP, Sony and Phillips also stand ready to compete with all these firms in the 'home entertainment' space.

The national rollout of digital television in the USA by large phone companies such as Verizon and ATandT using Internet protocol technology is beginning to ramp up the need by cable firms to deploy smarter interactive capabilities. Ed Grazyk, Marketing Director at Microsoft TV, Verizon's technology supplier, noted that all subscribers would get HDTV, DVR, VOD and an interactive electronic programme guide (EPG) as part of his firm's service. He added that the telcos will, over time, easily add various advanced, Internet based interactive services to the offering. In fact, technologies already available from Microsoft (the Xbox 360) Apple (Apple TV) and Oracle (by means of various Linksys products) allow viewers to personalize the programme guide, and to conduct programming searches and schedule recordings from PCs and other connected devices. They also allow individuals to incorporate Internet content and personal media into the viewing experience – allowing viewers, for example, to view the TV digital photos stored on a networked PC. Most important, from an advertising standpoint, they allow for sending of new forms of commercials to the home, and even the individual, on the home television set. One rapidly growing example involves the integration of brands into Internet linked video games. Companies such Massive (owned by Microsoft) and Double Fusion aim to change the commercial messages seen in the games dynamically, depending on what the game provider knows about the users.

But the arrival of an interactive, customizable domestic TV set is just the start of transformations in television technology that promise to further reshape programming and advertising. Although the Internet and the domestic TV set will increasingly be integrated, the stand-alone PC will increase as a vehicle for accessing programming created by both professionals and amateurs. Despite some employers' displeasure, the workplace has become a venue of major importance to advertisers who want to reach huge numbers of people who trawl through the web and buy products at times when their employers would rather they work. While some workplaces block the viewing of IPTV, in many places employees do go online to watch during the day. Media firms and their sponsors see the potential for customized programming and commercials in that space, based upon what they learn about their audiences. Already researchers are beginning to note differences in the VOD programming people choose to consume, depending whether they are watching on the web or on cable (Mandese 2007). As data about differences in viewing based on video platforms (and location) become part of the industry belief system, it will affect the kinds of audio-visual entertainment and targeted advertising that are presented in different venues.

And while new ways to merge advertising and programming on the home set and Internet are major concerns of programmers, technologists and marketing executives, the newest buzz centres on the 'third screen' – the mobile phone. In Japan, Korea and parts of Europe, developments in both programming and marketing have outpaced those in the USA, where 3G and other broadband mobile technologies are not as developed. The new audio-visual age is just beginning, but major media conglomerates are jockeying alongside entrepreneurial upstarts to decide what programming will work best on hand-helds, how to repurpose contemporary materials for mobile audiences, and how to create search engines that help people find what they want to watch at the time they want it. Not only are media firms and marketers deciding the best avenues for return on investment in this new area, they are confronting mobile phone companies that have a strong monetary interest in controlling access to their customers in order to charge media firms that want to reach them and to receive a cut of the advertising revenue. Tensions among wireless firms, media companies and marketers around these issues are likely to increase.

One valuable piece of information about customers that the mobile providers hold is their location as they move through the day. Media firms and marketers do have other ways to reach their favourite customers as they travel. People can text-message their postal address or postal code, for example; they can scan a barcode in a store; or they can point their blue-tooth enabled phone to a transmitter on a billboard. Whatever the method, being able to follow known individuals who agree to receive programming, information and discounts in places that matter to them takes the personalization of messages to an entirely new level. It is likely that people who agree to these sorts of relationships will knowingly, or unknowingly, offer up enormous amounts of information about their interests, backgrounds and movements in time and space. This is information marketers can use as they travel with consumers down the aisles of supermarkets, electronics stores and other retail outlets. It is here, at the point of product selection – what Procter and Gamble executives have called the 'first moment of truth', that marketers might find the ability to send coupons or engage in other tailored incentives particularly compelling media buys.

The social implications of television in the digital age

These developments augur a new era of consumer surveillance. At first glance, the customization of advertising might not seem at all objectionable. Individual consumers could, in fact, benefit, as marketers might give them tailored discounts for products and free entry to media events. Yet, the emerging marketplace might well be far more an inciter of angst over social difference than a celebration of American cultural diversity. Over the long haul, the intersection of large selling organizations and new surveillance technologies seems sure to encourage a particularly corrosive form of personal and social tension. Audiences will quite logically assume – in fact, they might even be told – that the customized advertisements, entertainment, news and information they receive reflect their standing in society. They might be alarmed if they felt that certain marketers have mistaken their income bracket, their race, gender, or their political views. They might try to improve their profiles with advertisers and media firms by establishing buying patterns and lifestyle tracks that make them look good, or by taking actions that make others look bad. There already is resistance to these developments, and there might be more. Yet, the competitive factors shaping database marketing and media technologies connected to it are so strong that social criticisms will not derail them. Instead, the public rhetoric about data driven personalization in marketing will probably be ever more rosy. All the while, in many societies the activities of database marketers are likely to find great interest from governments with an interest in exploiting both the information and the technologies to conduct surveillance on citizens for political purposes.

The trajectory traced here about television will undoubtedly also have consequences for the very make-up of the broader media system. The ability to move customized audio-visual advertising by means of hand-helds directly to the point of purchase might lead some advertisers to lessen their purchase of space and time on traditional media. It also seems likely that what media firms learn about the habits of individual consumers by means of out-of-home tracking might affect far more than decisions about the materials and advertisements they serve them in the mobile space. What they learn could well have implications for the spectrum of audio-visual news, information, entertainment – and the embedded marketing messages – that they confront at home as well.

Conclusion

Just a little into the twenty-first century, then, advertising and media practitioners see 'television' as part of a cross-platform activity that is part of the process of meeting the needs of marketers who want to be able reach customers at every turn. The traditional domestic television box is, in the short term, being used as a way to move target audiences to the Internet, where marketers can engage directly with them through the medium's increasing interactivity, targeted tracking, data mining and the cultivation of relationships. In the medium and long term, media and marketing executives aim to migrate these capabilities to the domestic TV box, as well as other large and small screens in and out of home. Whether all – or any – of these audiovisual technologies should be called 'television' will actually be one of the smaller issues confronting media and marketing practitioners, as well as the researchers who study the social implications of their work. The rethinking of television is both causing – and reflecting – changes in the way that society relates to itself. It is an ongoing process that deserves close attention.

Notes

1. This chapter was accepted in April 2007.
2. Roy M. Speer and Lowell W. Paxson created the first television shopping show, 'Home Shopping', in the Tampa Bay area of Florida in 1982, and in other parts of the country three years later. See Andrew Feinberg, 'Picking Up the Pieces in Home Shopping', *New York Times*, 28 September 1988, Section 3: 4.
3. See the Cable TV Privacy Act of 1984, Section 551, 'Protection of Subscriber Privacy', part c. Available at http://www.epic.org/privacy/cable_tv/ctpa.html.

References

Interviews

Conversation with Dana Runnells, Senior Marketing Manager, *Comcast Spotlight*, 11 February 2005.
Interview with Gerrit Niemeijer, 14 February 2005.
Interview with Pat Ruta, VP Business Development, *Visible World*, 11 February 2005.

Publications

Advertising Age (2007) 'Media Agencies Ready for Convergence?', 1 March.
Bennett, Martha (2002) 'Interactive Television: Moving Forward, at a Snail's Pace', *Forrester IdeaByte*. 1 November.
Elkin, Tobi (2002) 'Madison + Vine: Getting Viewers to Opt In, not Tune Out', *Advertising Age*, 4 November.

Feinberg, Andrew (1988) 'Picking Up the Pieces in Home Shopping', *New York Times*, 28 September, sec. 3.

Gnoffo, Tony (2005) 'Technology Forces Television Advertisers to Re-Evaluate Methods', *Philadelphia Inquirer*, 23 January.

Horovitz, Bruce (2007) 'Marketers Set Up a Screen Play', *USA Today*, 2 February.

Johnson, Bradley (2002) 'TiVo, ReplayTV View for Uncertain Prize', *Advertising Age*, 4 November.

Linnett, Richard (2004) 'AdAges', *Advertising Age*, 4 March.

Mack, Anne M. (2004) 'Interactive Quarterly', *AdWeek*, 20 September.

Mandese, Joe (2007) 'On-Demand Video Data Reveals Online, Cable Users Go To It Differently', *Online Media Daily*, 29 March.

Neff, Jack (2004) 'Addressable TV Meet with Agency and Marketer Resistance', *Advertising Age*, 15 March.

Riedman, Patricia (2000) 'Dot-Com Slump Crimps Marketing', *Advertising Age*, 29 May.

Schiller, Gail (2007) 'Bud.TV Hops To It with Originals', *Hollywood Reporter*, 2 February.

2
BBC and New Media: Legitimization Strategies of a Public Service Broadcaster in a Corporate Market Environment

Nancy Thumim and Lilie Chouliaraki

Introduction

This chapter explores the use of new media by the BBC as a strategy for the institution to sustain its legitimacy under a new regulative regime that favours open market competition. Even though the BBC, one of the major Public Service Broadcasting institutions worldwide, is not privatized, it is, nonetheless, now obliged both to adopt practices that originate in the private sector in order to remain competitive in the changing media environment, and, at the same time, continually to secure and consolidate its justification for public funding. We argue that one of the practices strategically employed by the BBC in this process is the use of new media for purposes of public participation and self-representation by ordinary people, and we focus on a particular case study of this practice: *Capture Wales*, a BBC Wales Internet-based project that pictures Wales from the citizens' autobiographical perspectives.[1]

Even though the BBC has established multiple user-generated content hubs, which are designed to host and selectively broadcast citizens' contributions, we choose to focus on *Capture Wales* because this online project best illustrates the institutional ambivalence of the BBC around its use of new technology as a strategy of legitimization. We define institutional ambivalence as the consequence of co-existing yet unresolved tensions within the BBC regarding the visibility and status of the project, as well as the BBC's broader vision of new media as a means to public participation. Our argument is that, even though tensions around public participation are historically ongoing in the BBC, the use of new media as the vehicle for institutional legitimization re-articulates these tensions around the idea of 'public value', refashioning the BBC's institutional identity in new, though not unproblematic, ways.

The chapter is organized in four sections. We begin by describing the context in which the legitimacy of the BBC in the new media market is debated, and locate the case study of *Capture Wales* in this context. We move on to a discussion of the rationale that informs the BBC strategy to connect the use of new media with projects of public participation, and we subsequently focus on two central tensions:

- The visibility of *Capture Wales* within and outside the BBC
- The BBC's broader vision regarding the use of new media for public engagement, as these emerge through stakeholders' accounts and other forms of empirical documentation.[2]

In conclusion, we point to the advantages and limitations of this strategy as it seeks to address at once the demands of the market, in terms of competitiveness, and those of civil society, in terms of publicizing the 'authentic voices' of ordinary people.

'Public value' and digital storytelling

Capture Wales is an award-winning digital storytelling project, which was set up as a partnership between BBC Wales and Cardiff University in order to facilitate people in the making of their digital stories:

> Everyone has a story to tell ... each story is as individual as the person who made it. (www.bbc.co.uk/wales/capturewales).[3]

Running monthly workshops between 2001–08, the project pioneered the training of ordinary citizens in the use of new media so as to tell their own stories, which were subsequently broadcast on the BBC Wales' website. Two elements are indicative of the rationale that informed the project: digital technology and real-life experience.

Whereas the former points to the centrality of digital media (cameras, mobile phones, ipods and so on) as vehicles of public engagement through and with the BBC, the latter points to the valorization of ordinary individual experience as a privileged domain of the BBC's online mediations.

The particular combination of these elements marks a shift from the past. The first – the amateur use of technology in videos of personal stories – has long been included in mainstream media, but often (with some exceptions) only as material within a particular genre of television entertainment; for example, in ITV's *You've Been Framed* home videos (Matthews 2002). At the same time, the amateur production of news through user-generated content has recently been welcomed as an opportunity for democratizing news flows (for example, Beckett 2008), but simultaneously treated as a threat to the journalistic values of validity and trustworthiness (for example, Bennett and Entman 2001). The second element, the valorization of ordinariness, has similarly been met with a certain ambivalence, as mediated representations of real-life are always caught in struggles over authority and prestige. They are either accused of popularizing content ('dumbing down') in genres such as talk shows or reality television (for example, Murdock 1999), or celebrated for democratizing content (for example, Van Zoonen 2001).

The BBC Wales digital storytelling project introduces a different dimension to these controversies, in that it seeks to professionalize the citizen's use of digital technology in their storytelling productions through BBC-run regular workshops. In so doing, it also seeks to re-valorize ordinary experience as an important part of its own institutional mediations:

> each Digital Story is made by the storyteller themself, using his or her own photos, words and voice. (www.bbc.co.uk/wales/capture-wales)

It is this shift towards teaching the digital and encouraging self-representation (one's own photos, words and voice) that points to the emergence of 'public value' as the dominant discourse for understanding the role of the BBC in the contemporary digital media milieu.

Public value reflects here an increasing concern within the BBC to abandon 'elitist complacence', whereby the delivery of high quality informational and educational content was regarded as automatically ensuring public trust and institutional legitimacy, and to regard public trust as something to be constantly aimed for and earned by the public (Born 2004). The rise of public value as a discourse that informs the BBC's key policy concerns is tightly linked with changing market circumstances. Coming to replace the 'public service provider' discourse with its universal license fee policy, the discourse of public value promotes a conception of the BBC as one among many competitors for public trust, operating in a mature open market of subscription-based providers and convergent media (McQuail 2000; McQuail and Siune 1998).[4]

In this new landscape, the public value discourse provides a novel rationale for the existence of the BBC, which both acknowledges the shifting terrain of media industries and re-asserts the continuing importance of the public as the key reference for service provision in the digital age. Public value performs this double act by merging consumer research methods measuring 'value' indicators among individual consumers – the public value test, with the public interest in delivering service that is beneficial to society as a whole – public value here projecting the BBC's traditional role as an institution of public education that today seeks to navigate its audiences into the digital future.

It comes, then, as no surprise that the new priority commitments of the BBC White Paper are reflected with precision in the *Capture Wales* project:

> sustaining citizenship and civil society; promoting education and learning; stimulating creativity and cultural excellence ... reflecting the UK's nations, regions and communities.[5]

Indeed, even though the launch of *Capture Wales* dates prior to the White Paper, it is chronologically located at the centre of debates around the new role of the BBC as an institution with a unique market position with respect to engaging with new technologies and promoting citizenship.

Specifically, *Capture Wales*' dual focus on the professionalization of digital skills and on the re-valorization of individual experience can be seen as a manifestation of the double claim to legitimacy that the public value discourse makes possible. On the one hand, the project provides a space for public education, in the form of skills training that generates public value in terms of enabling participation and self-expression; on the other hand, it is geared towards the production of concrete artefacts, in the form of digital content that can become the object of evaluation along the lines of a public value test.

This dual focus, however, is not without its tensions – tensions inherent in the public value discourse between a market logic of value measurement, which aims to deliver what we call instrumental benefit, and a social logic of the valorization of public participation, which aims to deliver what we call ethico-political benefit. In the next section, we unpack these tensions in the BBC's public value discourse, by referring to the ways in which BBC Wales' stakeholders argue for the potential benefit of *Capture Wales*: as strengthening civil society but also as justifying the organization's licence fee.

Discourses of benefit: Civil society and the licence fee

What is the benefit of introducing digital storytelling projects as platforms for civil participation in the BBC? There is no single response to this question but there is instead a cluster of discourses that provides different, often complementary but potentially conflictual, arguments around the benefit of such projects.

Specifically, two different discourses cluster around the question of what the BBC producers regard as the benefit of using new media to enhance public participation.[6]

- The first is ethico-political and sees the benefits of public participation in terms of public good, as enhancing the repertoire of voices in civil society
- The second is instrumental and sees these benefits in terms of institutional interest, as increasing BBC's chances for public funding.

To be sure, the ethico-political and the instrumental are analytical rather than substantial distinctions and, in practice, all strategic decision-making is informed by considerations of both. The distinction is useful, however, in drawing attention to potential discrepancies between the two, and particularly to the difficulty in fitting the instrumental benefit of using new media at the service of public funding in a celebratory rhetoric of the BBC as enhancing the dynamics of deliberation in civil society.

The ethico-political benefit for the BBC in running *Capture Wales* connects the use of new media with new opportunities for citizen participation in public debate. In so doing, it directly reflects the discourse of public value mentioned earlier. It does so insofar as public value refers to the BBC's capacity to go beyond 'traditional' concerns of equal citizen access and fair reporting, and move towards the idea of using new media as a vehicle for citizens to broadcast their own content:

> the importance of user-generated content is growing in the BBC. It's actually, we've come full circle in that it's suddenly got a really huge place because...there's a feeling that we actually don't connect with our audience, the fact that there are people out there that have just got great stories to tell.[7]

Whereas the BBC's user-generated hubs already testify to the institution's commitment to deliver public value by connecting with citizens and rendering their accounts of events legitimate newsworthy items, in fact *Capture Wales* goes beyond this in two ways.

On the one hand, content production goes hand in hand with new media skills training, that is, with such competences as scanning, uploading and editing still and moving images. In *Capture Wales*, the development of digital literacy skills by professionals, in the five-day workshops run by the expert team under the auspices of the BBC, is seen as a crucial form of empowerment that enhances people's capacity to use technology and perform in public. In this sense, the BBC community studio sessions, cyber café functions or Internet taster gatherings

> are part of a broader effort to...develop as many different kinds of tools as possible, to engage the public with programme makers more directly, in discussion, in contributing to programmes, and to engage people in projects around media literacy and creativity.[8]

On the other hand, participation goes beyond reporting and becomes self-representation; that is public storytelling organized around experiences of the self and its immediate environment.

Capture Wales is a digital storytelling project that follows a grass-roots rationale of 'digital technology at the service of the people' and, as such, understands the idea of people speaking about themselves to be part of the political vision of genuine democracy.[9] The idea of 'authentic voices' is central to this vision. This is partly because of the strong truth claim and emotional power that such voices bring to mediated content, but also, importantly, because of the strategic role that 'ordinary' voices can play in transforming the character of the BBC from a paternalistic institution – where, *sometimes, you get the sense in the BBC that authentic, real voices, need to be interpreted to be communicated* – to a contemporary institution that gives people control over the representation of their own lives – what BBC's Director of Nations and Regions called a *revolutionary* move.[10]

Such rhetoric brings together quite different positions of interest when, for example, in a similar vein to BBC management, the Creative Director of *Capture Wales*, Daniel Meadows, also used the language of revolution, echoing the (Marxian) radical discourse of people owning 'the tools of production':

> No one has ever given people the tools of production, they've only eked them out, little by little. Oh yes, well you can take a Handicam and film yourself, you know, crying over the loss of your boyfriend but we're going to edit it. You know, that's gone now and it's fantastic, you know. And that we've managed to achieve that is for me, that's where the ground's been broken, that's the difference we've made.

The defining moment around this shift of control lies in the elimination of editorial intervention on behalf of the BBC: the institution does not edit user content as, in the BBC's Director of Regions' quote above, the voices of the people do not any more 'need to be interpreted and communicated'. This radical rhetoric by the BBC management and the *Capture Wales* expert team provides some grounds for the celebration of participation but, as we shall see, leaves intact institutional tensions between, for example, management priorities and those of the creative team, or between individual and collective agency of media users.

Parallel to the ethico-political benefit, crystallized in this celebration of popular empowerment through new media, there is also a strong instrumental benefit for the BBC in launching *Capture*

Wales. The project's use of new media to engage the public seeks to re-affirm the relevance of the BBC to increasingly larger constituencies of audience, now potentially lured away by the abundance of digital content offers, and ultimately to justify its state funding through the licence fee. As part of a broader market-driven process of radical change in the BBC's online presence, *Capture Wales* can be seen as an example of content production that intends to *be made more distinctive, and to deliver more public value, in this developing and growing market*.[11] Specifically, it can be seen as reflecting a fundamental re-structuring, whereby the BBC closed down a number of websites on the grounds that *they would not meet our new test of public value*, whereas it re-oriented others, shifting their *focus on educating people about the creative process of film-making and allow audiences to share this*.[12]

Participation through new media appears again as a key word of this strategic discourse on benefit – though, this time, benefit is not understood in ethico-political terms as authentic self-expression but, rather, in instrumental terms as an innovative service that increases the BBC's competitive position towards other players in the digital market. This instrumental discourse on benefit correspondingly reflects a competing conception of public value, also mentioned earlier, which, rather than relating to public good, is oriented towards the measurement of user satisfaction. The main reference to this instrumentalist conception of benefit is online content, insofar as content is the only measurable indicator of product quality and user satisfaction in the context of *Capture Wales*.

Online content evidently refers to concrete stories as outputs of the project, and is directly linked to the funding of the BBC:

> The licence fee essentially is about content, so we felt it was really important that the workshops produced the kind of content that we could publish.[13]

This reference to 'publishability' contrasts with other examples of digital storytelling, where the outcome does not necessarily have to be published on organizational platforms,[14] and points directly to the institutional criterion of quality – so that *the kind of content we could publish*, in the quote, means high quality content capable of being displayed on BBC Wales' website. This precondition of quality is repeatedly emphasized by others involved in the production of *Capture Wales*:[15]

> I think one of the things the BBC has massively been able to do...is massively been able to inject a level of quality. You know, we have delivered the very best to the people who've made them in terms of our editorial experience, our teaching experience and our technical experience. That matters, the benchmark is high. People don't make crap digital stories when they work with us, but they still feel they're their stories.[16]

Whereas the quote firmly asserts the ethico-political view on story-telling as an expression of 'authentic' voices, in that people 'still feel they're their stories', it simultaneously reflects a concern with publishability, in that 'the benchmark is high, People don't make crap stories'. This captures a different concern with institutional standards and measuring quality – a concern that could potentially compromise the publication of 'authentic', that is unmediated and non-edited content.

The key to striking a balance between the two lies in the BBC seeing its public value provision not only as a matter of the story products themselves but, importantly, of the process of producing stories in the skills training workshops. This is evident in the quote asserting that the BBC has 'delivered the very best in our editorial experience, our teaching experience and our technical experience'. Clearly, here, the participants' sense of ownership goes beyond online content as prod-uct; ownership, rather, refers to the sense of community that the pro-ject seeks to establish among the local stakeholders that participate in the process of storytelling. This conception of community continues to evoke a grass-roots view of spontaneous creative encounters in local collectivities, reflected in the metaphor of the BBC's digital story-tell-ing projects 'as the digital campfire around which people gather to tell their stories'.[17] Yet again, however, the BBC's concern with qual-ity deliverables further reveals a more instrumental approach to the learning community as the aggregate of public preferences, which can be assessed in terms of the degree to which participants respond to or interact with expert input by the institution – the public value test measuring quality precisely in terms of 'responsiveness to refined preferences' (Horner et al. 2006: 44).[18]

In this context, measuring the public value of the BBC's digital storytelling crucially involves the organization's capacity to demonstrate that it can mobilize effective expert–user partnerships with a view to increasing the digital literacy capital of local users.[19] The importance of community here lies not so much in unleashing and promoting the creative resources of the public but, rather, in demonstrating the extent to which BBC Wales provides innovative services through stakeholder networking so as to justify and legitimize its public funding. To the satisfaction of the BBC governors, *Capture Wales* did, indeed, work to that effect:

> further development of the digital storytelling project *Capture Wales/Cipolwg ar Gymru*...and record attendance at community events and outside broadcasts...all helped deepen the relationship with license payers across the UK.[20]

The use of online content is, therefore, doubly defined by the instrumental discourse on public value: as process, referring to the expert team–media users collaboration in the community, and as product, referring to the outcome of the collaboration. Both these definitions reflect the requirement of the public value of discourse to monitor institutional quality in tangible terms, as authentic stories and as innovative networks. Yet, it is precisely the unresolved tensions between these institutional requirements and the parallel claims to public ownership, popular authenticity and community building, originating in the ethico-political discourse of public value, that produce a fundamental institutional ambivalence in the *Capture Wales* project. It is to these tensions that we now turn.

Institutional ambivalence around *Capture Wales:* Visibility and vision

Institutional ambivalence is evident in the ways in which the BBC staff refer to their own experience of *Capture Wales*. In this section, we explore the articulation of such ambivalence in terms of two central themes:

- The *visibility and status* of the project among BBC staff, including the BBC management and the *Capture Wales* creative team

- The *vision* around the project as articulated by these same stakeholders.

Visibility and status

Despite the BBC's enthusiastic endorsement of digital storytelling,
Capture Wales, together with the broader *Telling Lives* project in BBC
England, always remained insignificant in quantitative terms. On the
one hand, its hits were too low to be recorded by the Audience Research
Department of the BBC, so the project remained outside the range of
institutional visibility granted to projects with higher ratings.[21] At the
same time, its storytelling products only occasionally made it into the
prime time BBC Wales television network, thus restricting the external visibility of its content to the visitors of the BBC *Capture Wales*
website (although there is recently a more continuous presence as a
result of the development of BBCi and the inclusion of *Capture Wales*
and other user generated output such as *Video Nation*, 'behind the red
button'). Nevertheless, at least in 2004, according to the BBC's own
internal research into user-generated content, the wider public beyond
the project participants did not know about the project at all.[22]

Such problems with visibility inevitably reflect difficulties in the
overall status of the project within the BBC. Despite the enthusiasm
of top management, which included *Capture Wales* in one of BBC's
reviews towards the Building Public Value Charter renewal, publicity
and promotion staff found promoting the project challenging. This
might have been a consequence of the very innovative character of
Capture Wales, which left press officers with nothing similar with
which to compare this project:

> The BBC Wales' press office is set up to promote its television pro-
> grammes and radio programmes ... But ... when you're trying to get
> across to them ... a rather more wide ranging concept about some-
> thing, and what we're really trying to get is people to get person-
> ally involved in the BBC and to use the BBC to get their own
> personal messages across really, then we have press officers, who
> are not used to doing that, speaking to journalists who have never
> come across this before.[23]

The validity of such organizational justifications granted, the net
outcome of this lack of engagement has been that the visibility of the

project was severely restricted and its status remained local, thereby minimizing the dissemination of 'authentic' public voices.

Problems of publicity further indicate that it would remain challenging to integrate the different stakeholders of this innovative partnership within the BBC fully. As *Capture Wales'* Creative Director put it, the expert team's experience of community, youth work and education, as well as professional photography, functioned as a strength for the BBC, but, at the same time, it sustained a sharp distinction between themselves and the BBC:

> Well the BBC is a funny institution, it is sort of run on this cross between the army, public school and the civil service, in that everybody has a rank, you see. And it's terribly respectful of rank and, I mean, I could never work in it if I wasn't doing digital storytelling.[24]

As this quote suggests, the Creative Director, as well as other members of the expert team, seemed to distance themselves, at least to some extent, from the wider institution whose priorities they did not always share. According to one of the team members, if another funding source emerged, she was certain that the team would happily all leave the BBC. *Capture Wales* was, she implied, more important than the BBC affiliation. Indeed, there was a gulf between senior management's enthusiasm and the inability of the *Capture Wales* team to achieve a higher profile for the project – 'a gap between rhetoric and practice', in the words of the Creative Director. The clearest illustration of this gap is, perhaps, the fact that the English Region's *Telling Lives* was discontinued in March 2005, despite the senior BBC management's apparent enthusiasm for digital storytelling.[25]

To sum up, the institutional ambivalence around the visibility and status of *Capture Wales* refers to a discrepancy between, on the one hand, the celebration of online storytelling evident in BBC strategic documents and in the launch of this project (and similar ones) and, on the other hand, to the minimal visibility of the project within and outside the institution; to the unclear perceptions of the project among BBC publicists; to the difficulties of integration between the BBC and the *Capture Wales* creative expert team; and, finally, to the short-lived trajectory of its sister project and the ultimate discontinuation of *Capture Wales* itself in 2008. Whereas the celebratory rhetoric can be seen as reflecting the ethico-political discourse that permeates BBC official documents and management stakeholders, the multiple failures to integrate and formalize the project within the BBC could be interpreted as reflecting a certain reluctance on the part of the organization fully to embrace the project as a grass-roots initiative of public participation, sustaining it only to the extent that it serves the institution's instrumental benefit of monitoring its own public value in terms of innovative product and process.

Vision

The vision of the BBC's digital storytelling initiatives is to turn passive audiences into active communities, where everyone has the chance to tell their story and enjoy the stories of others:

> From *Voices* through *Video Nation* to *Digital Storytelling* and *Telling Lives*, hundreds of people with no previous broadcasting experience have taken the opportunity to tell their stories. For some, it has given them the skills and confidence to change their lives.[26]

Tightly linked to the discourse of public value, again, this vision both aspires to use new media as a form of citizen empowerment at community level and simultaneously to situate the organization at the heart of a competitive market of innovative transformations towards the digital future. As a consequence, similarly to the discussion on *Capture Wales'* visibility, the BBC's vision of the project is torn between the ethico-political interest on value, articulated in the grass-roots claims to social empowerment and community building, and the instrumental interest of value, best captured in perceptions of *Capture Wales* as an individualized and skills based endeavour that facilitates the BBC's public value test rather than strengthens civil society. We explore a key manifestation of this tension around the conception of self-representation in the *Capture Wales* project, particularly the potential of self-representation to contribute to online community building.

Self-representation is at the core of the practice of digital storytelling; in Rennie and Hartley's words: 'a digital story is something personal, generated from photo-albums and people's memories' (2004).

As we saw earlier, project stakeholders celebrate the elements of individual creativity and personal involvement that characterize such storytelling in *Capture Wales*, in particular emphasizing the people's access to tools of production and the lack of editorial control in the composition of content. This positive spirit is further reflected in BBC Wales' reporting on participants' workshop experiences:

> it's quite extraordinary on the feedback forms, you get this kind of, you know: how much experience have you got with computers to date? And you know, on a scale of one to five, that's often a kind of one or two, and then all the questions about the value people put on the experience are all, kind of, up at five, I mean, really it's extraordinary.[27]

Nevertheless, we need to keep in mind that self-representation texts, far from being the outcomes of unrestricted self-expression, involve an acute awareness of generic convention and a high degree of regulation:

> Short, personal and written with feeling and in the first person there's a strictness to their construction: 250 words, a dozen or so pictures, and two minutes is about the right length.[28]

This means that the pedagogic process of teaching skills to media users was simultaneously a process of tight control over the style, genre and length of their individual texts, with a view to securing the quality outcomes demanded by BBC Wales. Again, in the words of Creative Director Daniel Meadows:

> digital stories – when properly done – can be tight as sonnets: multimedia sonnets from the people.

In this manner, the highly structured workshop process ensures that a subtle gate-keeping mechanism is in place, whereby the rejection of self-representation stories is very rarely necessary because the creative workshop itself leads to the production of a very particular form of self-representation: 'family photographs and a first-person voice-over'. Participants did not deviate from this very specific repertoire of genres of self-representation, even if they might have felt restricted by the representational possibilities of such genres, because the participatory logic of 'having a voice' through BBC's digital storytelling went hand-in-hand with skills training in the production of a very specific textual genre.

The strict regulation of the workshop process by the creative team is clearly dictated by a sound educational rationale: the learning of a creative craft means – at least, to an extent – being subject to the power of the expert.[29] Yet, as is the case in all pedagogic power relationships, the vision of empowerment in *Capture Wales* that is allowing the users' 'authentic' voices to populate the BBC online content was achieved under a certain institutional condition: rather than authenticity meaning people 'gaining' some control over what to say and how to say it online, authenticity here involved a narrow definition of self-representation (family pictures plus voiceover) and of the content and style of people's storytelling (digital 'sonnets'). Whereas this institutional condition leaves some space for the articulation of the ethico-political interest to public value, as we shall see, *Capture Wales* (probably unavoidably) seems to privilege the instrumental interest insofar as the regulation of content guarantees the delivery of measurable products (quality outcome) without necessarily delivering the promise of 'democratizing' their content (the grass-roots aim of 'giving voice' and building community).

The ethico-political moment of the project seems to lie, in particular, in the empowerment that the project makes possible for its participants through the process of skills training itself – a process delivered by a creative team with top quality expertise and strong commitment to the cause of digital education. Together with the stories themselves, as the following quote implies, it is the quality of the team that defines the participants' experience of digital storytelling and their relationship to the institution itself:

> Whatever else happens, the experience of the people in the workshop, and their relationship with us, is crucial...Because that's what makes it special, that's what makes it different...that's why picking the team is very important.[30]

As a result of the BBC Wales' employment of a highly skilled team, the workshops, indeed, turned into a uniquely rewarding experience for participants. As BBC Wales' Head of Talent, Maggie Russell, put it:

> Now what is fantastic is, I haven't heard one story in four years of somebody having a bad experience making a digital story...I think it's to do with the quality of the team that are delivering it...it's to do with, we are probably one of the highest quality community media teams anywhere in the UK.

This strong quote clearly emphasizes the value of teamwork in the *Capture Wales'* training process, and the potential for individual agency in making stories that the project managed to mobilize (evident in the remarkable line that there seems to be no negative account of digital storytelling making). What is left out of this quote – and, indeed, from broader institutional considerations – is the dimension of collective agency in the *Capture Wales* project. A central part of the ethico-political interest of public value, which focuses on the strengthening of civil society and the democratization of ordinary voices through digital platforms, collective agency draws attention to the fact that the creation of community requires more than the sharing of autobiographical narratives. In the words of Rennie and Hartley (2004), it requires an effort to use new media platforms in ways that enable the 'narratives produced...to become more than the sum of their parts'.

With its current dual emphasis on 'capturing individual lives and creating community',[31] the project throws into relief the difficulties of sustaining the ethico-political interest. Such difficulties might have to do with the practical impossibility of keeping such communities going for any length of time beyond the five-day span of the workshops themselves – inevitably, here, the concern is with the former – *capturing lives*, rather than the latter – *creating community*. Yet, such a collection of individualized accounts on private lives can only be defined as a public in the narrow sense of being dispersed in the space of digital display rather than in the broader sense of sustaining communities of communicative action; that is, formations of collective deliberation over shared concerns with a sense of common purpose and commitment.

Along these lines, a more instrumental version of the vision on digital storytelling is put forward by BBC Wales's Head of Talent, when asked to reflect on the success of *Capture Wales*:

I mean the important thing for me is that we've done it, we've done it really well. It continues to be valid. As long as it continues to be valid, we'll continue to do it. But, you know, it may be that this has sparked off a new idea and we should be doing the new idea.[32]

This 'it's good as long as it continues to be valid' logic reveals a vision of *Capture Wales*, perhaps not shared by all stakeholders inside or outside the BBC, as just one 'idea' among many that signals the institution's commitment to the spirit of innovation, rather than a conscious investment on the power of new media to strengthen civil society.

The BBC in the digital cultural sphere

Our discussion suggests that the BBC is approaching digital storytelling as a tool to enhance its institutional legitimacy through expanded public participation, in terms of both educating the public by means of skills training, and providing voice to the public through new online content. Following its agenda to increase public value, this emphasis on digital storytelling is part of the BBC's broader move to incorporate audiences in its organizational practices through interactive sites and user generated content hubs as well as journalistic blogging. Such practices should be seen as the BBC's efforts to restyle itself away from its traditional elitist profile and closer to the contemporary profile of an innovative, open and inclusive organization. Simultaneously, the BBC is also making efforts to render itself competitive in an open market regime where the national audience cannot be taken for granted as the BBC's 'natural' constituency but, rather, needs to be persuaded in terms of the network's added value vis-à-vis other content providers.

By embarking on this self-restyling project, the BBC further contributes to a restructuring of the cultural public sphere, the sphere where citizenship is not exclusively about political deliberation but also about personal narrative, lifestyle choice and aesthetic appearance, precisely by renegotiating the boundaries between the expert and the ordinary, the private and the public (Couldry et al. 2007). Of course, the BBC has, throughout its history, been engaged in struggles for legitimacy (for example, Smith 1974), thereby constantly shifting and negotiating these boundaries but, as we have sought to show, the form this battle currently takes is particular to the current context of digital innovation and open market competition.

The use of new media in this process is strategic, in the sense that these media provide a central platform for the BBC's articulation of a public value discourse – a strategic discourse that makes a dual claim to legitimacy in terms of measuring the BBC's economic performance (value for licence fee money) and enabling the democratization of ordinary voice and agency. This duality, we argued, produces a fundamental ambivalence between instrumental and ethico-political conceptions of benefit – an ambivalence that we explored in terms of how the visibility and vision of the digital storytelling project *Capture Wales* figures in stakeholder accounts within the BBC.

Capture Wales, let us recall, has been a successful BBC Wales– Cardiff University initiative that brought together an expert creative team with a large number of media users to produce a series of highly praised short digital stories, thereby demonstrating how local partnership in skills training can offer an empowering experience of mediation for ordinary participants. Our discussion, however, indicates that the relatively low visibility of the project outside the circle of those already involved, as well as the systematic failures to integrate and formalize the project within the organization, might be seen as compromising the ethico-political benefit of the project, sustaining it only to the extent that it serves the institution's instrumental benefit of monitoring its own public value in terms of innovative product and process.

At the same time, the vision of *Capture Wales* to publicize autobiographical accounts that enhance civil society seems to be troubled by a narrow conception of self-representation (as family pictures) and a loose dispersion of individual voices in the digital space. What would further the ethico-political interest, in this context, would be a stronger sense of commitment from the BBC to a temporally sustainable project to publicize people's voices, or a reflexivity about how to turn this digital space into a space of collective deliberation over matters of common concern. In the light of our remarks, the interest, at the moment, seems to be restricted to the BBC demonstrating its capacity for innovative service delivery, a key assessment criterion for the organization's economic value, rather than maximizing ethico-political value.

What our discussion ultimately indicates is that, as a consequence of this ambivalence around the ethico-poltical interest in its public value claim, the BBC may be problematizing the traditional hierarchical boundary between the private and the public, but it does so, only to the extent that it enables individual users to disseminate private stories in public space, rather than in the sense of enabling collective participation in sustained projects of cultural citizenship, where the voices of individuals can be put to the service of (deliberating over) a common good. In this manner, the potential of digital storytelling to establish a space of publicness where new styles of communicative agency and new forms of authoritative discourse populate the cultural sphere – engaging with, but also challenging, the traditional hierarchies of broadcasting – was not fully realized. Clearly, a sense of empowerment for project participants lies in the opportunity they were given in the workshops to experience a brief glimpse of the world of media production and to act out the roles of the media presenter and/or performer. This is no small thing, insofar as it clearly demonstrates that the public value produced through technological innovation lies in re-negotiating the power relations between institutional authority and ordinary people – in allowing the latter to appropriate the 'means of media production' and to tell their own stories in public. For such sense of empowerment, however, to give rise to more complex forms of collective agency, the BBC's technological innovation needs to be embedded in communicative channels that make it possible for digital stories to be circulated effectively, and cited as powerful and legitimate chains of reference within broader projects of civil engagement.

Conclusion

In this chapter, we use the case study of *Capture Wales* in order to examine the role that the new media play in the innovation efforts of a major broadcasting organization, the BBC, in the context of the UK's de-regulated media market. We argue that the BBC's use of new media, as a privileged site for the users' engagement in digital storytelling, can be understood as a strategic legitimization move in the BBC's attempt to reposition itself in the digital cultural sphere. This attempt is based on the double-edged nature of the emerging public value discourse that the BBC is promoting for itself in the contemporary media market. Competing interests within the discourse, however, give rise to crucial tensions between ethico-political (serving society) and instrumental (justifying the licence fee) conceptions of benefit within *Capture Wales*, which in turn produce constant struggles over the visibility, as well as the vision, of/for digital storytelling by the stakeholders involved in its execution.

Notes

1. *Capture Wales* is part of the BBC's broader digital storytelling initiative that involved a number of similar projects across regional networks, entitled *Telling Lives* (http://www.bbc.co.uk/tellinglives/). Celebrating the potential of digital media to strengthen public participation, the *Capture Wales* project was initiated by BBC Wales New Media department and Cardiff university lecturer, professional photographer and Creative Director of the project, Daniel Meadows, and launched in April 2001 by Menna Richards, Controller, BBC Cymru Wales. Working with an adaptation of a Californian model of digital storytelling, this pioneering project has won four major awards, including a BAFTA Cymru.

2. The empirical material is drawn from N. Thumim's PhD thesis entitled 'Mediating Self-Representations: Tensions Surrounding "Ordinary" Participation in Public Sector Projects', London School of Economics (2007). Interviews were conducted between September 2003–04. See also, Thumim, N. (Forthcoming, 2009) for a related discussion.

3. There are several books and articles about digital storytelling; see, for example, *Digital Storytelling, Mediatized Stories*, in the Digital Formation series at (Peter Lang Publishing, 2008, edited by K. Lundby), *Story Circle. Digital Storytelling Around the World*, (Blackwell, 2009, edited by J. Hartley and K. McWilliam, Queensland University). See also: Kidd 2005; Burgess 2006.

4. For the emergence of the concept of 'public value', see Moore (1995), whose definition of public value as the delivery of a set of social, as well as economic outcomes that are aligned to citizen priorities in a cost-effective manner, has been very influential in subsequent developments of public value models. Cole and Parston (2006: xiv) have formulated two key questions for the delivery of public value by public service organizations, which focus on the social value of what these organizations are bringing to the public, and on the economic value of how effectively they are spending taxpayers' money:

     Why (or to what end) does this organization or programme exist? And, how will we know when the organization or programme has achieved its intended purpose or goal? (Cole and Parston 2006: xiv).

     It is largely these two questions that the BBC is seeking to address in launching digital-storytelling projects, such as *Capture Wales*.

5. BBC White Paper, 'A Public Service for All: the BBC in the Digital Age' (4 March 2006).

6. We use the term 'producers' to refer to staff members at BBC Wales who are involved in various ways, and to varying degrees, in the production of *Capture Wales*. The project teams are those most closely involved in the day-to-day production of the projects. In addition, personnel from different levels of the institutions are involved in the funding, production, marketing and display of the self-representations (Thumim 2007, Unpublished PhD thesis, University of London).

7. Carole Gilligan, Editor of the user-generated content website at BBC Wales, Video Nation.

8. Mandy Rose, Editor, *New Media*, BBC Wales.

9. See the development of oral history as a political force to counter dominant histories (for example, Perks and Thomson 1998).

10. Pat Loughrey, Director of BBC Nations and Regions at the International Digital Storytelling Conference, Cardiff, November 2003.

11. Michael Grade, BBC Chairman, CBI Conference, 2004.

12. Michael Grade, BBC Chairman, CBI Conference, 2004

13. Mandy Rose, Editor, *New Media*, BBC Wales.

14. For example, in the original initiative of the Center for Digital Storytelling in Berkeley, California, where emphasis falls on individual 'writing' and self-expression: 'our primary concern is encouraging thoughtful and emotionally direct writing'.

15. For example, by Daniel Meadows, Creative Director, *Capture Wales*; Gilly Adams, Head of Writers' Unit, BBC Wales, and leader of the *Capture Wales* Story Circle

16. Interview with Maggie Russell, Head of Talent, BBC Wales.

17. Michael Grade, BBC Chairman, ICM Conference, 2004.

18. Indeed, the instrumental conception of public value involves an understanding of the concept in terms of 'finding ways to harness professional expertise in order to shape and guide public preferences', thereby measuring public 'responsiveness to refined preferences' (Blauge et al. 2006). A clear example of this is the UK government's use of Jamie Oliver's TV documentary series, *Jamie's School Dinners* as a model example to show how 'public value can be created by responding to that shift [in consumers' preferences]' (Oakley et al. 2006).

19. The aim [of *Capture Wales*] is to work with local communities to generate material capable of being displayed on local websites, BBC websites and, selectively, on broadcast television (*Welsh Lives* – original *Capture Wales* proposal).

20. www.bbcgovernorsarchive.co.uk/annreport/report03/audiences.txt

21. Emma Trollope, Audience Research, BBC Wales, notes from a phone call.

22. Sparkler Report (2004), internal report about BBC user-generated projects; press articles copied and collected by David Cartwright, Head of Press and Publicity, BBC Wales.

23. David Cartwright, Head of Press and Publicity, BBC Wales.

24. Interview with Daniel Meadows, Creative Director, *Capture Wales*.

25. *Capture Wales* discontinued running workshops in 2008, although it continues to publish digital stories made by partner organizations on its

website. Given the commitment of the expert team, *Capture Wales* did manage to turn 'a two-month project...into a one-year pilot and then a three-year commission, which ultimately ended up lasting seven years' (Meadows personal website).

26. 'Building Public Value: Renewing the BBC for a Digital World', (BBC, June 2004: 72).

27. Interview with Mandy Rose, Editor, *New Media*, BBC Wales.

28. Daniel Meadows Creative Director of Capture Wales personal website.

29. This position reflects a particular type of institutional agency that *Capture Wales* makes available to its participants; namely, that of 'conditional freedom' (Chouliaraki 2008: 846). We use the term 'conditional freedom', in the context of our study, to refer to the function of institutional practices to regulate, but by no means determine, the participants' relationship to new media by opening up a restricted number of educational and creative possibilities with which they may engage. As an economy of institutional regulation, we argue, conditional freedom is not resolutely negative but, rather, inherently ambivalent – positive as well as negative.

30. Interview with Karen Lewis, Production Manager, *Capture Wales*.

31. This tension echoes Joe Lambert's (Director, CDS) book *title Digital Storytelling: Capturing Lives, Creating Community* (2002, CDS, Berkeley, CA) and is critically discussed by Beeson and Miskelly (2005: 5).

32. Interview with Maggie Russell, Head of Talent, BBC Wales.

References

Beckett, C. (2008) *SuperMedia: Saving Journalism So That It Can Save The World* (Oxford: Wiley-Blackwell).

Beeson, I. and Miskelly, C. (2005) 'Digital Stories Of Community: Mobilisation, Coherence and Continuity'. Available at *web.mit.edu/comm-forum/mit4/papers/beeson-miskelly.pdf*

Bennett, W.L. and Entman, R.N. (eds) (2001) *Mediated Politics: Communication in the Future of Democracy* (Cambridge: Cambridge University Press).

BBC (2004) 'Building Public Value: Renewing the BBC for a Digital World', June: 72.

BBC (2006) 'A Public Service for All: The BBC in the Digital Age', White Paper (London: Department for Culture, Media and Sport).

Blauge, R., Horner, L. and Lekhi, R. (2006) 'Heritage, Democracy and Public Value', Conference proceedings of 'Capturing the Public Value of Heritage', 25–26 January 2006, Royal Geographical Society, London.

Born, G. (2004) *Uncertain Vision: Birt, Dyke and the Reinvention of the BBC* (London: Secker and Warburg).

Burgess, J. (2006) 'Hearing Ordinary Voices: Cultural Studies, Vernacular Creativity and Digital Storytelling', Continuum, *Journal of Media and Culture Studies*, 20(2), June, 201–14.

Chouliaraki, L. (2008) 'Mediation as Moral Education', *Media, Culture & Society*, 30(6): 831–52.

Cole, M. and Parston, G. (2006) *Unlocking Public Value* (London: Wiley).

Couldry, N., Livingstone, S. and Markham, T. (2007) *Media Consumption and Public Engagement: Beyond the Presumption of Attention* (Basingstoke: Palgrave).

Grade, M. (2004) Keynote address, CBI Conference, Birmingham.

Hartley, J. and McWilliam, K. (2009) *Story Circle. Digital Storytelling Around the World* (Malden, MA: Wiley-Blackwell).

Highfield, A. (2006) 'BBC Makes Long-Term Plans for New Media', *New Media Age*, 13 April.

Horner, L., Lekhi, R. and Blau, R (2006) 'Deliberative Democracy and the Role of Public Managers', Final Report of the Work Foundation's Public Value Consortium, London, November.

Kidd, J. (2005) '*Capture Wales*: Digital Storytelling at the BBC', *Wales Media Journal*, 2: 66–85.

Lambert, J. (2002) *Capturing Lives, Making Creating Community* (Berkeley, California: Centre for Digital Storytelling).

Lundby, K. (ed.) (2008) *Digital Storytelling, Mediatized Stories. Self-Representations in New Media. Digital Formations*, 52 (New York: Peter Lang).

Matthews, N. (2002) 'Surveying the Self: Broadcast Home Video as Cultural Technology', in J. Campbell and J. Harbord (eds), *Temporalities Autobiography And Everyday Life* (Manchester: Manchester University Press).

McQuail, D. (2000) *Mcquail's Mass Communication Theory*, 4th edn (London: Sage).

McQuail, D. and Siune, K. (1998) *Media Policy: Convergence, Concentration, and Commerce* (London: Sage).

Moore, M.H. (1995) *Creating Public Value: Strategic Management in Government* (Boston: Harvard University Press).

Murdock, G. (1999) 'Rights and Representations: Public Discourse and Cultural Citizenship', in J. Gripsrud (ed.), *Television and Common Knowledge* (London: Routledge).

Oakley, K., Naylor, R. and Lee, D. (2006) *Giving Them What They Want: The Construction of the Public in 'Public Value'* (London: BOP Consulting).

Smith, A. (ed.) (1974) *British Broadcasting*, compiled and edited by Anthony Smith. (Newton Abbot: David and Charles Holdings).

Thumim, N. (2007) 'Mediating Self-Representations: Tensions Surrounding "Ordinary" Participation in Public Sector Projects', Unpublished PhD thesis, LSE, University of London

Thumim, N. (Forthcoming, 2009) ' "Everyone Has a Story to Tell": Mediation and Self-representation in Two UK Institutions', *International Journal of Cultural Studies*.

Van Zoonen, L. (2001) 'Desire and Resistance: Big Brother and the Recognition of Everyday Life', *Media, Culture & Society*, 23(5): 669–77.

3
Expansion and Autonomy: The Rise of the Business Press

Peter Kjær

Introduction

This chapter describes the rise of the modern business press. Its purpose is to characterize the overall expansion of what has become an important actor in the environment of business and to explore an important, yet understudied, dimension of the media-as-business intersection; namely, the autonomization of business news production, which has today emerged as a distinct field of practice.

The expansion of the business press over the past decades has been an expansion in several dimensions, including media platforms and outlets, circulation and readership, and the overall size of business news content relative to other forms of media content. The autonomization of business news production that has accompanied this expansion has involved two key dimensions:

- The professionalization of business journalism
- The parallel professionalization of sources.

A central feature of the modern business press that developed during the 1960s was an orientation towards a new and much broader market for business news. Rather than addressing the concerns and interests of the few – that is, stock market brokers or an elite of business leaders – the business press was to address 'decision-makers' throughout the economic and political sphere in society: top- and middle-managers in large corporations, individual shareholders, small investors, owners and managers of small and medium-sized firms, business school graduates and so on. This new market for business news held promises of an unprecedented expansion of the business press.

At the same time, the definition of business news changed. Rather than being guided by external criteria of quality and relevance – defined, for example, by the stock exchange, business associations or political institutions – business news was to be produced according to journalistic standards with a strong dedication to the newsworthy, as defined by the media. Instead of merely reproducing company statements or stock market information, the business press now was to offer its own stories and interpretations of economic processes, actors and outcomes. Hence, individual corporations could no longer expect favourable treatment but would have to face critical questioning and scrutiny by professional business journalists. This, in turn, required firms to open themselves up to the outside world and more readily share information with the public, a process that also required particular competencies on the side of business.

In other words, the rise of the business press was more than just an expansion into the media market. It also involved a transformation of the definition of business news and, potentially, even the interrelationship of business and media. In this chapter, I will describe this process of transformation.

My characterization of the rise of modern business press deals with the Nordic countries, but my overall claim is that, while there are important differences between industries, countries, regions and so on, there has been a general trend towards expansion in the business press in most industrialized market economies (see also Deephouse 2000; Carroll and McCombs 2003; Mazza and Pedersen 2004; Doyle 2006). At the same time, the analysis will also suggest that one needs to pay serious attention to the concrete ways in which business news is being defined and business–media relations are organized in particular contexts.

The analysis will be organized by a simple distinction between the *media order* and *the field of business news production*, inspired by Slaatta (2003) and Kjær and Slaatta (2007b: 16). The *media order* pertains to the organization of a field of mass media populated by particular media platforms and outlets occupying particular positions with regard to one another. In my account of the rise of the modern business press,

I will emphasize how media entrepreneurs in each country managed to change the business press and transform its overall position within national media orders from a peripheral position to its present position, which is characterized by an almost universal expansion.

The *field of business news production* (Kjær and Slaatta 2007b) pertains to the changing position of business journalism as it professionalized and as its counterparts in the business sector also embarked on a path of professionalization. The notion of 'field' attempts to capture, analytically, how a particular system of relations among actors emerges and becomes stabilized (see also DiMaggio 1991; DiMaggio and Powell 1991, Slaatta 2003; Benson and Neveu 2005; Grafström 2006). Here, my account will emphasize how business news production has become not only a recognized and relatively autonomous field as a result of parallel processes of professionalization, but also one that is characterized by a fragile negotiated order between journalists and their sources (Cook 1998; Kjær and Langer 2005).

The empirical basis for the analysis is historical data on the business press in Denmark, Finland, Norway and Sweden, which was collected as part of a Nordic comparative research project on the recent history of the business journalism (see Kjær and Slaatta 2007a). The Nordic project only indirectly dealt with the professionalization of sources, and I have therefore also drawn on existing studies of the development of the PR and communication industry in the Nordic countries (for example, Allern 1997; Ihlen 2004; Larsson 2005; Kjær and Morsing forthcoming) as well as information found on the webpages of the professional associations of the industry.

The four countries under study share a number of cultural and institutional features. They are all highly developed, export oriented, capitalist economies characterized by stable systems of parliamentary democracy, well-established welfare states that have been reformed over the last 20–25 years, a long history of corporatist policy-making and high levels of media literacy. There are also important cultural and linguistic differences between the four countries, as well as important differences in industrial structure; for example, in the relative prevalence of large firms, in the role of the agricultural sector, in foreign trade patterns and so on.

The similarities and differences might be important keys to explaining the pattern of expansion of the business press in the four countries. However, the ambition of the chapter is mainly descriptive, in the sense that it attempts to make a case for the relevance of considering the media-as-business in terms of how the business press has expanded and how business news production has become autonomized. Here, I will emphasize a few shared overall trends and not examine either national differences or their underlying causes in any systematic manner. However, I will consider, in the final section, the need for further and more detailed research into distinct characteristics of fields of news production within national media orders.

The creation and expansion of the modern business press

The modern business press emerged in the mid-1960s (Grafström 2006; Slaatta et al. 2007; see also Parsons 1989), and resulted, to a major degree, from the activities of a small group of entrepreneurs within national media contexts.

In Sweden, the Bonnier family, a media dynasty that had dominated the Swedish publishing industry for decades, was among the first to explore the potentials of developing a new approach to business coverage. They first focused on the magazine market, inspired by the success of *Business Week*, as well as the *Wall Street Journal* and the *Financial Times*. With the backing of Bonnier, the business weekly *Veckans Affärer* was launched in 1965 by four journalists and editors, none of whom had a background in business reporting. As an observer described it: 'The first editor in chief, von Platen, even disliked the whole idea of corporate news initially, and needed to be persuaded to work at the business weekly', but the shared idea was to 'transform business and economic information into journalistic products' (Grafström 2006: 91f.). *Veckans Affärer* proved to be a huge success that quickly out-performed its only rival, the old weekly *Affärsvärlden*, which had been re-launched the previous year.

The Swedish experience inspired Erik Rasmussen, a Danish journalist, who immediately attempted, unsuccessfully, to develop the business reporting of an old Copenhagen daily newspaper. Rasmussen was then hired by *Børsen*, a Danish business daily that had experienced a long period of decline. His job was to reform *Børsen*'s editorial profile, and soon Rasmussen and his companion Christian Lillelund mobilized the direct financial and managerial support of Bonnier, which became a large shareholder by 1969. In 1970, *Børsen* was re-launched as a modern business newspaper and soon experienced a dramatic growth in circulation.

In Norway, the modernization of the business press was very much associated with the work of Trygve Hegnar. An academic by training, Hegnar had a strong and enduring interest in journalism, and began developing ideas of a radically different type of business reporting while working for the established Norwegian business weekly *Farmand*. After having sought to reform *Farmand*, Hegnar started his own bi-weekly business and economy magazine entitled *Kapital*, which had a strong political and sensation oriented profile.

In Finland, the process of innovation began at the leading all-round daily *Helsingin Sanomat*, where, under the editor-in-chief *Aatos Erkko*, business reporting was strengthened in about 1970. Soon, the competitor *Uusi Soumi* followed suit by successfully launching a special weekly business section in 1972.

To the surprise of many sceptical observers, this early investment in business journalism proved a commercial success, and gradually the business press began a long process of expansion within the four national media orders. Both the new business magazines and the reformed business dailies experienced increasing sales, and soon a number of rivals and spin-offs were introduced (Slaatta et al. 2007: 48ff.). In 1976, a new Swedish business daily, *Dagens Industri*, was established that, after a slow beginning, became a major success story in the Swedish media market from 1980 onwards. In Denmark, the monthly *Erhvervsbladet* became a daily in 1974. In Norway, *Kapital* encountered competition from the rival *Økonomisk Rapport* from 1974 and from the old, but reformed, commerce daily *Norges Handels- og Sjøfartstidende* from around 1975. Finally, in Finland, the old business newspaper *Kauppalehti*, which had traditionally had a secure position in the market but was being challenged especially by *Helsingin Sanomat*, was successfully reformed in 1977 as was the business magazine *Talouselämä*.

From the mid- and late 1970s, the emphasis on business news spread to the mainstream press, where a number of newspapers established dedicated business pages, sections or supplements. In this context, business news proved key to the survival of ailing, old newspapers that, with the withering away of party loyalties and political regulation, were facing tough competition in the media market. Thus, apart from the Finnish newspapers mentioned, the Swedish *Svenska*

Dagbladet, the Danish *Jyllands-Posten* and *Berlingske Tidende*, and the Norwegian *Dagbladet* developed a more distinct business profile.

By the mid-1980s, the business press entered a phase of rapid growth in several dimensions. New outlets appeared in all four national contexts and an ever-increasing number of publications – such as business magazines, management newsletters, and financial dailies – found their way to the market. At the same time, circulation figures soared. Thus, in Sweden the circulation of the specialized business press (dailies and magazines) increased from about 10 million copies in 1984 to almost 50 million by 2000 (Grafström 2006: 50).

Around 1990, the expansion also came to include the electronic media as regular newscasts and programmes on business and economy were launched, by commercial broadcasters and, soon, also by public service broadcasters. Finally, towards the late 1990s, business news production moved on to both general and highly specialized Internet platforms offering both instant news reporting around the clock and in-depth analysis of news events, aimed either at the general public or on a subscription only basis (Grafström et al. 2006; Slaatta et al. 2007: 58ff.).

The expansion of business journalism was not only an expansion in outlets and readers, but even in the total and relative number of business news items in individual media outlets. Figure 3.1 depicts the number of articles per week dedicated to economic topics in eight newspapers in the Nordic countries between 1960 and 2000.

While also showing significant differences between individual outlets, Figure 3.1 indicates how the total number of articles has more than doubled.[1] Importantly, the figure also shows how the expansion in economic content was relatively modest, until the 1980s (Figure 3.2). The number of articles dedicated specifically to business topics also increased dramatically during the 1980s and 1990s relative to, for example, labour market coverage or coverage of economic policy.

Thus, from the perspective of national media orders, the position of the business press had been radically transformed over a 40-year period starting in the mid 1960s and culminating in the 1990s. There had been a development and expansion of outlets dedicated to business news. Similarly, the consumption of business news increased dramatically, and the production of business content had become an important concern in most media platforms.

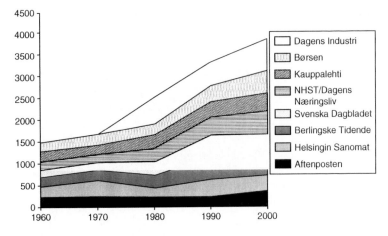

Figure 3.1 Economic content in Nordic newspapers (number of articles per week)

Source: (Kjær et al. 2007: 132).

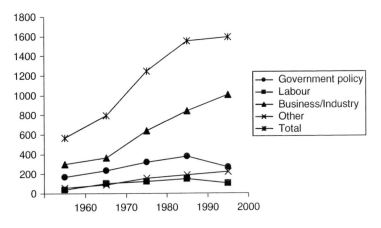

Figure 3.2 Dominant themes in economic content (number of articles per week)

Source: (Kjær et al. 2007: 146).

The field of business news production: Professionalization and counter-professionalization

Alongside the expansion of the business press in national media orders, the field of news production underwent a process of transformation. This transformation can be described as a process of autonomization of news production whereby journalists operating in the field attained professional independence, but also, importantly, a process whereby there was a reorganization and professionalization on the side of news sources. Taken together, these professionalization processes constituted a field of business news production as a field in its own right, but also introduced into this field a particular negotiated relationship between two groups engaged in a mutual production of business news.

Professionalization is here taken to denote the practices through which these groups sought to create and stabilize a position for themselves in relation to the production of news – by defining business news as a distinct field of activity governed by particular rules of the game, by seeking to define the competences required to engage in the field, and even by defining expectations with regard to other actors in the field and so on (see also Grafström 2006: 49ff.; Allern 1997: 20ff; Larsson 2005; Ainamo et al. 2006, for a discussion on journalists and corporate communicators as professions).

I first describe professionalization from the perspective of journalists, before turning to the viewpoint of the sources, and end with a consideration of the emergent field of business news production.

The professionalization of (business) journalism

In the context of journalism, business news production only gradually became a distinct and recognized activity. Early attempts to expand business coverage were met with scepticism, especially among journalists who saw business coverage as little more than free advertising. The innovators in the field, however, stressed how business reporters were to no longer to be 'the mouthpieces of business' but were to become independent and critical players in the field (Fonsmark 1996: 189). Also, the ideal business journalist 'wrote about business in an intelligible way' (Grafström 2006: 99). This required new competencies on the side of reporters.

Up until the 1960s, the existing business and economy desks had been staffed by a mix of people, few of whom had particular skills in business journalism. On one hand, there were journalists who, without having any particular insight into business issues, had taken on the responsibility of producing daily business reports. On the other hand, there were, more occasionally, economic or technical experts who had ventured into the media world but who had little training in news journalism. One of the first tasks facing the entrepreneurs in the business press was that of recruiting new staff or changing the competencies of the existing staff.

Two different strategies can be found (Grafström 2006):

- Some outlets focused on recruiting candidates with a background in economics or business studies, subsequently training them in journalism so as to foster a staff with a high level of expertise that could relate to the complexities of the world of business and finance
- Some outlets recruited skilled journalists and then trained them extensively in how to understand business and economy, producing a staff with a clear dedication to journalistic norms and standards. As there were no educational programmes in business journalism, the development of competencies in modern business journalism thus consisted of on-the-job-training.

At the same time, business journalists benefited from the general strengthening of journalistic training as schools of journalism and academic programmes for journalists were established from the 1960s onwards.

The modernization of business journalism also entailed a new relationship to the audience. While the new business journalists were rarely in opposition to the idea of capitalism or a market economy, they saw themselves as writing on behalf of a broader segment of the public, rather than only top-managers or powerful owners and investors. This was mirrored in the visual and textual formats of business newspapers and business magazines. There was an early emphasis on conveying some of the drama of the business world to the readers, while also providing complex information in an accessible form. Business newspapers and magazines quickly moved towards a visual aesthetics similar to that of the tabloid newspapers, and also were swift to make use of visual aids such as photographs, illustrations and so on. The most radical in this respect was probably Trygve Hegnar's *Kapital* in Norway, which pioneered in the use of 'ugly' posters in newsstands, and simple and dramatic headlines on front pages, but even *Dagens Industri*, *Kauppalehti* and *Børsen* adopted a visual profile that emphasized photos, large front page headings and other visual aids.

Finally, the modernization of business journalism entailed building new relationships to business and business sources; that is, a critical distance on behalf of the reader. Most fundamentally, this had to do with the right of journalists to 'pose questions' to business and the need for business representatives to provide answers to such questions – for the sake of business and society. Rather than merely being a passive relay, journalists were 'to take actively part and to take stands' (cf. Ainamo et al. 2006: 627). This required that the media and journalists be able to disregard their immediate financial interest in pleasing advertisers, as well as servicing outside institutions, by providing various forms of routine business information. Instead, they were to focus solely on newsworthy events, firms and so on.[2] It also required a basic attitude of openness on the side of business, and a willingness to disclose financial and other types of information publicly. This was by no means a given in the early years. The news oriented journalism was met with some degree of hostility by the business elite, who accused it of being sensationalist and directly harmful to business and industry (for example, Fonsmark 1996: 190f.). However, gradually an idea of independent business journalism took foothold and, from the 1980s onwards, business journalists also began pursuing investigative ideals of journalism. In the case of Denmark, this orientation was, among other things, indicated by the awards in journalism given to business journalism. Between 1980 and 2003, the most prestigious award, the Cavling Prize, was given to business journalists five times – each time, for investigative journalism (Schultz 2006). To be sure, investigative journalism only constitutes a limited part of modern business journalism, but – today, at least – no one seriously challenges the right of journalists to scrutinize financial statements, corporate strategies, mergers and acquisitions and so on, or the obligation of firms to present information to the public about key business issues and decisions.

The professionalization of corporate communication

Public relations and corporate communication underwent a parallel process of professionalization, especially during the 1980s and 1990s. Although the notion of public relations had already been introduced in the Nordic countries in the late 1940s,[3] it was not until the late 1960s that public relations gained recognition as a more distinct area of activity. In Sweden, the recognition of public relations was linked to the challenges posed to large corporations in relation to pollution problems and in relation to broader debates on economic democracy (Larsson 2005: 77ff). The initial expansion took place during the 1970s and early 1980s within large firms who established 'information departments' that produced press releases, information materials, staff magazines and so on.

All four countries experienced a period of rapid growth in the communication industry from 1985 until 1995, as the market for private consultants in PR experienced a period of intense expansion,[4] and the overall number of practitioners in the area of PR and communication increased from just a few hundred in each country to several thousands (for example, Allern 1987: 184ff.; Larsson 2005: 129ff.). With this expansion, a notion emerged whereby public relations and corporate communication was perceived as a distinct activity – having to do not only with the ongoing production of corporate information, but also with the overall organization of communication. Communication required a special strategic expertise that entailed direct access to management – first, in the handling of distinct problems such as investor relations, 'public affairs' and crises management (Larsson 2005: 117) and, later, as an approach to the management of all relevant communicative processes within a corporation, among other things known as 'integrated communication' (Christensen and Morsing 2005).

In this process, one sought to specify the expertise involved in communication by emphasizing the need for systematic competencies. Already, in the early years of PR-clubs and networks, the need for shared ethical guidelines had been stressed and, in the late 1980s, this concern resurfaced as both associations of communication workers and associations of PR consultancies passed new or revised ethical guidelines for members articulating both the overall ideals of public relations (that is, its contribution to democracy, transparency and efficiency), as well as the particular obligations and competencies of practitioners in relation to clients and customers. As the professional associations of communicators or information workers expanded, they began to offer seminars and courses on a systematic basis, introducing practitioners to news ideas and practices in the field. Also, prizes were awarded to distinguished practitioners to motivate competence-building and mutual learning. Finally, the industry was also concerned with the creation of academic degrees and programmes in the area of information and communication, which were established in all four countries from the 1970s and onwards.

The professionalization of PR brought with it a change in how information and communication professionals related to the media and to journalism – and to other actors in the field. There were several issues at stake, here. Until the late 1960s, the relationship between business journalists and corporate sources could be characterized as one of close ties and 'reciprocal trust', as it was described in the Finnish case (Ainamo et al. 2006: 624), while the following decades entailed a growing distance between the two sides as suggested by clashes between media and business over corporate reporting during the 1970s (Ainamo et al. 2006: 626; Fonsmark 1996: 190ff.).

Indeed, in the early years a key concern facing those wanting to promote PR practices was to demonstrate how this was not just an outgrowth of advertising, and how PR actually had to do with 'social contact'; that is, the relations between firms and 'society' (Ihlen 2004; Larsson 2005). In this context, it became pivotal to distance PR from marketing and narrow commercial interests. Although strong undertones of social obligation have persisted, the expansion of public relations during the 1980s and 1990s – along with the overall liberalization of the Nordic welfare societies, and the growing importance of investor relations – has entailed an easing of relations to marketing, as well as a stronger strategic orientation of PR. In other words, PR practices are now seen as an integral part of how firms relate strategically to the market, as well as to non-market stakeholders. In this context, the media are an important means with to manage corporate reputations (and identity), and are a strategic influence on other actors and conditions of action.

The trajectory of parallel professionalization – three phases of field formation

The dialectical processes of professionalization, of business journalism and PR, and of corporate communication, both constituted and transformed what can be described as an autonomous field of business news production. Based on the description above, at least three phases of field formation can be distinguished.

1. A phase of *nascent field formation*[5] in which both business communication and journalism began to be recognized as possible areas of activity – as signalled, first, by the development of early professional bodies in the field of PR during the 1950s, and by innovation within the field of business journalism during the 1960s. However, business–media relations were largely governed by the traditional and highly routinized bonds between big business, business associations and a loyal business press.

2. A phase of *emerging mutual independence and recognition*, during the 1970s and early 1980s, as journalists began to pursue more active strategies of journalistic news production, while large corporations began to build up capacities in the area of press relations and information handling. This phase was initially characterized by strong conflicts over the rules of engagement but, gradually, certain mutual expectations and routines emerged, signalling that business news was at least to be co-determined by journalistic criteria. As firms became accustomed to journalistic scrutiny, and began to realize the potentials of media visibility, the corporate contribution to news production became more organized.

3. A phase of *field autonomy* from the mid-1980s, in which business journalists experienced an unprecedented growth in their sub-field while also encountering a remarkable growth in the PR industry as a whole. Commercialization and popularization were important aspects of the expansion of business journalism, while PR and corporate communication practices on the side of business changed from being a largely practical concern that only incidentally became a managerial concern into a sub-field increasingly informed by a strategic management perspective. In this phase, the production of business news became a domain governed by professionals on both sides – both adhering to particular criteria, goals and strategic interests in mutual

interactions over news production (See also Grafström et al. 2006; Grafström and Pallas 2006).

Today, the field of business news production remains an important environment for both media and business. At the same time, a number of recent trends might challenge or transform the field in important ways.

Recent trends

One significant trend is what journalists and editors refer to as 'reader orientation'. A recent example of this is found at the Danish daily *Berlingske Tidende*, which, in the face of strong competition, decided to pursue a strategy of extreme orientation towards the needs of the reader, in terms of how news products were designed and newsroom practices were managed. Here, journalistic criteria of relevance might risk being challenged by ideas of usefulness or immediate relevance to the reader, and by the need for branding of media products in a highly competitive media markets. In this context, as one editor phrased it, readers might not want 'hair-in-the-soup' stories offered by business journalists. The recent expansion of various forms of consumer journalism seems to point in the same direction, where emphasis might shift from business news to other types of media products, such as rankings, quality tests and so on.

Another challenge to the field arising from the side of business sources has been the increasing professionalization of investor relations and the role of securities analysts. With the booming stock markets and the growing interest in financial investment, securities analysts not only play an important role as media sources (and commentators), but also, on the part of corporate communicators, come to take precedence as targets of corporate communication efforts. A Swedish analysis of the publication of quarterly reports thus showed how large corporations increasingly downplayed media relations and, rather, emphasized the more 'direct' access to the marketplace provided by the analysts (Grafström et al. 2006).

A final trend, which is related to both those already given, is the increasing specialization of circuits and platforms of communication as the Internet becomes increasingly important to all the actors involved. On the part of the media, this has led to highly specialized news services catering to very distinct audience segments with very particular needs: immediate financial updates, quick news analyses, market evaluations and so on. On the part of business, this has entailed the creation of distinct media platforms by large firms – sometimes, as an outgrowth of corporate websites or investor newsletters but now providing not only corporate messages, but also more general news about the industry, markets and regulatory initiatives (Kjær 2007b).

All three trends challenge the autonomy of the field, no so much by shifting the balance of power from one side to the other – as is often suggested by observers (for example, Davis 2000) – but, rather, by challenging the notion of business news as something that is produced in a particular organized interaction between journalists and their corporate sources. Suddenly, it seems that journalists might not need corporate sources to meet readers' needs, and firms might not need journalists to communicate with the market. Rather, other actors and relational arrangements might become important to news production and communication, the nature of which remains to be investigated in greater detail.

Conclusion

The rise of the modern business press has now been described as a process of expansion and autonomization. It has been described as an expansion within national media orders, whereby the business press has undergone a prolonged and highly successful expansion in terms of outlets, readers, and the total and relative volume of content. It has been described as a process of autonomization, whereby a journalistic sub-field has emerged governed by its own professional standards and, on the other hand, a sub-field of corporate communication has experienced a parallel process of professionalization. Taken together, the professionalization of business journalism and sources constitute an autonomous field of business news production.

By stipulating the existence of an autonomous field of business news production, we are alerted to a number of pertinent issues for further research and discussion. Most importantly, by interpreting business–media interactions from a field perspective, the relation of journalists to their sources cannot simply be examined and evaluated in light of a general model of public opinion but should include an understanding both of the particular rules of the game and the particular positions occupied by the two sides in the relationship. Certainly, professionalization involves ideas of both higher purpose and independency, but the meaning of those terms is specific to the field. They might also vary over time – as the field matures, or as positions change in the field – and they might, of course, also vary between various national or regional contexts. In a Nordic context, one has just begun to pay serious attention to the emergent rules of the game in the journalist–source nexus (see Slaatta 2003; Kristensen 2005; Larsson 2005; Grafström 2006).

There is also a need to understand, in detail, how relations actually play out between the two sides. Although attempts have been made, it is extremely difficult – at an aggregate level – to measure the balance of forces in the field. Heuristically, contrasting the number of journalists with the number of corporate communicators makes good sense and suggests how journalists are being pressured by increasingly professionalised sources (Allern 1997). At the same time, one should take into account the unique resources held by journalists in the particular relationship – as co-producers of symbolic capital (Slaatta 2003; Tsoukas 1999) in a highly competitive economy of attention – and also consider the particular strategies pursued by the two sides in particular areas of the field. The source-relations of a high profile business magazine editor might, thus, differ significantly from those of a journalist of a business supplement of a small daily newspaper. Ericsson et al.'s (1989) idea of examining the negotiation of news between journalists and their sources should definitely be pursued vigorously, even in the field of business news, with detailed attention being paid to actual processes of news-making in media organizations and in corporate communication departments (see also Grafström and Pallas 2007; Pallas 2007).

Finally, there is a need to understand, in a field context, the particular discourses of economic activity that are being produced and circulated in the form of economic news – and the effects these discursive frameworks might have (see also Gavin 1998). The business press and the field of business news production have been permeated by different ideas of what 'business' or 'the economy' is, how it should be represented and how it should be acted upon. Historically, a *doxa* informed by the notion of productive enterprise in a national economy has given way to notions of firms as financial assets in a global economy (Kjær 2007a). There might also be important variations between, for example, news discourses emphasizing wealth, conspicuous consumption and personal finance, as opposed to discourses emphasizing leadership, investment and market change (cf. Slaatta 2003: 183ff. and Tienari et al. 2007). In a Nordic context, there now exists a number of analyses that have begun to study both the 'embeddedness' of news discourses in larger discursive and ideological frameworks, as well as the field-specific character of the meanings offered by the media – in terms of forms of legitimization, identification and means-end frames (Vaara and Tienari 2002; Tienari et al. 2003). Here, a field perspective would entail an interest in the constitutive effects of such meanings, both on the side of the media and on the side of business (Morsing 1999; see also Chen and Meindl 1991; Mazza and Alvarez 2000; Hayward et al. 2004; Rindova et al. 2006).

Taken together, exploring these three paths of research might hopefully lead to a well-founded conceptual understanding of the role of the business press and the conditions under which business news is being produced, as well as an appreciation of the highly contextual nature of the business–media relationship.

Notes

1. In terms of the share of space, the expansion of economic news was even more dramatic. Although our data here are less reliable, it appears that, due to the growth in the size of individual articles, the space taken up by business and economy news grew by 300 or 400 per cent from 1970 onwards.
2. In several instances, this collided with the readers' mundane interest in stock market quotations and so on, and other traditional offerings of the business press. After first doing away with such routine content, dailies such as Børsen in Denmark were forced to reintroduce it after strong protests from readers (Fonsmark 1996).
3. In Finland, Sweden and Norway, 'clubs' or networks for PR practitioners (or press officers) were established as early as 1947–50, although the membership basis appears to have been quite limited in the early decades. A Danish PR association was established in 1961.
4. Comparative data for all four countries are not available, but the expansion of the consultancy field is, in part, mirrored by both the establishment of associations for PR bureaus in all four countries during the 1980s and 1990s (Finland 1983, Denmark 1988, Norway 1988, Sweden 1990) and the growth in membership of these organizations.

5. The notion of a 'nascent field' comes from Grafström's (2006) analysis of Swedish business journalism.

References

Ainamo, A., Tienari, J. and Vaara, E. (2006) 'Between West and East: A Social History of Business Journalism in Cold War Finland', *Human Relations*, 59(5): 611–36.

Ainamo, A, Tienari, J. and Vaara, E. (2007) 'The Professionalization of Business Journalism in Finland', in P. Kjær and T. Slaatta (eds), *Mediating Business. The Expansion of Business Journalism* (Copenhagen: Copenhagen Business School Press).

Allern, S. (1997) Når kildene byr opp til dans. Søkelys på PR-byråene og journalistikken (Oslo: Pax).

Benson, R. and Neveu, E. (2005) *Bourdieu and the Journalistic Field* (Cambridge: Polity Press).

Carroll, C.E. and McCombs, M. (2003) 'Agenda-Setting Effects of Business News on the Public's Images and Opinions about Major Corporations', *Corporation Reputation Review*, 6(1): 36–46.

Chen, C.C. and Meindl, J.R. (1991) 'The Construction of Leadership Images in the Popular Press: The Case of Donald Burr and People Express', *Administrative Science Quarterly*, 36(4): 521–51.

Christensen, L.T. and Morsing, M. (2005) *Bagom Corporate Communication* (Copenhagen: Samfundslitteratur).

Cook, T. (1998) *Governing with the News: The News Media as a Political Institution* (Chicago: University of Chicago Press).

Davis, A. (2000) 'Public Relations, Business News and the Reproduction of Corporate Elite Power', *Journalism*, 1(3): 282–304.

Deephouse, D.L. (2000) 'Media Reputation as a Strategic Resource: An Integration of Mass Communication and Resource-Based Theories', *Journal of Management*, 26(6): 1091–112.

DiMaggio, Paul J. (1991) 'Constructing an Organisational Field as a Professional Project. US Art Museums 1920–1940', in Walter W. Powell and Paul J. DiMaggio (eds, *The New Institutionalism in Organisational Analysis* (Chicago: Chicago University Press).

DiMaggio, Paul J. and Powell, Walter W. (1991) [1983] 'The Iron Cage Revisited – Institutional Isomorphism and Collective Rationality in Organisational Fields', in Walter W. Powell and Paul J. DiMaggio (eds), *The New Institutionalism in Organisational Analysis* (Chicago: Chicago University Press).

Doyle, G. (2006) 'Financial News Journalism: A Post-Enron Analysis of Approaches towards Economic and Financial News Production in the UK', *Journalism: Theory, Practice and Criticism*, 7(4): 433–52.

Ericson, R.V., Baranek, P.M. and Chan, J.B.L. (1989) *Negotiating Control: A Study of News Sources* (Milton Keynes: Open University Press).

Fonsmark, H. (1996) Børsens Danmarkshistorie 1896–1996 (Copenhagen: Børsens Forlag).

Gavin, N. (ed.) (1998) *The Economy, Media and Public Knowledge* (London: Leicester University Press).

Grafström, M. (2006) 'The Development of Swedish Business Journalism. Historical Roots of an Organisational Field', Doctoral thesis no. 121, Department of Business Studies, Uppsala University.

Grafström, M., Grünberg, J., Pallas, J. and Windell, K. (2006) Ekonominyhetens väg: Från kvartalsrapporter till ekonominyheter (Stockholm: SNS Medieforum).

Grafström, M. and Pallas, J. (2007) 'The Negotiation of Business News', in P. Kjær and T. Slaatta (eds) *Mediating Business. The Expansion of Business Journalism* (Copenhagen: Copenhagen Business School Press).

Hayward, M.L.A., Rindova, V.P. and Pollock, T.G. (2004) 'Believing One's Own Press: The Causes and Consequences of CEO Celebrity', *Strategic Management Journal*, 25: 637–53.

Ihlen, Ø. (2004) *Informasjon and samfunnskontrakt: Perspektiver og praksis* (Oslo: Fagbokforlaget).

Kjær, P. (2007a) 'Changing Constructions of Business and Society in the News', in P. Kjær and T. Slaatta (eds), *Mediating Business. The Expansion of Business Journalism* (Copenhagen: Copenhagen Business School Press).

Kjær, P. (2007b) 'Erhvervsjournalistikkens Ekspansive Evolution', Published 10 October at http://www.kommunikationsforum.dk/default. asp?articleid=12858

Kjær, P. and Langer, R. (2005) 'Infused with News Value: Management, Managerial Knowledge and the Institutionalization of Business News', *Scandinavian Journal of Management*, 21(2): 209–33.

Kjær, P. and Morsing, M. (forthcoming) 'Corporate Reputation and the News Media in Denmark', in C. Carroll, *Corporate Reputation and News Media all over the World*.

Kjær, P. and Slaatta, T. (eds) (2007a) *Mediating Business. The Expansion of Business Journalism* (Copenhagen: Copenhagen Business School Press).

Kjær, P. and Slaatta, T. (2007b) 'Mediating Business. Toward a Relational Perspective', in P. Kjær and T. Slaatta (eds) *Mediating Business. The Expansion of Business Journalism* (Copenhagen: Copenhagen Business School Press).

Kjær, P., Erkama, N. and Grafström, M. (2007) 'Transforming Business News Content. A Comparative Analysis', in P. Kjær and T. Slaatta (eds) *Mediating Business. The Expansion of Business Journalism* (Copenhagen: Copenhagen Business School Press).

Kristensen, Nete Nørgaard (2005) 'Kommunikationsbranchens medierelationer – professionelle netværk, kommunikationsfaglige perspektiver og mediedemokratiske konsekvenser'. Modinet Working Paper 19 Copenhagen University, Copenhagen.

Larsson, L. (2005) *Upplysning och propaganda. Utvecklingen av svensk PR och information* (Lund: Studentlitteratur).

Mazza, C. and Alvarez, J.L. (2000) 'Haute Couture and Prêt-à-Porter: The Popular Press and the Diffusion of Management Practices', *Organisation Studies*, 21(3): 567–88.

Mazza, C. and Pedersen, J.S. (2004) 'From Press to E-media? The Transformation of an Organisational Field', *Organisation Studies*, 25(6): 875–95.

Morsing, M. (1999) 'The Media Boomerang: The Media's Role in Changing Identity by Changing Image', *Corporate Reputation Review*, 2(2): 116–36.

Pallas, J. (2007) 'Talking Organisations. Corporate Media Work and Negotiation of Local Practice', PhD Dissertation, Uppsala University.

Parsons, W.D. (1989) *The Power of the Financial Press. Journalism and Economic Opinion in Britain and America* (Aldershot: Edward Elgar Press).

Rindova, V.P., Pollock, T.G. and Hayward, M.L.A. (2006) 'Celebrity Firms: The Social Construction of Market Popularity', *Academy of Management Review*, 31(1): 50–71.

Schultz, I. (2006) *Bag nyhederne* (Fredriksberg: Forlaget Samfundslitteratur).

Slaatta, Tore (2003) *Den norske medieorden. Posisjoner og privilegier* (Oslo: Gyldendal Akademisk).

Slaatta, T. with Kjær, P., Grafström, M. and Erkama, N. (2007) 'The Nordic Business Press and the New Field of Business Journalism (1960–2005)', in P. Kjær and T. Slaatta (eds), *Mediating Business. The Expansion of Business Journalism* (Copenhagen: Copenhagen Business School Press).

Tienari, J., Vaara, E. and Björkman, I. (2003) 'Global Capitalism Meets National Spirit: Discourses in Media Texts on a Cross-Border Acquisition', *Journal of Management Inquiry*, 12(4): 377–93.

Tienari, J., Vaara, E. and Erkama, N. (2007) 'The Gospel According to the Global Market. How Journalists Frame Ownership in the Case of Nokia in Finland', in P. Kjær and T. Slaatta (eds), M*ediating Business. The Expansion of Business Journalism* (Copenhagen: Copenhagen Business School Press).

Tsoukas, H. (1999) 'David and Goliath in the Risk Society. Making Sense of the Conflict Between Shell and Greenpeace in the North Sea', *Organisation*, 6(1): 499–528.

Vaara, E. and Tienari, J. (2002) 'Justification, Legitimization and Naturalization of Mergers and Acquisitions: A Critical Discourse Analysis of Media Texts', *Organisation*, 9(2): 275–303.

Part II
Media in Business

4
Strategic Auto-Communication in Identity–Image Interplay: The Dynamics of Mediatizing Organizational Identity

Annemette Kjærgaard and Mette Morsing

Introduction

Through a longitudinal study, we explore how organizational identity change is influenced by external stakeholders. We analyze how a strategic auto-communicative process, in terms of a company's stimulation of mass media attention, serves as a catalyst for identity construction within the organization. Our findings demonstrate the importance of mass media for influencing identity and for creating strong member identification. Moreover, they illustrate the process by which the mediatization of organizational identity, which at first sight might seem oriented towards external audiences, could have significant influence on internal audiences and their self-description. Our empirical data derive from a 10-year study of the Danish hearing instrument provider Oticon A/S, which has been celebrated by the media for its organizational transformation from a steep hierarchy to a matrix organization in a process that seemed to happen overnight. While Oticon's overwhelmingly positive massive media attention is perhaps difficult to replicate, we suggest that it acts as a critical case through which to investigate how mediatization influences organizational identity dynamics in general.

This chapter is organized as follows. First, theories on identity and strategic auto-communication are presented and related to the media. Next, the case study of Oticon is described, and we discuss the contribution of our findings. Finally, conclusions are drawn and implications for management in the context of the media and further topics of research are suggested.

Identity

Organizational identity contributes to the daily sense-making in organizations and helps answer the questions: 'Who are we?' and 'Where are we going?' In this study, we draw on Pratt and Rafaeli's definition of identity as the self-categorizations individuals use to denote their sense of belonging (that is, identification) with particular human aggregates or groups (1997). In our case, we identify a clear shift in members' self-categorization. This shift does not derive from a change in their sense of belonging to different human aggregates or groups but, rather, from a change in the way they discursively construct themselves as members of the same organization. We empirically observe how, over a 10-year period, managers and employees upheld a strong sense of belonging to the same social group – Oticon A/S. What did change during this time was the way they made sense of the group. Initially viewed as old corporate elite, distinguished and noble – a kind of tacit untouchable, it transformed into a rejuvenated and energetic innovative cutting-edge firm – an internationally profiled corporate brand. In this renewed process of self-categorization, language becomes a central concept for the understanding of identity change. Astley and Zammuto (1992) state that language is at the face of identity, while Fairclough (1992) says the importance of language is intensified, as language shapes action and thereby becomes inseparable from action. Our study demonstrates how the mediatization of an organizational identity change enacted the identity change in a process where the very incorporation of a new language of identity played a major role.

To further understand how Oticon's identity change came about, we address Dutton and Dukerich's definition of identity as 'the way insiders think outsiders perceive the organization's construed external image' (1991). Although we take an interest in unfolding the media's perceptions of Oticon over time, our interest is not so much the media's construction of the broad palette of narratives about the same company but, rather, how organizational members choose to make sense of this broad palette, and how their own sense-making influences ongoing identity construction. Dutton and Dukerich's identity definition brings attention to the role of external stakeholders in internal identity construction in contrast to other identity theorizing that emphasizes how members, isolated from institutional influence, make sense of themselves (for example, Albert and Whetten 1985). Our study of Oticon's identity change demonstrates the importance of this 'inside-out and outside-in' perspective, as we observed how insiders, in particular, made sense of themselves when confronting their own representation in the media. Moreover, our study shows the importance of language as a means of identity change, as we observed how members began referring to themselves in ways that mirrored or reflected the ways Oticon was represented in the media. As such, we build on the social constructionist idea that who we are is a self-reflective process, shaped as a function of how we see ourselves in relation to others (Berger and Luckman 1966). Our study is an illustration of how organization members construct their 'selves' by comparing and contrasting themselves with 'significant others' (Mead 1934).

Our case study also brings attention to how identity is a self-reflective question, as also suggested by Albert and Whetten (1985) and, more importantly, how not only actors, but also actants (Callon 1987) stimulate self-reflective questions. Although theorization on organizational identity often argues that identity is an ever-ongoing construction, in practice, organizations experience how slowly old values and norms die (Schein 1986). The question is to what extent the self-reflective questions are asked by the organization itself and, moreover, if they are asked by someone (actor) or something (actant) to whom organizational members attribute sufficient authority and legitimacy. Are they 'significant others' or just 'others'? Do organizational members pay attention to the questions, and do the questions have any significant impact on their identity? Prior research (Gioia and Chittipeddi 1991; Ginzel et al. 1993; Elsbach and Kramer 1996) has shown how insiders might have a tendency to reinforce their identity as they are faced with a different and slightly less positive perception of the company as presented by outsiders. While agents of change – in the shape of management consultants or rankings – are frequently used in practice, our study brings attention to how the media might very effectively ask organizational members self-reflective questions that stimulate identity construction. Dutton and Dukerich's study of identity change at the Port Authority of New York and New Jersey was the first identity study to point at the potential role of the media for identity change (1991). They showed that organizational members did not change their perception of themselves until the media depicted the organization in a less favourable light. Building on their study, we suggest that, in contemporary organizations, the media serve as a 'significant other' that raises self-reflective questions, and thereby engages organizational members in identity construction.

Strategic auto-communication

In this chapter, we add a twist to prior studies on the media's role in organizational identity, as we observe how the company itself stimulated the media attention. In Dutton and Dukerich's study, as well as in other identity studies where the media influences ongoing identity construction (Gioia and Chittipeddi 1991; Ginzel et al. 1993; Elsbach and Kramer 1996), the media's representation of the respective organization springs from its own research and is not stimulated from 'within'. Drawing on the theory of auto-communication, we develop a model conceptualizing the processes through which a company from 'within' strategically communicates a desired new identity in the media with the intention of influencing organizational members' own perceptions of their identity. In 1983, Broms and Gardberg pointed out the auto-communicative elements in all corporate messages – that is, that while external stakeholders are the target audience, reception by organizational members is part of the sender's considerations in composing the messages (Broms and Gardberg 1983). In his legendary article from 1997, Lars Christensen drew attention to the limited awareness in the few existing studies of auto-communication concerning 'the fact that organizational self-talk is legitimized and approved by way of the environment' (1997: 203). He emphasizes the meta-text as a vital element of auto-communication – that is, that corporate messages do not exist in an environmental vacuum, and that their auto-communicational importance has more to do with the context in which they appear than the messages themselves. Messages are sent from a 'corporate I' to a variety of stakeholders and, as they return to the 'corporate I', they have been given a new and stronger status. When companies communicate about themselves as an 'ideal corporate we' – for example, as a 'green company' – they tell themselves, and perhaps reconfirm, that they are 'green'. However, and equally important according to Christensen (1997), they show that they adhere to institutional expectations for contemporary organizations, and that they can expect to be recognized as legitimate partners in society (DiMaggio and Powell 1991). The external audience's acknowledgment of the messages transforms the messages from texts to meta-texts, as they are attributed an external authority and status. The organization manages to tell itself how it should look ideally and, at the same time, it also shows itself that it is capable of interacting with other concurrent discourses, expressing itself in the appropriate media. In other words, the organization demonstrates to itself that it is respected 'out there' (Christensen et al. 2008).

In theory, the meta-text is activated every time a corporate message is sent out to external stakeholders and simultaneously read by organizational members. According to Christensen and Cheney (2000), the process of auto-communication happens despite the sender's lack of knowledge about the positive or negative reactions of external stakeholders: the 'age communicates through its very existence' (Christensen and Cheney 2000: 252). In fact, Christensen and Cheney claim that often the corporate messages are of higher relevance for the sender than for the external receivers. They provide the convincing example of corporate websites where many companies spend multiple resources on continuously designing and updating their websites without any specific guarantee that anyone out there is reading the messages at all. Other examples are corporate value statements or corporate social responsibility (CSR) reports (Morsing 2006). While external stakeholders might take some interest in corporate websites, value statements and CSR reports, the theory of auto-communication posits that organizational members are the primary readers of these corporate messages. Members read and identify with their own corporate messages with great interest, as their reputation and recognition are at stake. In this way, the processes of auto-communication serve to establish and reinforce corporate self-images and identities.

While organizational members are the key stakeholders of auto-communicative projects, this does not mean that external stakeholders are superfluous. External stakeholders provide authority and legitimacy to corporate messages, and thereby assist their transformation into significant meta-texts, hence reinforcing the organizational identity as the messages return to employees. According to the theory of auto-communication, which takes an analytical approach, this process happens as a passive endorsement as companies send out corporate messages that return to organizational members (Morsing 2006).

In this chapter, adding a strategic approach to the theory, we argue that the theory of auto-communication underestimates how insiders might strategically target other insiders as their primary audience, as they design and communicate messages that appear to be oriented toward external stakeholders. In our case study, the CEO of Oticon systematically engaged the media in publishing articles about a new organizational identity he envisioned in order to change employee perceptions of themselves. In this sense, auto-communication is used strategically to stimulate the enactment of an identity change among employees according to a CEO's vision. Acknowledging the instrumental desire to stimulate a positive cycle of auto-communication with positive member identification, this chapter points to how managers emphatically speak to their employees through the media. The managerial messages are provided with another type of status and public legitimacy as employees are exposed to them in the media, and receive them other than merely directly from the manager at an internal company meeting.

The empirical study

The ongoing construction and reconstruction of a celebrity firm

Our findings build on a longitudinal study based on qualitative interviews supplemented by a tracking of Oticon being mentioned in the media from 1992 to 2000. The data, which show how the CEO presented a new desired identity and framed the company as a celebrity firm, also show how the media ascribed celebrity status to the organization by highlighting different features throughout the course of many years. We accentuate how this ongoing celebrity status influenced the way members made sense of their organizational identity. Building on Goffman's theatre metaphor (1969), we argue that the identity construction often analyzed in the identity literature as an internal organizational affair, in our case, happened largely in the interplay between the external audiences' reception of the company's appearance 'on stage' (that is, in the media) and the organizational members' sense-making 'behind the scenes' (that is, off-stage) of the on-stage performance. In Goffman's words: 'identity emerges as you experience how you think others perceive of you'.

Oticon's spaghetti organization

During the 1990s, Oticon became a celebrity company known as 'the spaghetti organization'. CEO Lars Kolind created the metaphor as he described his organizational ambitions to a journalist by saying that it meant having an organization that is 'changeable like a portion of newly boiled spaghetti, which never stays the same but sticks together anyway'. Immediately becoming a popular description inside and outside the firm, 'the spaghetti organization' involved a staff of 130 persons working in Oticon's headquarters in Copenhagen. The operational aim was to increase the innovation rate of products and services by improving motivation, flexibility and communication among the staff working in marketing and sales, research and development, distributor support, and accounting. As Kolind explained: 'Oticon managers and employees are our intellectual capital. We are absolutely dependent upon them to survive against the future competition.'

In order to realize this kind of transformation, Kolind told everyone at Oticon that they were expected to act more independently on their own initiative. Everyone was to have equal opportunities to act in order for the new organization to be efficient. Managers and employees were to shift from a narrow functional optimization perspective to a general and more holistic view comprising the entire organization. As Kolind envisioned: 'The organization must become a brain rather than a machine ... and the last thing the brain resembles is a hierarchy'.

Kolind presented Oticon's new organizational identity to managers and employees as a set of key principles.

The spaghetti vision:

1. The philosophical cornerstone: personal dialogue and volunteering
2. Multi-task job profiles
3. Multi-disciplinary project teams with no fixed hierarchical positions

4. Moveable and open offices
5. Electronic offices: the paperless office

His vision involved a completely new perspective on the organization's identity. Each element of the vision was designed to support the other elements to create the new spaghetti identity. An important aspect was the implementation procedure. The materialization of the vision was to take place in one comprehensive change process – not in the step-by-step procedure that most organizational practice adheres to and most normative organizational change research recommends. At Oticon, the move to a new headquarters was to take place simultaneously with the implementation of the other physical and structural changes. Everything was virtually turned upside-down overnight.

The media's construction of Oticon

What turned out to be a central aspect of the implementation procedure was the media attention. Although this was not part of the design programme, the media's celebration of Oticon's spaghetti organization soon became a taken-for-granted feature of the new identity. Moreover, although the celebration of Oticon started with a fascination with the uniqueness of the spaghetti vision, the media continued to attribute celebrity status to Oticon for a decade, by celebrating other features related to Oticon's organization.

To stimulate the identity change, Kolind systematically invited the press to document the organizational change, and a number of journalists took an immediate interest in the project. The impact was that Oticon was suddenly, and conspicuously, mentioned in the media as a 'revolutionary organization' and an 'organizational experiment'. Within a few months, the media's perception of Oticon had changed dramatically. Table 4.1 illustrates the overall change.

The change between these two identity descriptions was a comprehensive, intense and relatively short process. However, what is interesting for our case study is the endurance of the massive media mention, and how members of the organization were actively involved in the ongoing identity construction and re-confirmation of Oticon as a celebrity firm as they also became subjects of the media's inquiry. Oticon became a celebrity firm in the national media, and enjoyed being mentioned positively in the media to a considerable degree in the following decade. Two issues characterized the media

Table 4.1 The media's changed descriptions of Oticon

Old identity: who are they?	New identity: who are they?
Science and engineering	Playful, experimental
Silent	Networkers
Reliable	Creative
Stable	Dynamic
Follower	First-mover
Traditional	Daring, visionary
Isolated/closed	At the centre of things/open.
	'The Oticon Way' as role model

Source: Inspired by Morsing and Kristensen 2001.

mention: first, a number of different issues dominated the description of Oticon over time; second, the media mention was almost always supportive and positive.

Our study examines two national Danish daily newspapers' mention of Oticon over the course of 10 years, *Børsen* and *Politiken*, to explore the ways in which the media managed to sustain continued interest in staging Oticon as a celebrity firm for so long. *Børsen* is a politically right-wing daily business newspaper targeting corporate managers, while *Politiken*, which targets urban dwellers, is a politically moderate daily newspaper with an intellectual slant. *Børsen* published 445 articles mentioning Oticon, and *Politiken* published 246. The articles were categorized according to which aspect of Oticon was highlighted in the article. Figures 4.1 and 4.2 depict those aspects highlighted in the positive media attention to illustrate the weight that the two newspapers put on the different features of Oticon.

Although the two newspapers are rather different with respect to target audience, political orientation and topical interests, they highlight the same four aspects of Oticon: office design, structure, social responsibility and reliability, and, for the intellectually ambitious *Politiken*, CEO Lars Kolind is also featured in the paper. The fact that visible features embedded with symbolic notions, such as office design and structural aspects of Oticon, are highlighted in the period demarcating the beginning of the spaghetti identity era seems to have added to the media attraction and celebrity status attributed to Oticon. Indeed, they caught the attention of the media. Another notable aspect of the media mention is the large number of

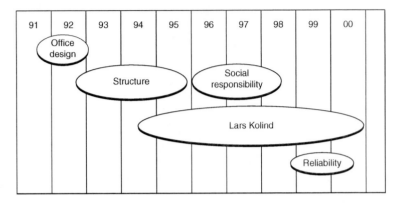

Figure 4.1 Newspaper mention of Oticon: Topics in Politiken

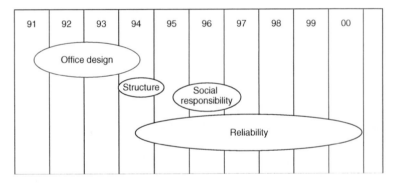

Figure 4.2 News paper mention of Oticon: Topics in Børsen

photos and other types of illustrations of Oticon occupying news-paper space that visualize for the reader the nature of Oticon. For example, a transparent plastic tube containing shredded paper from upstairs symbolized transparency and the idea of the paperless office. The electronic information system and meeting rooms built out of glass bricks reminded everyone about organizational transpar-ency. Informal places to drink coffee and broad staircases functioned as encouragement to meet and talk. And open, mobile offices and drawers on wheels for all managers and employees symbolized the flexible and minimal office hierarchy: Oticon easily made a good story for the press, as well as for academia. Pictures were also shown of the new headquarters in an old building that was formerly a soft drink manufacturing factory that had been completely renovated with fashionable interior design.

As of 1994, economic reliability became a key issue in *Børsen*, which underlines the interest of the target audience: corporate managers. *Politiken*'s pages were open to CEO Lars Kolind as of 1994. This was, in part, inspired by an invitation to Lars Kolind from the Minister of Social Affairs to join a national network of corporate CEOs to discuss the issue of social integration of minorities in the workplace. Kolind's personal commitment to this issue became associated with his role as Oticon's CEO, as the vision behind Oticon's spaghetti organization was judged to fit very well with this social cause. In practice, social integration was in no way an aspect of Oticon's spaghetti organiza-tion, neither was it discussed at a strategic level. However, having become such a strong icon of the spaghetti organization, Kolind's personal key issues were now also seen to be Oticon's.

While the data in Figures 4.1 and 4.2 do not directly show the positive celebrity status attributed to Oticon by both newspapers, they demonstrate how the media managed to reinvent Oticon by highlighting different features and continually arguing that it was a company of high interest to readers. We argue that Oticon's con-struction of many different features of its organization contributed to the media's continued interest. In fact, we argue that, had CEO Lars Kolind not ensured a variety of unique features attributed to Oticon, the media would have found it more difficult to uphold its celebration.

Members' identity construction

Initiated from inside the organization, the identity process was set off by Kolind's strong, ambitious and encompassing 'spaghetti vision', which spurred the interest of Danish – and, later, also the international – media. In fact, Oticon's spaghetti organization turned out to receive unpredicted positive attention in the liberal as well as the socialist press, which provided headlines such as: 'The Company of the Future Looks Like Spaghetti', 'The Soccer Team Replaces the Pyramid' and 'Competition on Intellectual Capital'. Even trade union magazines discussed Oticon's organizational project in positive terms.

While the media attention started with a few personal portraits of Kolind and his vision, they were quickly followed by interviews and articles about a number of other organizational members, telling about their lives in the spaghetti organization. The public interest in Oticon grew during 1991 and 1992, with the CEO spending many hours talking to journalists from small and large newspapers and magazines, first Danish ones but, later, also international ones. He was invited to give numerous lectures in other organizations, business schools, unions, and so on to talk about 'the cultural revolution in Oticon'. One example that illustrates the comprehensiveness of the media attention and its influence on other companies was when a large telephone company used Oticon as 'testimonial' in a nationwide media campaign in the autumn of 1991. The advertisement showed a picture of an Oticon project manager sitting in the new high-tech, open office space at Oticon's headquarters with the headline 'What did Oticon do on 8–8–91?', followed by an explanation of why Oticon chose to use this particular telephone company to deliver its telephone system.

As the interest and subsequent demand for interviews grew too large for Kolind to manage himself, other organizational members were encouraged to give talks to different audiences about Oticon's change process and the resulting organizational structures. The number of visitors that wanted to inquire about the organizational experiment, and interview managers and employees, also grew. The visitors wanted answers to questions such as: 'How do you manage your time when nobody monitors you?', or 'How are you able to work in new fields where you have no prior experience?', and 'What aspects of your job have changed with the spaghetti organization'. They were looking for specifics and for the areas in which Oticon distinguished itself from other organizations. When confronted with questions framed in the 'spaghetti frame of reference', managers and employees found themselves answering within that same framework's terminology, using the diction and arguments of this new organizational philosophy: 'Oh, it's a bit confusing to start with, but you get used to the anarchy after a while. And you become your own boss', or 'You have to be outgoing yourself and a bit adventurous to survive this organization, and that includes taking on new tasks. Things that you previously had no idea about', and so on. Answers to the questions show a notably increasing organizational reflexivity; as one employee explained, for example,

'Maybe I can't come up with a good answer to the question immediately, but I have often experienced a good answer the same night
or a couple of days later.' Questions about everyday work life, daily
routines and attitudes towards organizational life are seldom asked
directly, and it turned out that managers and employees were eager to
invite external observers and to talk to them.

Employees read the articles and were visibly seduced by this massive media attention. They watched themselves appear in newspapers and on national television with bold statements about the
many improvements that had come about with the introduction
of the spaghetti organization. They found themselves exaggerat-
ing the organizational improvements as they were confronted with
the media inquiry and, as we interviewed them afterwards, some of
them expressed how they were stunned to find themselves almost
hyping the descriptions of the spaghetti organization as they were
confronted with an external audience. One project manager, who
regarded himself as being relatively critical towards the spaghetti
hype, reported how he suddenly found himself lecturing on the spaghetti organization at business schools and corporate networks, and
being confronted with questions such as 'Is everybody at Oticon as
enthusiastic about the spaghetti organization as you are?'

By autumn 1991, the international media had already become interested in Oticon. The BBC and CNN produced television segments
about Oticon, and management guru Tom Peters made a video and
later wrote a chapter about Oticon in *Liberation Management* (1992).
Furthermore, quite a few professors from abroad – for example, from
Harvard, the Cranfield School of Management, Insead, Imede and
the University of New South Wales in Australia – visited Oticon in
order to produce cases or articles about the spaghetti vision. Interest
in Oticon also produced a few Danish management books about
Oticon's organizational vision and the change process, including
Holistic Management (Lyregaard 1993), and *Think the Unthinkable*
(Poulsen 1993). Also among this literature is our own research on
Oticon's change process (Morsing 1995, 1999) and a later publication
related to Kolind's resignation in April 1998 (Morsing and Eiberg 1998;
Kjærgaard and Vautz 2008). 'The Oticon way of organizing' gradually
became an institution among Danish business managers.

In this way, the media provoked the self-reflective questions among
managers and employees that Albert and Whetten define as a strong

identity element, as members were specifically asked self-reflective questions by journalists and other external visitors. The visitors brought the vision one step closer to the individual organizational member. The external visitors became external observers or organizational anthropologists, watching and asking questions about all sorts of topics. They came to Oticon to visit and see the spaghetti organization with their own eyes, and to talk to some of its inhabitants, its managers and employees. They entered the organization filled with curiosity, questions and the expectation of finding evidence of almost futuristic organizing. Their questions were designed to frame and obtain good examples of Oticon's vision in practice. The external observers looked for evidence of 'spaghetti' – and they found it. Confronted with a positive 'external inquisition', it proved difficult to maintain a sceptical attitude toward one's own organization. No matter how sceptical managers and employees felt about the vision and its materialization, their loyalty towards the company's image was greater. An 'escalation of commitment' (Staw 1981) to the vision hit managers and employees as they were directly confronted by external observers.

During this evolution, organizational members surfaced and put into words important aspects of the spaghetti identity in a discrete yet forceful process. This period of inquiry was most forcefully played out from 1990 to 1993, as the media attention was new and still unusual for members. As organizational members were interviewed by journalists and other non-members about the company's activities, they found themselves participating in the discursive construction of the 'spaghetti identity'. The ongoing media attention, however, contributed to maintaining the self-reflection among members. Oticon's managers and employees became used to their celebrity status, and continued to describe themselves in the media as a spaghetti organization. A tacit agreement seemed to permeate the organization that Oticon was 'something special'; that is, an organizational experiment that inspired many other companies and, hence, deserved much attention. Consequently, the media became a forceful player in the ongoing identity construction of Oticon among organizational members.

While the media interest in the features of the spaghetti organization changed during the 10 years of our analysis, managers and employees continued to be interviewed by journalists and they continued to characterize the company in positive and unique phrases. As the media interest changed from focusing on office design and structure to social responsibility, reliability and to Kolind himself, managers and employees continued to speak favourably about the company as they were interviewed by the media. Internally, some members continued the positive interpretations of the media's representation of Oticon, while some members were more critical. Whether they were enthusiastically reconfirming or acting critically towards the media attention, our point is that managers and employees discussed themselves and their organizational practice in light of how they were mentioned in the media. They discussed to what extent they perceived the media representation as fair and correct, and to what extent it mattered if it were, indeed, fair and correct. Among enthusiasts as well as sceptics, the celebrity status was upheld. The media attention evoked a silent pride. As one Oticon employee stated 10 years after the media boom started, 'as an Oticon employee, you were almost certain to find yourself in the centre of attention at any dinner party. People wanted to know "What's it like to work in a spaghetti organization", "Is it true that your organization now looks more like ravioli?" and "What was it like to work for Kolind?", Alternatively, you could be drawn into discussions as an expert of new cross-organizational working methods, or the latest information technology.' Organizational members experienced an unprecedented interest in their opinions and experiences from Oticon, thus creating a sense of significance and pride.

The opportunity to articulate the philosophy of the vision gradually was brought to Oticon's managers and employees by means of the external observers. The discourse that previously belonged exclusively to the CEO was now permeating organizational members' own discourse. Employees found themselves arguing about the many opportunities available for personal development – for taking on challenging tasks, and for gaining more influence and so on – that were embedded in the vision. Sceptics reported their surprise at their own enthusiasm when telling others about the vision. This articulation of a new set of interpretive schemes moved the vision one step closer to being reality. The words, expressions, arguments and accounts of organizational events, myths and rituals, which had been induced by top-down communication, were, through the local articulation process, changed from a passive to an active asset. The articulation was not exclusively managerial rhetoric imposed on an organization but, rather, it became a process of raising organizational consciousness and reflectivity about the past and future in a shared vocabulary. In this sense, the spaghetti language shaped a mental picture of an organizational reality that became real in the local articulation.

Discussion and implications

This study set out to investigate the role of the media for identity construction. Strong empirical evidence demonstrates the influence of the media on identity construction, and for maintaining a self-description as an attractive and agenda-setting firm for which to work. The media's influence on organizational identity has been mentioned in other studies on the relationships between identity and image (Dutton and Dukerich 1991; Dutton et al. 1994; Elsbach and Kramer 1996), but it has not previously been explored in a case study on identity construction. Moreover, in our case, media becomes a discursive amplifier between management and employees in their ongoing identity construction. Our case also adds insights into some of the mechanisms that stimulate ongoing positive media mention, as Oticon's vision embraced a broad palette of important issues for the media to refer to and discuss in public, with the result that Oticon never sank into anonymity

The media did not play an active role in identity construction at Oticon until Kolind presented the spaghetti organization and caught the interest of journalists. Kolind stimulated the media attention and was a significant source of influence for the agenda-setting position that Oticon reached in the media.

Our interest in exploring the strategic use of auto-communication brought about the question of whether, with the media mention, Kolind was looking for more customers to buy more hearing instruments. Our answer is that he most likely was not. The state-driven market for hearing instruments was equally shared among three Danish providers, and Oticon's most important markets were found internationally. Hence, our answer to the question 'Who does the media mention target?' points internally towards the managers and employees of Oticon. Kolind had told managers and employees about the spaghetti organization's office structure, design, social responsibility and reliability, but this information achieved another status and significance when presented by the media. The auto-communicative effect of the media mention provided Kolind's messages with an authority and prestige he could not have given his messages had he told them directly to his managers and employees.

Kolind's construction of the identity features moved from his desk to the press and back to organizational members and, in that process, contributed to the ongoing identity construction. An additional feature of the auto-communicative effect at Oticon is the role of members as active co-constructors of the media mention. As many members were interviewed by journalists, students and other visitors, they were confronted with Oticon's identity and reconfirmed it in their desire to present Oticon as attractive when confronting an external audience.

Our study shows how auto-communicative processes attract, move or seduce managers and employees in a more implicit way than a direct managerial message. In that sense, strategic auto-communication becomes a strong managerial tool – and could also be seen as a form of manipulation. In his analysis of 'normative control' (Kunda 1982), Gideon Kunda describes how employee norms and values are indirectly and implicitly posed as institutional expectations on managers and employees in non-transparent yet forceful ways that they cannot escape without being perceived as powerless and weak. The methods of normative control are not revealed to managers and employees. Their force lays precisely in their non-transparent nature. Similarly, the auto-communicative process at Oticon is not revealed to managers and employees as a means of directing or changing their identity. We might even be inclined to think that auto-communication is effective because it is *not* presented as a strategic managerial manoeuvre but because it appears almost as a third party endorsement: the media independently appreciates corporate members and their activities. Therefore, future research on identity construction needs to take into account the ways in which strategic auto-communication raises concerns about ethicality. To what extent is it ethical to manipulate organizational members through mediatization?

Finally, the claim can be made that Oticon is a unique case that is impossible to copy. As in any case study, the exact duplication of the many social and cultural variables is unrealistic. However, we argue that Oticon's case can inspire other identity researchers to incorporate the media as an influential external player for internal identity construction in their research. Although Oticon's strategic and conspicuous use of auto-communication might not be repeated at the same systematic level, we think that future organizational identity research will benefit from focusing systematically on the dynamics of mediatization.

References

Newspapers

Aktuelt, September 14, 1991
Berlingske Tidende, August 4, 1991
Information, June 15–16, 1991

Publications

Albert, S. and Whetten, D.A. (1985) 'Organisational Identity', in L.L. Cummings and B.M. Staw, *Research in Organisational Behaviour*, vol. 7 (Greenwich, CT: JAI Press): 263–95.

Astley, W.G. and Zammuto, R.F. (1992) 'Organisation Science, Managers, and Language Games', *Organisation Science*, 3: 443–60.

Broms, H. and Gardberg, H. (1983) 'Communication to Self in Organisations and Cultures', *Administrative Science Quarterly*, 28: 482–95.

Callon, M. (1987) 'Some Elements of a Sociology of Translation: Domestication of the Scallops and the Fishermen of St. Brieuc Bay', in P. Luff, G. Nigel Gilbert and David Frohlich, *Computers and Conversation* (London: Academic Press).

Christensen, L.T. (1997) 'Marketing as Auto-Communication', *Consumption, Markets and Culture*, 1: 197–227.

Christensen, L.T. and Cheney, G. (2000) 'Self-Absorption and Self-Seduction in the Corporate Identity Game', in M. Schultz, M.J. Hatch and M.H. Larsen, *The Expressive Organisation: Linking Identity, Reputation, and the Corporate Brand* (Oxford: Oxford University Press): 246–70.

Christensen, L.T., Morsing, M. and Cheney, G. (2008) *Corporate Communications: Convention, Complexity, and Critique* (London: Sage).

DiMaggio, P.J. and Powell, W.W. (1991) *The New Institutionalism in Organisational Analysis* (Chicago, Il: University of Chicago Press).

Dutton, J.E. and Dukerich, J.M. (1991) 'Keeping an Eye on the Mirror: Image and Identity in Organisational Adaptation', *Academy of Management Journal*, 34: 517–54.

Dutton, J.E., Dukerich, J.M. and Harquail, C.V. (1994) 'Organisational Images and Member Identification', *Administrative Science Quarterly*, 39: 239–63.

Elsbach, K.D. and Kramer, R.M. (1996) 'Members Responses to Organisational Identity Threats: Encountering and Countering the Business Week Rankings', *Administrative Science Quarterly*, 41: 442–76.

Fairclough, N. (1992) *Discourse and Social Change* (Cambridge: Polity Press).

Ginzel, L.E., Kramer, R.M. and Sutton, R.I. (1993) 'Organisational Impression Management as a Reciprocal Influence Process: The Neglected Role of the Organisational Audience', *Research in Organisational Behaviour*, 15: 227–66.

Gioia, D.A. and Chittipeddi, K. (1991) 'Sensemaking and Sensegiving in Strategic Change Initiation', *Strategic Management Journal*, 12: 433–48.

Goffman, E. (1969) *The Presentation of Self in Everyday Life* (London: Penguin).

Kjærgaard, A.L. and K. Kautz (2008) 'A Process Model of Establishing Knowledge Management: Insights from a Longitudinal Field Study.' *OMEGA* 36(2): 282–297.

Kunda, G. (1982) *Engineering Culture: Control and Commitment in a High-Tech Corporation* (Philadelphia: Temple University Press).

Lyregaard, P.E. (1993) 'Oticon: Erfaringer og faldgruber' [Experiences and Pitfalls], in S. Hildebrandt and L.H. Alken, *Mod holistisk ledelse – billeder fra praksis* (Århus: Ankerhus).

Mead, G.H. (1934) *Mind, Self, and Society* (Chicago: University of Chicago Press).

Morsing, M. (1995) *Approaching Paradise? Oticon in the Process from Hierarchy to Spaghetti*, in Danish (Copenhagen: Copenhagen Business School Press).

Morsing, M. (1999) 'The Media Boomerang: The Media's Role in Changing Identity by Changing Image', *Corporate Reputation Review*, 2(2), spring: 116–35.

Morsing, M. (2006) 'CSR as Strategic Auto-Communication – On the Role of External Stakeholders for Member Identification', *Business Ethics: A European Review*, 15(2): 171–82.

Morsing, M. and Eiberg, K.U. (eds) (1998) *Managing the Unmanageable for a Decade* (Copenhagen: Oticon A/S).

Peters, T.J. (1992) *Liberation Management* (New York: Alfred A. Knopf).

Poulsen, P.T. (1993) *Think the Unthinkable: The Revolution at Oticon*, in Danish (Copenhagen: Schultz).

Pratt, M.G., and Rafaeli, A. (1997) 'Organisational Dress as a Symbol of Multilayered Social Identities', *Academy of Management Journal*, 40: 862–98.

Schein, E. (1986) *Organisational Culture and Leadership* (Boston: Jossey-Bass).

Staw, B.M. (1981) 'The Escalation of Commitment to a Course of Action', *Academy of Management Review*, 6: 577–87.

5
Challenges in the Mediatization of a Corporate Brand: Identity-Effects as LEGO Establishes a Media Products Company

Esben Karmark

The LEGO Group (LEGO), one of the world's leading toy companies known primarily for the famous LEGO brick construction toy, decided to enter into the market for children's media products in the mid-1990s. Consequently, in 1996 LEGO established a subsidiary to develop and market media products for children, LEGO Media International. This initiative was part of LEGO's overall corporate branding strategy: LEGO would become a true corporate brand, meaning that the LEGO name and values should no longer be connected mainly with LEGO's main product – the brick – in the minds of consumers and employees but, rather, with the wider set of LEGO values related to children's play and development. Through the strategy to take the LEGO brand into the media business areas – which further included children's clothes, amusement parks and lifestyle products – the company's top management sought to realize the ambition to become the world's most well-known brand among families with children between the ages of 0–16 by the year 2005. By seeking to incorporate media products (which, in Lego's case, meant interactive software, music, film, television and magazines for children) into the product line, it could be argued, following Hjarvard (2004), that the LEGO Company and corporate brand were increasingly mediatized.

Mediatization is defined as a process in which a company's products are increasingly:

- Narrativized – such as LEGO engaging in licensing agreements with the makers of S*tar Wars* and *Harry Potter;*
- Imaginatized – such as LEGO creating fictional universes for play, and;
- Virtualized – such as LEGO transforming the physical building brick into simulations on computers.

By 2004, however, LEGO's top management announced a strategic shift in the company that meant that LEGO's product offerings should, once more, be closely related to the company's core idea, and that 'development projects not directly linked to the company's core business, such as electronic games, will be outsourced to licensee partners' (LEGO Annual Report 2004: 9). As a result of this strategic development (although electronic games would still be part of LEGO's product line) LEGO Media International was no longer responsible for the development of LEGO's media products and, in effect, ceased to operate. This development towards what we might call a de-mediatization of LEGO was partly related to a severe financial crisis in LEGO at the time, and the return to a focus on the core business was the company's strategic response to the crisis. As this chapter will show, however, another equally important factor in the process further related to the problems LEGO encountered as an organization that attempted to integrate a media company into its existing organizational culture and identity. Thereby, the case of LEGO and LEGO Media International demonstrates that meditization goes beyond changes in product and strategy. Rather, mediatization efforts crucially also involve issues of organizational culture and identity – that is to say, the organizational members' question: 'Who are we as an organization?' (Albert and Whetten 1985; Hatch and Schultz 1997).

This chapter builds on the case of LEGO Media International, and investigates the inter-relationship between corporate branding and the media, particularly the roles played by culture and identity in processes towards the mediatization of a company and of a corporate brand. Specifically, the chapter will show that organizational culture and identity can act as challenges to mediatization attempts, and will explain how a company such as LEGO is not readily 'transformed and shaped' by media interests, precisely because of culture- and identity-based resistance in the organization (for discussions on organizational change and resistance see Hatch and Schultz 2008; Christensen et al. 2008).

The case of LEGO attempting to extend its brand to media products raises important issues about the interconnections between media and business. In so doing, it throws into relief the importance of the process of mediatization, which has, so far, been seen as a 'black box' in the identity and corporate branding literature – where the media have been seen almost solely in terms of their role in shaping external perceptions of a corporate brand, such as corporate image or reputation[1] (for example, Dutton and Dukerich 1991; Morsing and Kristensen 2001; Fombrun and Van Riel 2004). I discuss the implications of this gap in 'The media as black box in identity and corporate branding literature' below. Mediatization, then, in the context of this argument, comes to draw attention to the internal aspects of the organization, its culture and identity, insofar as mediatization is also linked to further processes of change through which such internal aspects are transformed and shaped by the media it seeks to incorporate. The rest of the chapter will continue with a brief account of LEGO, its company culture and identity, before focusing on the mediatization of LEGO, and the subsequent processes of change and change resistance that mediatization brought about in the company.

The media as a 'black box' in identity and corporate branding literature

Corporate branding has received much attention among marketing practitioners and academics in recent years (for example, Hatch and Schultz 2001; Balmer and Gray 2003; Olins 2003; Schultz et al. 2005). Corporate branding differs from classical product branding in a number of ways, but the main difference lies in the foundation for the brand. In product branding, the product itself is the foundation for the brand. For one of the world's most well-known product brands – Coca-Cola – this means that branding revolves around the product. Here, product branding manifests itself in, for example, the 'always Coca-Cola' tagline, and the red and white colour scheme on the packaging. In corporate branding, on the other hand, the entire company or organization becomes the foundation for the brand. For one of the world's most well-known corporate brands – Disney – this means that everything the company does revolves around one core value: entertainment, as well as the supporting values of quality, variety and fun. In corporate branding, such values are seen as intrinsic to the company – in other words, they are part of the company's organizational culture and identity (Schultz 2005).

Another difference between product branding and corporate branding is related to the target audience. Whereas product branding usually focuses on the consumer as its target audience, corporate branding concerns itself with all the company's stakeholders: consumers as well as the media, NGOs, suppliers, shareholders, employees and regulatory bodies. The media as a stakeholder, thereby, is a key concern in relation to corporate branding, and it has even been suggested that the current 'fad' for corporate branding is closely linked to the companies' need to establish visibility and legitimacy in an overcrowded communication environment (Christensen and Cheney 2000). This point is further supported by the fact that 'business news' is on the rise, rendering anything related to business newsworthy – as is demonstrated by the recent high-profile corporate scandals exemplified by the Enron downfall (Kjær, Chapter 3.). Despite the increasing significance of the media in the emergence of corporate branding, the relations between the media and corporate branding are only addressed to a very limited extent in the relevant literature. The media are still seen as simply a stakeholder, as a partner for establishing 'relations', or as an outlet for the brand message (for example, Olins 2003; Schultz 2005).

Mediatization and corporate branding in LEGO

Mediatization, as suggested above, is a concept that we can employ to link the media and corporate branding, in order to fill in the black box, and explore the role of the media in influencing identity in organizations and corporate branding. Hjarvad proposes that corporate branding is, in itself, a mediatization process as '(corporate) branding is about making a product, a service or an entire company communicable, i.e. assume media form' (Hjarvad 2004: 4).

For LEGO, the corporate branding strategy to include actual media products in its product line served the purpose of changing the image

of both the product and the organization. The main aim was to recon-
nect with consumers, who were beginning to drift away from the traditional toy industry and towards the new and ever-increasing field of
media consumption. It is this exclusive strategic focus on products
and external image that rendered the organization's internal culture
and identity a black box for LEGO itself during its process of mediatization. This primarily external focus runs contrary to most recent
models on corporate branding, where, as mentioned, the significant
role of organizational culture and identity in corporate brand development is emphasized. For instance, Schultz (2005) argues that the inclusion of a new organizational unit, such as a subsidiary, in a redefined
brand organization often causes resistance in the existing culture
towards the new sub-culture. Based on the assumption that the intern-
ally- and externally-directed aspects of a corporate brand are linked,
Hatch and Schultz (2001) propose a model (see Figure 5.1) in which a
corporate brand consists of three separate, but connected, elements:

- The company's organizational culture and identity
- The top management's vision for the company
- The company's image among external stakeholders.

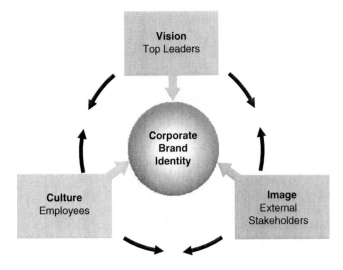

Figure 5.1   The culture–vision–image model
Source: Hatch & Schultz, 2001: 131.

In the model, corporate brand identity occurs at the juncture between vision, culture and image, and defines how 'we perceive ourselves as an organization'. Identity underpins the corporate brand – partly by the feedback from stakeholders and partly by the organization's self-insight. Such organizational claims about its self-identity are often defined as core values, beliefs or central ideas.

Building on the Corporate Branding model in Figure 5.1, we can assume that in order for a company to become mediatized as a consequence of a corporate brand strategy, such a process would necessarily go beyond changes in product and strategic vision to also include the organizational culture and identity, as expressed for instance in the company's values and core ideas. In the case of LEGO, as mentioned in p. 113, the company's 2004 annual report stated that products such as electronic games, introduced in 1996, were no longer considered part of LEGO's core idea and core business. Such a statement points to the fact that, during those eight years, a significant clash had taken place between LEGO's historical values and traditional organizational identity, on the one hand, and the changes in this organizational identity that were initiated by the mediatization of LEGO – a clash that ultimately made it necessary for LEGO to discontinue the development of its media products and abandon LEGO Media International. Let us see why.

LEGO: Culture, values and corporate brand

LEGO has always branded its products on the basis of the company name and values. Ever since the company was established in 1932, the corporate brand has been linked to the founding Kirk Kristiansen family's values regarding children and play: The LEGO name, in itself, is an abbreviation of the two Danish words 'Leg' and 'Godt' – which translates into 'good play'. From 1958 onwards, after the invention of the LEGO 'brick', LEGO became almost synonymous with that particular product, and the values and culture of the company developed accordingly. For example, during the 1970s the father of the current owners (known in the company as CKC) formulated the '10 LEGO characteristics' that LEGO products were meant to encapsulate. These characteristics included: 'Unlimited play possibilities'; 'Imagination, creativity, development' and 'Leading safety and quality', which all fitted the so-called 'LEGO System' of play based on the LEGO brick. LEGO extended the brand in the 1970s with products such as the Duplo range for toddlers, or the LEGO System range for more advanced LEGO models. However, these brand extensions were still closely linked to the original brick, and continued to carry the pedagogical values inherent in the 10 'characteristics'.

In the 1990s, the current owner and CEO, Kjeld Kirk Kristiansen, followed the company tradition in LEGO, but also sought to implement his own vision for the development of LEGO culture and corporate brand values. This vision placed less emphasis on the brick-related attributes of the LEGO brand and, instead, built the brand around the main LEGO value of 'creativity' and its related values of 'limitless', 'fun' and 'pride'. The main reason for the new brand strategy in LEGO was that the company was confronted with changing consumer patterns: the market for construction toys was declining, and LEGO was faced with an image problem in the children's market. The emergence of new electronically based entertainment for children was beginning to make LEGO look boring and old-fashioned. The shift in brand strategy, however, also signalled a much stronger focus on the potential of the LEGO brand itself. From the mid-1990s, LEGO's top management began considering the LEGO brand, rather than the product, as the company's strongest asset. Consequently, it began to place strategic focus on the position of the LEGO brand in rankings such as Young and Rubicam's 'Brand Asset Valuator'. This focus was further reflected in the formulation of LEGO's vision, which was for LEGO to become the world's most well known brand among families with children by the year 2005 – in effect, surpassing such mega-brands as Disney and Coca-Cola. What its top management envisioned, in this sense, was a change in the culture and identity of LEGO from its historical and deeply rooted product-based culture to a novel brand-based culture.

In order to achieve this vision, LEGO needed to be more visible to consumers, and thereby expand its product categories beyond the construction toy category. To this end, top management set out to establish the LEGO brand in new business areas – among them media products, such as computer software and electronic toys for children. A further shift in the company's strategic orientation was that it began to develop products that were connected to storytelling content around already familiar toys and mini-figures based on media products such as the *Star Wars* films, as well as the *Harry Potter* books and films. The rationale for these changes was formulated as follows:

> In principle the LEGO brand can appear in any context that helps stimulate creativity. So products and services marketed under the LEGO name can take many forms [such as] creative software as long as the software is loyal to the values of the LEGO brand, allowing children to explore and express themselves. (LEGO Brand Book 1999: 9)

The first step in this process of change was to establish the subsidiary LEGO Media International. LEGO Media International (LEGO Media) was established in 1996, and grew out of a Strategic Business Unit called Darwin, which was set up in the early 1990s with the aim of taking LEGO into the expanding software market. The Darwin project had links in London, which was seen as the centre of the software industry in Europe. When LEGO Media was established as a LEGO subsidiary, London was chosen as the location for this reason. By 1999, the company had grown to a staff of about 100 people. The stated purpose of LEGO Media was to develop interactive software and other media products for children – such as music, film, television and magazines – and market them on a worldwide scale. LEGO Media was staffed with primarily young people (the average employee age was 23; the managing director was aged 32) with a background in the publishing or the software industry. By 1999, LEGO estimated that LEGO Media could contribute about US$160 million to the LEGO turnover, although the company was still 'struggling to make a business of it' in the words of the managing director (Karmark 2002: 24).

Indeed, despite the fact that LEGO's top management saw children's media as a natural part of the brand's universe, extending its philosophy of play, imagination and creativity to the electronic and digital worlds of entertainment, by 2004 LEGO had significantly scaled down its ambition in the media products area. The development of electronic games was outsourced to external developers, and the plans to go into other areas of children's media – such as TV production and magazine publishing – went unrealized. It has been noted that this shift away from a media product strategy was, to a large extent, caused by LEGO's financial crisis in 2003 and 2004 (for example, Hjarvad 2004; Soendergaard 2004). This crisis led to a realization in LEGO that an over-reliance on the license based products linked to media hits such as *Star Wars* and *Harry Potter* made the company too vulnerable and unprepared for the market conditions in the years in which no such media sensations were forthcoming. Moreover, the inclusion of a media-based subsidiary also proved a significant challenge for the company to absorb because of culture and identity-based differences.

Organizational challenges to mediatization in LEGO

The concept of mediatization, let us recall, currently tends to focus on the company's product, strategy and external image. When establishing LEGO Media International, however, LEGO went further than simply adding media products to its product line in order to change the image among young consumers. Rather, it engaged in a process of substantial organizational development by including a new organizational unit, which, in terms of culture and identity, was substantially different from the main culture in LEGO. As Schultz (2005) argues, we can expect that a strategy to develop the organization's corporate brand identity through the inclusion of a new organizational unit with new responsibilities will be met with resistance and conflict within the organization. Indeed, this proved to be the case in LEGO, where conflict and resistance were specifically driven by certain key aspects of the corporate brand identity:

- Organizational culture and identity
- Product technology, as well as organizational vision.

Let us examine each in turn.

Organizational culture and identity

The first significant factor that influenced the mediatization development in LEGO was directly related to *organizational identity* or conscious reflections of 'who we are as an organization' (Albert and Whetten 1985). Such identity reflections are usually taken to occur in the context of organizational culture (Hatch and Schultz 1997). In this case, LEGO Media employees – young, London-based and with backgrounds in publishing and software development – established a counter-culture that was radically distinct from the historical values of this traditional, Denmark-Based, family-oriented company. Specifically, the culture of the LEGO Media organization was seen by its employees as a younger, wilder and less pristine culture, free of the restrictions of the 'only working with toys' culture, as one LEGO Media manager expressed it. However, rather than seeing this as a contrast to traditional LEGO, the LEGO Media employees perceived themselves to be more connected to the original values that the LEGO Company represents – that is, caring about children and creativity – than the dominant culture at LEGO headquarters. In other words, LEGO Media employees were persuaded that their media oriented understanding of 'who we are as an organization' was more connected to LEGO's core values than the symbolic brick-based toy was, and that they were closer to the 'original LEGO identity' – or to 'what the owners intended LEGO to be', in the words of another LEGO Media manager.

As a consequence, LEGO Media members perceived the dominant culture at LEGO's headquarters to be sceptical of the new organization. Indeed, members at LEGO headquarters in Denmark expressed strong reservations towards the LEGO Media organization, which were based on differences in organizational identity. In general, employees and managers at headquarters were not convinced that the employees in LEGO Media were closely connected to the LEGO values and identity. LEGO's headquarters was somewhat self-deprecatory, referred to as 'Mount Parnassus' by one manager, but that expression underlines the perception that LEGO headquarters was the only true carrier of the LEGO values such as 'caring' and 'connectivity' – values that managers at LEGO headquarters did not see readily realized in a media-based organization. Furthermore, the identity of the LEGO Media organization was perceived to be more connected to 'business'; that is, more concerned with marketing and 'things that sell' than with the LEGO values.

The cultural and identity-based differences between LEGO head-quarters and LEGO Media were, to a large extent, also based on perceived differences in *business culture* between the 'old' culture based on the market for construction toys and the 'new' culture based in media products. Several LEGO Media managers expressed the view that the LEGO Media organization had the potential to revitalize the LEGO company and brand because of the Media organization's link to a new market. To LEGO Media employees, the main characteristics of the media business culture were fast and cool. Fast in terms of the 'compressed cycle times' of product development, and cool in terms of media products' image among young consumers. In LEGO Media, the general perception was that these aspects of the media business culture were neither properly understood nor appreciated by the managers at LEGO Media headquarters. For instance, when referring to the 'cool factor' of the media products, one LEGO Media manager pointed out that LEGO Media had the potential to make LEGO into something for older kids. The manager pointed out that 'kids nowadays want cross-media reference', meaning that if a company's products are also available in media-form – such as on a Play Station – 'they think it is cool'. (Karmark 2002: 139).

LEGO Media managers, however, were sceptical of LEGO's reluctance to accept the media-based business culture – a reluctance that they saw as hindering the LEGO brand's potential. For instance, in terms of advertising, Media managers felt that LEGO Media products were not integrated into an overall communication strategy, thereby foregoing the potential to make the LEGO brand desirable to kids playing with Sony or Nintendo products. Another LEGO Media employee expressed doubts as to whether LEGO had sufficient understanding of the media business or the financial readiness to operate successfully in this business. Such perceived lack of understanding and acceptance of the media business culture meant that, according to the LEGO Media employees, the LEGO brand was managed in a restrictive way, often withholding the potential of the LEGO brand to expand in the media field and thus become more vibrant and creative, and less boring and conservative.

As a result of these cultural and identity-based differences between LEGO Media and the main LEGO organization, LEGO Media employees' identity perceptions were dual: they perceived themselves to be simultaneously 'more LEGO than LEGO' and 'not accepted as LEGO'. The 'more LEGO than LEGO' identity was driven by perceptions that, in many ways, employees in LEGO Media were more in tune with the LEGO brand values than employees at LEGO headquarters, whereas the 'not accepted as LEGO' dimension was driven by perceptions that the LEGO Media organization was not properly accepted as part of the LEGO corporate brand identity. As one LEGO Media manager said:

> LEGO has a great heritage, but I think that in the company there is a need to compare things with what we did before and there is

an unwillingness to include new business areas such as Media.
(Karmark 2002: 119)

Product technology and organizational vision

New product developments play a significant role in the conceptualization of mediatization as a catalyst for change: the product – the
LEGO brick, for instance – is not only the company's traditional core
product, it also represents a key symbol of organizational identity.
When deciding to go into the market for media products, therefore,
the established perception of 'who we are as an organization' was
challenged, as LEGO was faced with a different type of product and
technology. Despite the top management's position that the LEGO
brand and not the product (the brick) were at the core of the LEGO
strategy, this was not the experience of the LEGO Media employees.
First, they perceived that Media products were still alien to the established LEGO identity. For instance, LEGO Media members spoke
about the LEGO owner, and then CEO, Kjeld Kirk Kristiansen's 'eyes
lighting up' when talking about the Mindstorms product (a merger of
computer technology and the LEGO brick), whereas he was seen as
being much less enthusiastic about the new software products. One
reason for this reluctance might be the fact that media products
involve radically different time frames (the compressed cycle times
that software needs to get to the market swiftly, see p. 122), which
countered the dominant cultural norm in LEGO, where every toy had
to be tested repeatedly over a longer period. Employees at LEGO headquarters in Denmark did, in fact, voice concern over the way in which
the new products and technologies in LEGO Media affected the LEGO
Corporate Brand. For instance, one Denmark-based manager said:

> [LEGO Media] is where we are experiencing the most difficulty
> with the understanding of the [LEGO corporate] values. It might
> have something to do with the product; I guess software is more
> difficult. If you take the LEGOLAND theme parks, for example,
> they are almost LEGO all to themselves. But with LEGO Media it
> is more difficult – the physical identity of the product is not LEGO.
> (Karmark 2002: 112)

Such scepticism was inevitably further reflected in the company's
vision, where another clash between LEGO headquarters and its

Media subsidiary developed. The company's headquarters were aware of the fact that the LEGO Media organization promoted a future strategy whereby LEGO could move much further into the marketing of storytelling content, as done by the Disney Corporation. In the words of a Denmark-based manager, the LEGO Media organization wished for LEGO to become 'this fantastic power-house in storytelling' (Karmark 2002: 113). According to the headquarters management team, however, this was far from the reality of LEGO, which 'is not Disney' and which does not have studios or video distribution. In other words, storytelling was not considered part of the 'LEGO DNA' – the LEGO organizational identity – at the LEGO Group's headquarters, and was never pushed forward as part of its corporate vision. As a result of discrepancies in understanding product development and future direction, the LEGO Media employees saw themselves as being relatively marginalized within LEGO.

Mediatization and de-mediatization

There is no doubt that the media business appears to be an attractive solution to organizations such as LEGO, which are faced with the need to transform their brand image, both at product and company levels, among consumers. The mediatization thesis assumes that the media have the ability to 'transform and shape' an organization and a corporate brand just as they have the power to shape and define the characteristics of our individual identities – the way we see ourselves (Giddens 1991). Along these lines, Hjarvad (in Soendergaard 2004) noted that the emergence of media based products left LEGO in a 'no way back' situation because of the massive influence of media culture not only on software games, but also on the products that LEGO considered to be closer to traditional toys. Media products, such as *Star Wars* or *Harry Potter* figures, he argues, represent a double-edged sword for a company such as LEGO, because 'You cannot get the advantages of allying yourself with strong media brands and not be affected by their vulnerability' (Hjarvad, quoted in: Soendergaard 2004). This is certainly true, but, as the case of LEGO and LEGO Media International has shown us, there are further dimensions to the mediatization process within an organization that pose serious limits to the power of media and media products to shape traditional organizations and corporate brands.

So, what specifically does the process of mediatization in LEGO tell us about the interplay of media and business? The chapter argues that, in order for us to get a fuller picture of mediatization and its effects on a corporate brand, we should consider the culture and identity based responses to this process in the organization. The media and media based products are characterized by a dual image: consumers and employees in media based organizations might see them as 'fast and cool', while employees and executives in companies that are not traditionally media based such a LEGO might equally well regard them with scepticism. This is because the speed and coolness of the media are seen to be in opposition to more traditional corporate values such as quality, and even 'caring' (that is, being meticulous and thorough). Organizational members might also regard the media as simply a new technology that has some influence on the product line, but which does not necessarily affect established perceptions of 'who we are as an organization', or, indeed, the way in which external constituents perceive the corporate brand. Introducing media based products into the product line, therefore, does not necessarily mean that the organization or corporate brand is 'transformed'. Neither does it mean that, for a company such as LEGO, the road towards mediatization is inevitable. Certainly, LEGO went a long way to convince both internal and external stakeholders that LEGO's media based subsidiary would 'faithfully apply' both product characteristics (that is, design elements) and cultural values (the concept of constructive play) to the media products. Evidently, LEGO found it necessary to convince key stakeholders that the company and the corporate brand identity remained the same, despite the inclusion of media based products in the product line.

But can we say that LEGO was *de-mediatized* as a result of the culture and identity based reluctance towards the media products and recent strategic developments in the company (that is, a return to a focus on core products and markets)? Yes, but not entirely. In fact, the company recently presented its latest product in the computer games product line: a computer game based on the Indiana Jones movie character. Evidently, LEGO has sought to strike a mediatization balance. It has scaled down efforts that might have led to a transformation of the company and corporate brand identity (that is, the inclusion of a media based culture in the existing culture) while retaining some of the market and image advantages the company can experience from being present in the expanding market for children's software.

If the influence of the media and media based products is, indeed, becoming increasingly inevitable, we might expect that LEGO's mediatization balance may be the way in which similar companies choose to approach media based products. Certainly, the high profile media mergers such as AOL–Time Warner, which was seen by many as the merger of 'old' and 'new' media, have not be unproblematic. Their problems arise precisely because of difference in culture and identity, between the 'techno true believers' (such as in AOL) and the 'establishment intractability' (such as in Time Warner) (*Business Week* 2003). Treading a cautious ground within internal culture and seeking to avoid such identity based clashes might well be a sounder way to deal with mediatization.

Conclusion

This chapter has considered mediatization as a concept that might bring us closer to an understanding of the inter-relationship between business and media, particularly when considered in relation to corporate branding. Whereas corporate branding research tends to consider the media as a 'black box', the concept of mediatization, in turn, tends to ignore key aspects of corporate branding such as organizational culture and identity. An analysis of the process towards mediatization of the LEGO company and corporate brand demonstrated that these aspects of corporate brand identity play a significant role in the way in which mediatization attempts are received in the organization. Conflict and resistance, in particular, arise over differences in organizational identity and business culture, as well as product technologies and vision for the organization. Mediatization balance may be an appropriate and safe strategy for organizations to apply, whereby thier media products are included in the product line of a company without disturbing core aspects of its corporate brand identity.

Note

1. Corporate image is most commonly taken to be about how a company is perceived, in a broad sense, by external constituents such as consumers, the media, NGOs and regulatory bodies. Corporate reputation is seen as a

more strategic construct as the result of a company's accumulated images among various stakeholders over the long term.

References

Albert, S. and Whetten, D. (1985) 'Organisational Identity', in L.L. Cummings and B.M. Staw (eds), *Research in Organisational Behaviour*, vol. 7 (Greenwich: JAI Press).

Balmer, J.M.T and Gray, E.R. (2003) 'Corporate Brands: What are They? What of Them?', *European Journal of Marketing*, 37(7/8): 972–7.

Business Week (2003) 'Can Dick Parsons Rescue AOL Time Warner?', 19 May.

Christensen, L.T. and Cheney, G. (2000) 'Self-Absorption and Self-Seduction in the Corporate Identity Game', in M. Schultz, M.J. Hatch and M.H. Larsen, *The Expressive Organisation: Linking Identity, Reputation, and the Corporate Brand* (Oxford: Oxford University Press): 246–70.

Christensen, L.T., Morsing, M. and Cheney, G. (2008) *Corporate Communications. Convention, Complexity and Critique* (London: Sage).

Dutton, J. and Dukerich, J. (1991) 'Keeping an Eye on the Mirror: Image and Identity in Organisational Adaptation', *Academy of Management Journal*, 39: 517–54.

Fombrun, C. and Van Riel, C. (2004) *Fame and Fortune* (New York: Prentice Hall).

Giddens, A. (1991) *Modernity and Self-Identity – Self and Society in the Late Modern Age* (Oxford: Blackwell).

Gjoels-Andersen, P. and Karmark, E. (2005) 'Corporate Brand Stretch – Brand Extension in a Corporate Brand Perspective', in M. Schultz, Y.M. Antorini and F.F. Csaba, *Corporate Branding – Purpose, People Process* (Copenhagen: CBS Press).

Gjoels-Andersen, P. (2001) 'The Internal Dimensions of Branding – A Case Study of Change of Brand Strategy in LEGO from a Focus on the Famous Building Brick to Introducing a Broad Variety of LEGO Products in the Children's Universe', PhD series, Copenhagen Business School.

Hatch, M.J. and Schultz, M. (1997) 'Relations between Organisational Culture, Identity and Image', *European Journal of Marketing*, 35.

Hatch, M.J. and Schultz, M. (2001) 'Are the Strategic Stars aligned for Your Corporate Brand?', *Harvard Business Review*, February: 128–34.

Hatch, M.J. and Schultz, M. (2008) *Taking Brand Initiative – How Companies can Align Strategy, Culture and Identity through Corporate Branding* (San Francisco: Dossey-Bass).

Hjarvard, S. (2004) 'Brand New Toys', Paper presented to the International Colloquium 'Pluridisciplinary Perspectives on Child and Teen Consumption', Angoulême, France, March 25–26.

Karmark, E. (2002) 'Organisational Identity in a Dualistic Subculture – A Case Study of Organisational Identity Formation in LEGO Media International', Ph.D. series, Copenhagen Business School.

LEGO (1998) *LEGO Media Company Profile* – Internal LEGO Group Publication

LEGO (1999) *LEGO Brand Book* – Internal LEGO Group Publication

Morsing, M. and Kristensen, J. (2001) 'The Question of Coherency in Corporate Branding – Over Time and Across Stakeholders', *Journal of Communication Management*, 6(1): 24–40.

Olins, W. (2003) On Brands (London: Thames & Hudson).

Schultz, M. (2005) 'A Cross-Disciplinary Perspective on Corporate Branding', in M. Schultz, Y.M. Antorini and F.F. Csaba, *Corporate Branding – Purpose, People Process* (Copenhagen: CBS Press).

Schultz, M., Antorini, Y.M. and Csaba, F.F. (2005) *Corporate Branding – Purpose, People Process* (Copenhagen: CBS Press).

Soendergaard, U. (2004) 'LEGO: 'Fra Byggeklodser til Bytes til Byggeklodser'' (in Danish), www.kommunikationsforum.dk, 6 May.

6

Making Sense of a Crucial Interface: Corporate Communication and the News Media

Joep P. Cornelissen, Craig E. Carroll and Wim J.L. Elving

In this chapter, we provide an overview of how news organizations work, and develop a theoretical account of communicative interactions between corporate communication professionals representing commercial companies and journalists working for news organizations. This account conceptualizes these interactions as a discursive process in which professionals and journalists construct and negotiate frames about an event or issue related to a company. This process tends to be guided on both sides by the individual's professional identity (as a communication professional or a journalist) and the identity of his or her organization.

Introduction: Sense-making in news organizations and corporate communication

Communication professionals return to work each day to disseminate information, explain, negotiate and generally garner support for corporate decisions with those groups that matter to the company: stakeholders. Workers, members of the communities in which the company operates, customers, environmental groups, investors and government officials on every continent are making their expectations about corporate conduct heard. For the benefit of the company, it is necessary to communicate with these stakeholders. After all, the profitability and livelihood of companies depend on strong reputations as well as inter-actions with each of these stakeholder groups (for example, Fombrun and Van Riel 2007). The strategic importance of cultivating, insofar as possible, the corporate reputation of the company with these stake-holders has been recognized by CEOs and senior executives in the USA, Europe and elsewhere (Argenti et al. 2005; Murray and White 2005). As a result of this recognition, both the academic and professional worlds have been overwhelmed with principles and frameworks that prescribe ways in which companies can identify their most important stake-holder groups (for example, Mitchell et al. 1997) and how to communi-cate with them (for example, Cornelissen 2008; Fombrun and Van Riel 2007). Most of these principles and frameworks are focused on what are often considered the 'dominant' stakeholders: employees, custom-ers and prospects, activist groups, NGOs and the financial community. One important constituent, the news organization, has often been overlooked in the corporate communication literature, despite evi-dence that the news media can actually make or break a company's reputation (Carroll 2004; Dutton and Dukerich 1991). Hence, we think that understanding how news organizations operate, and how they can be engaged from the perspective of communication professionals and consultants, is vastly important. We suggest that such an under-standing is particularly essential, given the emphasis placed by CEOs and top executives on strategic corporate communications during cor-porate crises and in dealing with the media, and their views that there is a huge under-performance in the communications profession in the USA, the UK and continental Europe because of a limited understand-ing of how companies should engage with constituents such as the media (Argenti et al. 2005; Murray and White 2005).

Our aim in this chapter, therefore, is:

- To provide a broad overview of how news organizations work; and
- To develop a conceptual framework of communicative inter-actions between communication professionals of commercial organizations and journalists that might help professionals in identifying viable repertoires of action for their own dealings with the news media.

In doing so, we aim to contribute to an increased awareness and reflexivity of communication professionals about how they can most effectively communicate with the news media. The conceptual framework itself is rooted in a tradition of research that recognizes the crucial role and ability of communication professionals to articulate an understanding of a corporate event, decision or issue in ways that resonate with potential readings of that same event, decision or issue by the media (and, by extension, by the general public). This tradition of research has been labelled differently ('discourse', 'framing', 'sense-making', 'practical authorship') dependent on the discipline (for example, communication studies, social psychology, management, organizational sociology) within which the writing or research is based.

In this chapter, we primarily use the term 'sense-making' and draw on writings in organization theory. Sense-making is a central organizational construct that describes how individuals within an organization come to make sense of events and issues within and outside their organizations that need to be made intelligible to themselves and others (for example, Weick 1995; Weick et al. 2005). In these situations, individuals engage in sense-making activities (for example, categorizing, bracketing and labelling an experience) to provide an account – a discursive narration or framing of an event, decision or issue – that has a semantic function as an interpretation or explanation (for themselves) as well as a performative function, in that it provides a basis for influencing and shaping the interpretations of others and for negotiating a common understanding with them (Quinn and Dutton 2005). We argue that this is also essentially what happens when communication professionals engage with journalists from various news media. They have to make sense of an event, decision or issue for themselves and others within the organization (sense-making), but they then also need to frame the event, decision or issue in such a way that it is likely to be accepted by stakeholders outside the organization, including different news media (framing). Framing processes in regard to the media are of particular importance because of the amplifying effect of the media on a company's reputation when 'good' or 'bad' news is reported (Carroll and McCombs 2003). Such framing, and the sense-making processes that precede it, also require an intimate understanding of the workings of news media. On this basis, we argue that, when corporate media and communication professionals see themselves as communication 'technicians', they might focus on the dissemination of information rather than engaging in prolific dialogue with the media and other stakeholders. We illustrate this tendency with/through an example of a nuclear fuels company's response to/communication management in connection with a leak.

Overview of the news media: Roles, identity and reputation

The news media involve a variety of organizations where core operational processes include the production and dissemination of news content through various media (newspapers, radio, TV, the Internet). Deephouse and Carroll (2006) adapt the Shoemaker and Reese (1996) framework that outlines five levels of influences on the actual production of news content, from the journalist who does the fieldwork gathering materials all the way up to the ideology of the country hosting the news organization that disseminates the produced content. The model adapted to business news is important for corporate communication professionals because it illustrates the variety of influences on the production of news content, and points to the limited degree of control that journalists producing stories about organizations actually have on the whole process, which includes the final printed words constituting the news story with each level subsumed by the higher levels. The five levels from Shoemaker and Reese (1996) are:

- Journalist
- News routines
- News organization
- Issues external to the organization
- The overarching ideology of the news organization.

At the *journalist level*, Deephouse and Carroll (2006) suggest that journalists have very little control over the final words that are printed. Journalists might talk to sources, cover a beat and write a story but not recognize their own story when the story goes to print. This is because, at the routines level, there are many other people involved in the writing process who affect the printed story, such as the fact checker who verifies the correct spellings of the people, organizations and places mentioned. Copy editors might check that quotes are appropriately attributed to sources in a way that min-imizes conflict and controversy. Layout and design specialists might be concerned that news stories do not go over a certain word limit, and that the story is designed within the format of the outlet and probably with an idea of how to attract readers and/or consumers. Moreover, the newspaper editor might decide that what was once a business news story should be a front-page article for a much wider range of audiences. In such a case, the lead paragraphs would need to be re-written from a business or strictly financial perspective to a public interest perspective so as to attract a much wider reading audience typical of the front page. Business journalists detest this organizational reality, as it creates additional work (having to rewrite part of their story) and prevents them from moving on to the next story.

At the *news routines level*, it means that the journalist is, to an extent, writing toward the needs of the editorial desk to which they are assigned: the national news desk, local news desk, the financial/business news desk, or perhaps even the international news desk or the arts desk. For journalists, writing to the needs of the desk or to their peers is their way of ensuring that their story makes it into print. While no journalist writes a story for sheer waste or with the intent of not getting picked up, whether the story is published is not his or her call. Moreover, journalists do not have a say on the final printed story, what the headline of the story is, or what photographs will be included (if any) with their story. Those decisions lie with their numerous editors, including the front-page editor, national, business/financial, arts/community, and others.

The *organizational level* of analysis suggests that, when a reporter switches from the *Financial Times* to *The Wall Street Journal Europe*, the journalist's professional training might help the reporter under-stand some expectations because of their professional experiences, but they will still be expected to learn the corporate culture and adjust to the operational styles of the newspaper. For example, *The New York Times* has been characterized as 'the editor's paper' while *The Washington Post* isthe 'reporter's paper', referring to the levels of bureaucracy that exist between them.

The level *external to the news organization* refers to the influences on the news organization from outside the organization. This is not sim-ply 'environment' in an abstract sense, but involves the web of relationships of which the news organization is a part. This can include board interlocks, sources, advertisers and general issues of public relations with other stakeholders of the news organization – even their view of 'audience'. Corporate communication professionals often play an important role at this level as sources who are asked for comments on an aspect of their organizations. According to some (Merten 2004; Elving and Van Ruler 2006), communication professionals prompt as much as 80 percent of news reports about companies.

Then, finally, *ideology* is the highest level of analysis. Ideology refers to the underlying process the news media use to produce meanings and ideas. It can also refer to media, cultural and political systems of the country in which the news organization resides. For example, published news reports might have different meanings when they are published primarily as a commodity, or as a means of nation-building, or out of a connection to theocracy – as is the case in a few Middle Eastern countries (Sriramesh and Verčič 2003) capitalist countries that are generally sympathetic toward businesses, one could argue that, on the whole, businesses are given the benefit of the doubt regarding their intentions, until there is evidence that the business has violated social norms. As Gans comments:

> The underlying posture of the news toward the economy resembles that taken toward the polity: an optimistic faith that, in the good society, businessmen and women will compete with each other in order to create increased prosperity for all, but that they will refrain from unreasonable profits and gross exploitation of workers or customers. (Gans 1979: 41)

Issues of identity and reputation

An important point that is related to these five levels is that news media are characterized by their own issues of identity (Carroll 2004). Journalists, for example, have their own roles. For journalists, these identities are bound up in how they see their individual roles as reporters, and also in their roles as professionals. In this sense, their identities cross levels to include the aspect of news routines. At the level of the individual journalist, their internalized roles and professed professional identity can be such as a *watchdog*, a *lapdog*, a *neutral disseminator of information*, a *community/public journalist*, an *advocate*, or a *sentinel*. Each of these various identities implies a set of values and procedures for how the journalist carries out his or her job. At the level of news routines, the professional role attributed to a journalist (for example, as an investigative journalist, a business journalist, a political news reporter, an environmental reporter) equally carries with it a particular professional identity and, hence, particular routines that accompany the enactment of the identity. For one thing, each type of reporter will answer to a different editorial desk. The deadlines might be different. The rules for verification and corroboration of their sources might be different. The questions they ask their subjects are also likely to be different. The journalist might also have identity characteristics tied up in the nature of the news medium (that is, being a broadcast journalist, being a print journalist, or being a magazine journalist) that has also routine-level implications. Writing for these different media forms involves different timetables, deadlines and reporting styles. The print journalist will employ the pyramid-organizational scheme, where the most important information is shared first in the article, then, as the article increases in length, the information appearing further down in the news article will be deemed less important. In contrast, the radio journalist will try to share the information early on. Moreover, a reporter who is assigned to a business or financial desk will be concerned about angles from the perspective of business audiences, the implications for financial performance, stock performance and so on. The public affairs reporter will be more concerned about the public angle. A feature writer will be more concerned about the human interest angle.

The role of identity in news organizations continues at the news organization level in terms of the image or reputation that the news organization aims to uphold. Such an image or reputation might be tied to expectations of their audiences, readers and listeners. The *Guardian* newspaper in the UK, for example, aims to uphold its reputation as a newspaper that is trusted as a reliable source for breaking news and commentary on political and environmental issues. Carroll (2004) has argued that, where companies often reply on corporate communication professionals and PR consultants to build their reputations, the news media typically attempt to manage their reputations themselves directly through a variety of strategies, including the ombudsman, the public editor, letters from the editor and publisher, the publication of correction, and many other techniques that the news media use, but these are sufficient to make the example. The point is that the news media build and maintain their reputations through the core process of publishing stories.

Finally, besides the various levels to the production of business news and the different issues of identity and reputation related to news organizations, there are also clear distinctions between different kinds of news media. For instance, in the USA there is a clear distinction between, say, Fox News, CNN and *The New York Times*. In the UK, the famous tabloids all differ greatly from so-called quality newspapers such as the *Times*, or the *Guardian*. These differences matter, particularly from the perspective of a corporate communication professional who is interacting with representatives of these different news organizations. Another point to be made is the time frame of the different news media. Television and the Internet are 'fast' media, in the sense that when a topic or an article is published directly when it is finished. In contrast, newspapers are slower, in that they wait until the next deadline for publication. Magazines have an even longer waiting period for Internet and television is important to corporate communication professionals, because the chance of incorrect reporting probably would be greater for these fast media.

Corporate communication and the media

Traditionally, literature has described the relationship between communication professionals and journalists as adversarial. Journalists were identified as having a negative opinion about communication professionals, in part because they felt that there was a clear divide between their interests: according to journalists, communication professionals think about the needs of their companies first and what journalists need last. Traditionally, research also found that journalists felt that professionals withheld information, were not always objective and did not focus on issues of public interest (Belz et al. 1989). On the other hand, professionals have been found to be less negative about journalists; they often have a positive view of journalists and are eager to work with them (Neijens and Smit 2006). While positive, professionals also realize that journalists have their own agenda and might frame news about the company in line with their news routines. Both professionals and journalists have different agendas, thus, different angles regarding on news related to a company; however they do realize that they are interdependent. Journalists need, and often use, information provided by professionals and, equally, professionals and the companies for which they work often need the media as a conduit to generate coverage on the company, and to reach important stakeholders such as the financial community, customers, prospective employees, the government and the general public. The realization of this interdependence has led to a further specialization of media or press relations within corporate communication. Many large companies have a dedicated press office or media team that deals with the general media that subsumes, or is separate from, the investor relation professionals who deal with financial media such as *The Wall Street Journal* and the *Financial Times*. As a result, organized efforts to subsidize *The* news media should lead to significant correspondence between the corporate agenda and the news media agenda (Carroll and McCombs 2003).

Similar to journalists, communication professionals also tend to be guided by their own professional identity (the constellation of attributes, beliefs, values, motives, and experiences with which individuals define themselves in a professional role) and by routines associated with their roles. Research suggests that corporate communication professionals who have completed a degree at a university, or who have been working as a communication professional for a number of years, have some values and beliefs in common. In essence, they have been trained and are expected to operate as communication 'technicians' from the start of their careers (for example, Argenti et al. 2005; Grunig et al. 2002). Communication technicians are professionals who are responsible for the production and dissemination of communication materials. Dozier and Broom (1995: 22) defined a technician as 'a creator and disseminator of messages, intimately involved in production, [and] operating independent of management decision making, strategic planning, issues management, environmental scanning and program evaluation'. In this role, when a communication professional deals with journalists, he or she will be primarily concerned with the supply of information he or she gives a journalist. Press officers, for example, typically only tend to write press releases or organize press conferences that provide journalists with the necessary information. However, over time, communication professionals may progress to a managerial role in corporate communication (Dozier and Broom 1995). In this role, they are expected to perform a whole range of tasks (for example, counseling managers at all levels of the organization, developing a corporate social responsibility or citizenship program, supervising the work of others, and managing crisis situations) and to make sense of events that affect the corporation (for example, accidents, activist protests, strikes) that lie beyond their initial skills set as technicians. When acting as 'managers', communication professionals often also assume the role of a boundary-spanner between the organization and its environment, helping to gather, relay and interpret information from the environment as well as representing the organization to the outside world (Grunig et al. 2002). The implication of this role for dealing with journalists is that it often demands professionals to look beyond the press release toward the relationship with the journalist and the news organization that he or she represents, and even beyond that to the audiences and stakeholders that will be reached by the news medium. Spokespersons for a company or a director of media relations, for example, will often have to consider the wider ramifications of a news item for the company's reputation with different stakeholder groups.

Besides the difference in these roles, both 'technicians' and 'managers' aim to control the supply of information directed at journalists. They do so not only to represent their company in the best possible light, but also to ensure and verify that accurate information is being communicated. Amongst communication professionals, communicating accurate information is often seen as an important professional value and one that contributes toward maintaining good relationships with journalists.

Making sense of interactions between communication professionals and journalists

Building on from the characteristics of professionals and journalists, we argue that it is useful to conceptualize dimensions of the interaction between them. To do so, we start from the position that the meaning of events, corporate decisions or issues related to companies is discursively constructed and negotiated between both parties (Fiss and Hirsch 2005). This negotiation process is strongly guided by the identities of professionals and journalists and their beliefs about the significance of an event or issue to a wider public. Both parties discursively construct particular frames of an event, decision or issue, and negotiate between them the relevance and details of these frames. Framing involves the mobilization of discursive templates that provide coherence to a set of ideas and constitute 'schemata of interpretation' that 'organize experiences and guide action' (Snow et al. 1986: 464) and shape how people view the world by delimiting subject matter and focusing attention on key elements (Hallahan 1999; Carroll 2005). For journalists and the news media, framing deals with the construction of news items so they are more noticeable, meaningful and memorable to an audience (Entman 1993).

For communication professionals, this theoretical starting point means that 'problems do not present themselves to the practitioners as givens. They must be constructed from the material of problematic situations which are puzzling, troubling, and uncertain' (Weick 1995: 9). That is, professionals themselves decide first how they make sense of a particular event or issue in a plausible way dependent on the cues they receive about the event, decision or issue. The sense-making accounts that they construct for themselves and others in the organization, then, often provide the basis for the frames that they communicate to journalists. Journalists, in turn, might accept the frame that is provided to them, although, when they do, the frame is likely to be modified by journalists and editors in the process of news production (as outlined previously). In some cases, after negotiation with a professional, journalists might even disagree with a particular frame, either because they look at the issue or event from a different angle or because they simply disagree with the provided frame. We will elaborate on this theoretical framework of sense-making, frame construction and negotiation by reference to an empirical example. This empirical example provides the gist of the theoretical framework and allows us to build further detail into it.

Sense-making in action

In March 2005, a leak of nuclear material was detected in one of the plants of a nuclear fuels company in Northern England. The leak involved highly radioactive nuclear fuel dissolved in concentrated nitric acid and contained about 20 tons of uranium and plutonium fuel. As the leak was contained within the plant, it was of no danger to the public. When it happened, the media manager of the company was charged with communicating about the accident, putting him in a position where he had to make sense of the consequences of the leak for all of the company's stakeholders. He subsequently reasoned not only that the leak was physically 'contained' within the plant (which was the cue that he had received from company scientists and senior managers) and posed no direct health or security threat, not even to residents near the site, but also that the issue (of the health and safety implications of the leak) itself was 'contained' and under control. The company had started an investigation into the cause(s) of the leak and, hence, a due process was being followed. Because it was, in his view, a contained issue that posed no direct danger to the public, the incident was primarily an internal organizational matter with a very 'local scope' – meaning that only 'local' stakeholders needed to be informed that the incident had happened. Interpreting the incident in this way, his view was that 'the message only needed to be brought across' to the local media and the local government who, in turn, would inform the local community and that he should 'not release any further speculation about the cause of the accident', especially, not to the national media. The media manager particularly wanted to avoid some of the left-leaning newspapers because of their consistently negative reporting on the nuclear industry. He subsequently enacted this set of interpretations by sending a press release to selected local media and by briefing local government counselors. The local media accepted his framing of the incident as an internal organizational matter and reported that the incident posed no direct security or health risks to residents living near the site. However, one of the left-leaning national newspapers, which he had ignored at first, found out about the leak and printed a full-page feature on its front page two weeks later. The national newspaper framed the incident as a national disaster which raised serious questions about the safety and reliability of this company as well as the nuclear industry in general. This story was subsequently picked up by other national newspapers and damaged the image of the company and of the entire nuclear industry in the UK.

In this example, then, while journalists from the local media had accepted the framing of the professional, one of the national newspapers decided to frame the incident in a different way. Unsurprisingly, this national newspaper has a long record of opposing nuclear energy in its reporting and in public debates, which appeared to have motivated its own framing of the incident. In other words, the *identity* of this newspaper and that of its journalists primed a particular frame to help make sense of the incident (Weick 1995). Equally, the original frame that was constructed by the media manager was also guided by his own identity and that of his organization. His own professional identity was one of being a technician; this identity primed his sense-making of trying to lay low and of disseminating only the minimum amount of necessary information to local constituencies. Similarly, his company, as a recently privatized and science-based company, tends to emphasize faults or defects in the production process as simply an internal matter. As an internal matter, incidents such as the leak of nuclear material are seen as effectively addressed through an emergency protocol and a commissioned internal investigation. Because of his own and the company's identity, the professional was biased toward a frame that described the incident as a technical matter *within* the organization, that is of little to its stakeholders. The national newspaper, however, framed the incident as a crisis of legitimacy for the company by questioning its capability to operate in a safe and reliable way – a frame that resonated with the general public and has since then been present in public debates on the role of nuclear energy as a viable source of energy in the UK.

Figure 6.1 provides a summary of our theoretical account of the discursive negotiation of frames between a communication professional and a journalist from a particular news medium. As illustrated with our example of the nuclear company, the crux of what matters is the negotiation of frames as interpretations of events, decisions or issues. In the example, however, there was, no direct communication intially and therefore, no direct negotiation between the media manager and the journalist from the national newspaper. The media manager – influenced by the cue that he had received about the leak (namely that it was 'contained') and by his own professional identity – did not feel that the issue required an engagement with the national media. This decision effectively violated a principle of transparency

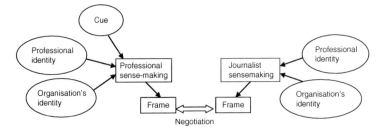

Figure 6.1 Sensemaking, framing and frame negotiation between professionals and journalists

Source: Author's figure

of information on the issue and meant that the company had not informed the journalist and his newspaper of its responses to the leak or of the background of the leak. One consequence of this lack of communication was that the initial news story reported factually incorrect data on the scope of the leak. In general terms, then, how the issue was framed by both parties as well as the lack of communication between them was affected by their professional identities and the identities of their organizations (see Figure 6.1). In the nuclear company, there is a genuine distrust in this left-leaning newspaper. Equally, the newspaper has been a vocal opponent of the nuclear industry. In addition, the professional's identity as a technician meant that he did not sufficiently reflect upon his own framing of the issue, the likelihood of the news media accepting his frame, and his narrow response in terms of only communicating to local constituencies. Professional identity (the constellation of attributes, beliefs, values, motives and experiences with which individuals define themselves in a professional role) thus played an important role in his sense-making. While his title is that of a media manager, it appears that he had not yet fully internalized the skills, attitudes and repertoires of behaviors associated with the professional identity of a communication 'manager' and had difficulties in elaborating or creating new repertoires of possibilities (Ibarra 1999). The more general implication arising from this example is that there might be a need for mentoring and job rotation schemes that facilitate the transition of professionals from the role and identity of 'technician' to that of 'manager' and, in doing so, increase their ability to identify new ways of making sense and new possibilities for framing an issue. In this case, the actual framing of the issue as a 'contained', 'local' and 'internal' matter taken from the cue that he had received, his own identity and that of his organization, as well as from his anticipation that the newspaper in question would not 'buy' the company's account of the issue and was likely to cast the accident in a negative light.

As such, there was little direct communication between the two parties, and, therefore, no opportunities to negotiate their respective frames. As a result, the initial story itself elevated the accident to a major crisis of legitimacy for the nuclear company in that it questioned the company's ability to operate in a safe and reliable way. The newspaper has since not redressed its account of the accident and, in its reporting, has continued to question the legitimacy and operational safety of the company's nuclear plant.

Conclusion

We started this brief chapter with an overview of news organizations and the production of news content. We continued our discussion with a theoretical account of the communicative interaction between communication professionals and journalists, illustrated by an extensive case example/study. We believe this account has the following practical implications for communication professionals.

First, the chapter points to the importance of understanding the process through which news is produced in different news organizations and, particularly, the considerations of identity that influence a journalist's perspective on company news ranging from issues and events to more 'standard' news such as quarterly or annual results.

Second, we argue that the communicative interaction between professionals and journalists can be seen as a discursive process of constructing and negotiating frames on company news. We think this sense-making perspective (Weick 1995) is a useful starting point for theorizing about and explaining examples such as one discussed above. For communication professionals this sense-making perspective suggests that they have to be reflective of how issues or events can be framed and the likelihood of acceptance of such frames by journalists from different media.

Finally, we point to the potential dangers for a company's reputation when a professional, because of his identity as a 'technician', is not sufficiently reflective of frames and potential media responses to a critical incident. In such cases, hasty or wrong decisions might be risky. In the example we discussed, the professional decided to ignore certain media and to adopt a linear process of information dissemination, whereas a two-way process of dialogue with the media and with concerned community residents might have been more appropriate. In making these suggestions, we hope that this chapter might serve as a foundation for further theorizing and research on corporate communication and the news media.

References

Argenti, P.A., Howell, R.A. and Beck, K.A. (2005) 'The Strategic Communication Imperative', *MIT Sloan Management Review*, 46(3): 83–9.

Belz, A., Talbott, A.D. and K. Starck (1989) 'Using Role Theory to Study Cross Perceptions of Journalists and Public Relations Practitioners', *Public Relations Research Annual*: 125–39.

Carroll, C. (2004) 'How the Mass Media Influence Perceptions of Corporate Reputation: Agenda-Setting Effects within Business News Coverage', Unpublished doctoral dissertation, University of Texas, Austin, Texas, USA.

Carroll, C.E. (2005) 'Frame', in R. Heath (ed.) *Encyclopedia of Public Relations* (Thousand Oaks, CA: Sage).

Carroll, C.E. (forthcoming) 'Corporate Reputation and the News Media', Unpublished manuscript.

Carroll, C.E. and McCombs, M.K. (2003) 'Agenda-setting Effects of Business News on the Public's Images and Opinions about Major Corporations', *Corporate Reputation Review*, 6(1): 36–46.

Cornelissen, J. (2008) *Corporate Communications: Theory and Practice*, 2nd edn (London: Sage).

Deephouse, D.L. and Carroll, C.E. (2007) 'What Makes News Fit To Print: A Five-Level Framework Predicting Media Visibility and Favorability of Organisations', Working paper.

Dozier, D.M. and Broom, G.M. (1995) Evolution of the Manager Role in Public Relations Practice', *Journal of Public Relations Research*, 7(1): 3–26.

Elving, W.J.L. and Van Ruler, A.A. (2006) 'Trendonderzoek communicatiemanagement' [Trend research communication management], Amsterdam, University of Amsterdam.

Entman, R.M. (1993) 'Framing: Toward Clarification of a Fractured Paradigm', *Journal of Communication*, 43(4): 51–8.

Fiss, P.C. and Hirsch, P.M. (2005) 'The Discourse of globalization: Framing and Sensemaking of an Emerging Concept', *American Sociological Review*, 70(1): 29–52.

Fombrun, C.J. and Van Riel, C.B.M. (2007) *Essentials of Corporate Communication, Building and Implementing Corporate Stories Using Reputation Management* (London: Routledge).

Gans, H.J. (1979) 'The Messages behind the News', *Columbia Journalism Review*, 17(1): 40–5.

Grunig, L.A., Grunig, J.E. and Dozier, D.M. (2002) *Excellent Public Relations and Effective Organisations* (New Jersey: Lawrence Erlbaum).

Hallahan, K. (1999) 'Seven Models of Framing: Implication for Public Relations', *Journal of Public Relations Research*, 11(3): 205–42.

Ibarra, H. (1999) 'Provisional Selves: Experimenting with Image and Identity in Professional Adaptation', *Administrative Science Quarterly*, 44: 764–91.

Merten, K. (2004) 'A Constructivist Approach to Public Relations', in B. van Ruler and D. Vercic (eds), *Public Relations and Communication Management in Europe* (Berlin: Mouton de Gruyter): 45–54.

Mitchell, R.K., Agle, B.R. and Wood, D.J. (1997) 'Toward a Theory of Stakeholder Identification and Salience: Defining the Principle of Who and What Really Counts', *Academy of Management Review*, 22(4): 853–87.

Murray, K. and White, J. (2005) 'CEO Views on Reputation Management', *Journal of Communication Management*, 9(4): 348–58.

Neijens, P.C. and Smit, E.G. (2006) 'Dutch Public Relations Practitioners and Journalists: Antagonists No More', *Public Relations Review*, 32(3): 232–40.

Quinn, R. and Dutton, J. (2005) 'Coordination as Energy-In-Conversation: A Process Theory of Organizing', *Academy of Management Review*, 30: 38–57.

Shoemaker, P.J. and Reese, S.D. (1996) *Mediating the Message: Theories of Influences on Mass Media Content* (2nd ed.) (White Plains, NY: Longman.

Snow, D., Rochford, E.B., Worden, S. and Benford, R. (1986) 'Frame Alignment Processes, Micro-Mobilization, and Movement Participation', *American Sociological Review*, 51(4): 456–81.

Sriramesh, K. and Verčič, D. (2003) *The Global Public Relations Handbook: Theory, Research, and Practice* (Mahwah, NJ: Lawrence Erlbaum).

Weick, K.E. (1995) *Sensemaking in Organisations* (Thousand Oaks, CA: Sage).

Weick, K.E., Sutcliffe, K.M. and Obstfeld, D. (2005) 'Organizing and the Process of Sensemaking', *Organisation Science*, 16: 409–21.

Part III
Business in the Media

7
Place Branding and Globalization. The Media is the Message?

Peter van Ham

Introduction: The emerging art of place branding in a mediated world order

The unbranded state has a difficult time attracting economic and political attention. Territorial entities such as cities, regions, and states are now branded in the same way as companies and products. It is well known that the corporate brand has become an essential part of business identity that helps audiences to identify with the company and – lest we forget – encourages them to buy its products and services. In a similar way, branding has become essential to create value in the relationship between territorial entities and individuals. This comes at a time when the role and power of states (and other territorial actors) is changing. States, as well as international organizations (IOs), need to justify their existence and have, therefore, embarked on a renewed quest for the hearts and minds of people, both at home and around the world.

Image and reputation have become essential parts of the state's strategic equity. As with commercial brands, they are built on factors such as trust and customer satisfaction. Place branding is required to make a country's image work for its economy and its citizens. One could think, for example, about the so-called country-of-origin effect, which plays an important role in consumers' purchase decisions (that is to say, 'German cars' and 'Japanese cameras'). Since many companies remain associated with their countries of origin, the images and reputations of brands and states tend to merge in the minds of the global consumer. In many ways, Microsoft and

Coca-Cola *are* America, just as Nokia *is* Finland (and vice versa). Now that the market has moved manufacturing to the developing world where labour is cheap, what distinguishes the West from the rest is the simple fact that 'we' have the respectable brands; many other states do not. The West has everything that counts, it has all the right labels, from 'market economy' and 'stability', to 'democracy' and 'security'; most other states do not.

Place branding is no static game – quite the contrary. In order to do their job properly, politicians all over the world have to find a brand niche for their state, engage in competitive marketing, assure customer satisfaction and – most of all – create brand loyalty. Most democratic states (and other territorial entities) can no longer make use of established mass media to reach their audience(s). The classical sender–message–receiver model lacks relevance in today's complex, multi-dimensional media environment. The ICT revolution – based on electronic media, mobile communication and the Internet – has created what Ronald Deibert calls 'hyper-media.' As Deibert suggests, this emerging media order 'points *away* from single mass identities, linear political boundaries, and exclusive jurisdictions, centred on territorial spaces, and *towards* multiple identities and nonterritorial communities, overlapping boundaries, and nonexclusive jurisdictions' (Deibert 1997: 15). To adapt to this new media landscape, most states try to shift both the mode and the means of communication, realizing that the challenges of competitive identity management can no longer be addressed by old-fashioned communication means (such as brochures and advertisements in printed media).

Numerous professional branding consultants offer their services to cities, regions, states and IOs, all of whom doubt whether they can survive the demands of a mediatized global society without adopting new strategies and tactics. These branding agencies tell their customers that anything for which one can construct a mental inventory is, in principle, a 'brand'. Their argument is straightforward: 'Contemporary brands succeed by getting close to the dreams of their audiences. They promise a better world, and they strive to deliver one. Since nation states today need to reengage popular support and understanding, they should use the power of branding to deliver a message about their value and values to the widest possible audience.' (Olins 2002).

Brand managers offer four arguments why branding is both necessary and beneficial for commercial and political actors alike:

- Products, services and locations have become so alike that they
  can no longer differentiate themselves by their quality, reliability
  and other basic traits. Branding adds emotion and trust to these
  'products', thereby offering clues that make consumers' choices
  somewhat easier
- This emotional relationship between brand and consumer ensures
  loyalty to the brand
- By creating an aspiration lifestyle, branding offers a kind of *ersatz*
  for ideologies and political programmes that are losing their
  relevance
- The combination of emotions, relationships and lifestyle (values)
  allows a brand to charge a price premium for their products, services and locations, which would otherwise hardly be distinguish-
  able from generics.

(van Gelder 2002)

Although these four branding qualities apply most directly to commercial products and services, political actors find themselves in an
environment dominated by almost similar pressures and parameters.
Cities, regions and states now adopt pro-active branding strategies in
the knowledge that, as a strong, attractive place brand, they can
charge higher prices, achieve higher profit margins, and expand
their market and political share by creating a brand premium. The
argument is quite simple. By managing their location's brand equity,
politicians do two things. Externally, they aim at attracting more
clients, charge more for their products/services, and generate overall
economic/political advantage for themselves. Internally, they are
making their citizens feel better and more confident about themselves by giving them a sense of belonging and a clear self-concept.
Branding, therefore, is about power and identity, and it is necessary
to keep these two sides of place branding in mind during our
analysis.

It is the intersection between media and brand management, and
the world of international politics that is of interest to me in this
chapter. These are paradigms that have little contact with each other,
although they share an interest in concepts such as globalization,

identity and power. After setting place branding in its proper historical and conceptual context, I will, first, examine the challenges
facing the European Union (EU) in branding itself as a relevant actor,
both abroad and 'at home'. Second, I will analyze Washington's
branding efforts to deal with its collapsing image in the aftermath of
its failing 'war on terror' and the botched military intervention in
Iraq. This chapter closes with some reflections on the challenges of a
new political and media dynamic whose emphasis on interactivity
and connectivity poses particular challenges for states (and other territorial entities) to link up with their multiple audiences.

Propaganda, place branding and public diplomacy

Place branding stands in a long tradition of reputation management,
spin-doctoring and propaganda. But the very idea that states are – let
alone should be – considered as brandable entities, still sets many
people's teeth on edge. 'Our beloved nation' should be beyond branding, it is argued, since it carries specific dignity quite unlike a marketed product. This is a questionable and certainly ahistorical
proposition.

Images and reputation have been important throughout history,
where early, pre-digital media channels have been used as modes of
communication. Germany's perceptions about Russia were shaped
decisively in the sixteenth century by reports about the despotic rule
of Czar Ivan IV ('the Terrible') (Kunczik 1997). Since then, Russia's
image in Germany has long been that of a cruel and servile people.
Moreover, all states have invented and re-invented themselves over
the centuries, replacing the *Fleur de Lys* with the *Tricolour*, celebrating
the German *Kulturnation*, or changing from Ceylon to Sri Lanka,
from Gold Coast to Ghana, from Southern Rhodesia to Zimbabwe,
from the Ottoman Empire to Atatürk's modern Turkey, from the
USSR to the Russian Federation. To reflect these changes, these states
have rebranded themselves, using (and abusing) all the parapherna-
lia of statehood by all the media available, and pursuing these efforts
relentlessly.

Since the world can be understood as a massive and complex media
network with multiple transaction streams (for example, tourism,
business, immigration and so on), attempts at influencing image and
reputation are both difficult to achieve and nigh impossible to

measure. Over the centuries, a great many events at the international level have had an indisputable symbolic communicative character, and states have done their best to improve their image abroad for specific reasons. Propaganda can therefore be considered a rather unsophisticated forerunner of the place branding we see today. But, just as merely selling a product through advertising differs from current commercial branding practices, traditional propaganda is a world apart from today's branding strategies. Especially, the media-genic creation of emotional ties between the citizen-*cum*-consumer and the (place) brand has unique qualities that make any comparison with past efforts of image management problematical.

However, this novelty, and the lack of an unmistakable ideological content, does not make branding a harmless and naive practice, especially since corporate branding and (economic) imperialism have often gone hand-in-hand. The comparison with Nazi Germany and the Soviet Union – with their strong logos (swastika, hammer and sickle), slogans, emotive identities, and ideological manifestos – comes to mind. Leni Riefenstahl's movies are an example of how media and film have had a glorifying effect on Nazism and remain so powerful that their distribution is restricted in some countries out of fear that they still touch people's souls. (Strangely enough, most Soviet emblems have quickly disappeared, also from our collective minds and sensitivities). But the conceptual link between propaganda and (place) branding seriously tinges the latter's credibility, especially with a wider public. Propaganda equals disinformation, lying and deceiving. And it is an interesting paradox that the concept of 'branding' has a rather bad image itself.

Due to this blotted track record, place branding consultants are, almost without exception, subjected to much opprobrium. Most notably, Naomi Klein (herself a remarkable anti-branding brand) has warned of the emergence of 'a fascist state where we all salute the logo and have little opportunity for criticism because our newspapers, television stations, Internet servers, streets and retail spaces are all controlled by multinational corporate interests.'[1] The place branding specialist Simon Anholt realizes that the public's suspicion towards his line of work is not new, and that since the publication of Vance Packard's *The Hidden Persuaders* (in 1957), 'the population has always been ready to believe that there is something innately corrupt or even sinister about an industry that panders so effectively to people's vanity, aspirations and simple desire to better themselves. Somehow, when these fiendish tricks are applied to something as sacred as the nation-state, all hell breaks loose. Insults are heaped on the head of brands, marketers and policy makers alike – "spin", "gloss" and "lies" are the most commonly heard in this country. In my own work, helping to improve the prospects of emerging markets through better branding of the country and its products, I am often accused of "rewriting history," "social engineering," "exploitation," "condescension," "neoimperialism" and worse' (Anholt 2002: 229ff.).

Closely associated with the notion of place branding is public diplomacy, which appeals to the core values of foreign audiences by using new techniques that are frequently directly derived from commercial practice. In order to be successful, public diplomacy – as do commercial marketing and PR – needs to identify target audiences in each country and/or region, and tailor strategies and tools to reach these audiences in a variety of different ways. For both place branding and public diplomacy, a key element is to build personal and institutional relationships and dialogue with foreign audiences by focusing on *values*, setting it apart from classical diplomacy, which primarily deals with *issues*. The theory and practice of place branding is part of a wider discourse that also involves strategic communications, reputation management, and PR. All in all, it embodies a new direction in the evolution of diplomacy and international politics taking place in a novel technological, media and political context.

For both place branding and public diplomacy, this implies that they have to adjust to a new media paradigm, which has shifted from a mass communication approach that is inherently information-centred, to a network communication approach based on message exchange, relationship building and network creation (Zaharna 2007). In an era where governments were the main media-owners, propaganda could be effective. Especially during the Cold War, information dissemination was vital and the mass media were the channel of choice, generating (soft) power for the state. Today, however, media power is not derived from control, 'getting the message out', or 'staying on message' but, instead, by entering into effective, interpersonal and open relationships. The emerging hypermedia environment constitutes a real 'revolution in diplomatic affairs' (Arquilla and Ronfeldt 1999), in the sense that accessibility and interactivity have become of central importance (Rafaeli 1988). Interactivity is 'the user's ability to dynamically select, manipulate, integrate and format the information to suit particular and changing needs' (Meyer and Zack 1996: 49). But interactivity also implies connectivity, which is now increasingly found in networks (Castells 1996). The main challenge for states is, therefore, to make this shift and to approach 'messaging' as a creative, participatory process.

The following two short case studies are situated in the context of a media and communication landscape and examine the role and place of soft power tools such as place branding within an international politics realm still dominated by more traditional hard power concerns. The cases of the EU and the USA show that the brand of these two key players in international politics are shaped by history and images, as well as their foreign policy agendas and actions. They also illustrate that these brands might change, and should be managed. Whereas the EU remains reluctant to take its brand in its own hands, the USA is more aware of the need for reputation management, and more at ease with branding and its policy implications. Both cases also indicate that the EU and the USA are using place branding and public diplomacy in order to adapt to the new media setting.

Branding Europe

Obviously, the EU is not a state but, rather, a community of member states. But as with states and regions, IOs have their own image and brand. Where NATO stands for (military) security, the EU is the ultimate affluence brand, radiating material comfort and family values (van Ham 2005). Knowing that Europe is unlikely to acquire a similar affection from its citizens as once enjoyed by the nation-state, the EU faces a serious challenge to brand itself by developing emotional ties between its citizens, as well as with the outside world.

A central role will be played by the (news) media in shaping society's understanding of what constitutes 'Europe', and what place the emerging Euro-polity will come to play in the political discourse. By providing an essential forum for public debate on matters politic, media have an important legitimization function in the evolution of a European civic society, and potentially in enhancing the feelings of community and solidarity. We should not forget that, in the construction of the modern nation-state, news media have played a similar role, and that the freedom of the press was perceived not only as a vital element of democracy, but also, first and foremost, as a symbol of the democratic *state*. Benedict Anderson has claimed that, in the conceptualization of the nation-state, the printing press was essential in the development of nationalism, and that the newspaper was a 'technical means for "representing" the kind of imagined community that is the nation' (Anderson 1983: 25). This is still very much the case today: media are still for and of their own country, focusing on national issues for a national (or linguistically defined) audience. Even a cursory examination of Europe's mediascape testifies that its institutions are still very much nationally specific, dominated by national regulatory regimes and political determinants. But it is also clear that the link between the news media and 'their' nation-state is no longer exclusive.

Although still confined by linguistic borders, newspapers such as the *Financial Times* and the *International Herald Tribune* are printed around the globe, reaching millions of readers with a 'global' message. CNN and Internet based news bulletins and magazines have an equally global reach. A truly European mediascape is not yet in sight, but modern distribution systems (such as satellite and cable) are calling for more intra-European cooperation between Europe's media enterprises and a subsequent demand for more European programmes. Trans-frontier satellite broadcasting, which started in the late-1970s, has from the onset represented a serious challenge to national media sovereignty (Humphreys 1996). Both the EU and the Council of Europe have animated the development of European TV programming by encouraging new productions and cross-boundary media cooperation.

Apart from cultural objectives, these initiatives have been driven by a certain industrial logic in an attempt to open up Europe's closed national markets, and to develop a wider European audiovisual space. Initial attempts by the European Broadcasting Union (EBU) to develop pan-European media channels have failed, as did short-lived experiments to launch Europa TV (which collapsed after one year's operation, in 1986). Other EBU sponsored channels, such as Eurosport and Euronews, have been more successful. Euronews, in particular, (launched in 1993) clearly reflects the desire to air a 'European' perspective of European and global economic and political developments.[2] Euronews now broadcasts in seven languages (English, French, German, Italian, Portuguese, Russian and Spanish), and reaches about 189 million households in 121 countries.

The European Commission's Green Paper, *Television Without Frontiers*, published in 1984, was explicitly aimed at opening intra-Community frontiers for national television programmes, and to contribute to the development of a single European broadcasting space. The Paper argued that information 'is a decisive, perhaps the only decisive factor in European unification... European unification will only be achieved if Europeans want it. Europeans will only want it if there is such a thing as European identity. A European identity will only develop if Europeans are adequately informed. At present, information via the mass media is controlled at [the] national level.'[3]

Philip Schlesinger has rightly pointed out that this perspective assumes a rather simplistic causal relationship between media consumption and the formation of a collective identity along European lines (Schlesinger 1993). Using radio and TV as the cultural instruments of nation-building is an outdated, obsolete 'modern' notion that has little chance of effectively forging a stronger European consciousness and brand. Such a European audio-visual space should certainly not be confused with more reporting on European issues through the national media. It would, however, imply that newspapers, magazines, radio and TV channels would offer information, entertainment and other programmes for a Europe-wide market, thereby trying to create a nation-state-transcending communicative context. This implies, of course, that Europe's multiple language barriers can be overcome. Europe's linguistic diversity might not lend itself easily to a general, homogeneous approach (Laitin 1997). Since communication is inevitable linked with language and linguistically mediated interpretations of the world, European opinion-forming will remain problematic, and European citizens will remain unduly participatively handicapped. In an age of hypermedia, different approaches and tools are required, opening up political space for EU-wide place branding.

The starting point for the EU is certainly promising. As with NATO, the EU has a powerful logo (a blue flag with a circle of twelve, yellow, five-pointed stars), which is inconspicuously omnipresent across Europe. It has a currency named after it, which makes it one of the most frequently used names across the continent ('That will be two Euros and fifty cents, please'). The numerable Euro-prefixed products and events (ranging from the Eurostar-train, the Euro 2008 soccer championships, to the Eurovision Song Contest) make Europe one of the most competitive place brands in the world.

The EU is a master brand, offering its name, style and character to all the policies, events and ideas it generates. It has a highly visible identity, offering many possibilities to position itself on the competitive market place of ideas. As a place brand, the EU stands for the idea of 'Europe' that is associated with a wide variety of concepts and notions, ranging from Christendom and the Enlightenment, to the Holocaust and football hooliganism. Historically, the story of *Europa* has been an inspiration for politicians, artists and entrepreneurs. After summarizing the Greek myth of the captured and raped Europa, the historian John Hale exclaims, 'what a subject this was! Sex, and violence, seascape, landscape, beauty and the beast, gestures of alarm and affection. In every medium, from painting to pottery, relief sculpture to enamel, the story soared on' (Hale 1993: 48).

Institutionally, as well, the European project is progressing, albeit not unproblematically. But it is widely acknowledged that Europe's task is to find a new *raison d'être* that inspires its own populace and appeals to the wider world as well. And this is where branding comes in. There is no denying that younger generations no longer buy Europe's founding myth: 'European integration brings peace'. This myth is dead now that the prospect of another Franco-German war (or basically *any* intra-EU war) is too improbable to serve as Damocles' sword begetting both discipline and respect. For most non-Europeans, the EU's influence derives from its affluence, its continuous peace and prosperity. But, for most Europeans, any attempt to resuscitate the story of the EU as the zone of Kantian peace is futile. Europe's younger generations are predominantly post-materialist, which implies that they are sufficiently well off to highly value tolerance and diversity, and all care more about self-expression than deference to authority. European citizens long for an EU that reflects and stands up for their values, be it gender equality, the abolition of the death-penalty, or avoiding market access to GMOs. Branding the EU is, therefore, a major identity-shaping project.

The European Commission – and EU Commissioner for Communications Margot Wallström, in particular – briefly considered obtaining the input of brand consultants to evaluate the EU's image and brand identity. In May 2006, Simon Anholt, one of the leading British brand specialists, was asked to shed his light on Europe's identity and to think through the possibilities of devising a strategy for improvement.[4] But when the story hit the news that the EU was engaged in rebranding, the Commission spokesman immediately denied this idea, calling it imaginary (Sain 2006).

Rolf Annerberg, Ms Wallström's head of cabinet, made it clear that 'the EU is a brand but it is competing with 25 national brands. It is very seldom you use them as a unit. The Ryder Cup golf that plays against the US is about the only case.'[5] It is already quite something to acknowledge that the EU – and 'Europe', in particular – is a major brand to be used as a valuable policy asset. Still, branding plays second fiddle to more conventional communications strategies within the European Commission. In 2006, following the failed effort to get a European Constitution, Ms Wallström launched a so-called 'Plan D – Debate, Democracy, Dialogue', which aims at reconnecting the EU with its citizens using modern media such as Internet chat sessions, as well as recruiting sports and music celebrities as EU ambassadors. This culminated in the European Commission's interest in setting itself up in the *Second Life* virtual community (of some 5 million members in 2007), in order to bring the EU closer to young people and make them more aware of its policies and objectives.

The European Commission's White Paper *Communicating Europe in Partnership* (2007) consolidates the EU's policies towards using new media, advocating two-way communication, involving active participation of citizens (witness the www.europa.eu/yourvoice website), as well as a shifting emphasis from Brussels based to a 'going local' approach. Still, especially member states seem reluctant to create a European masterbrand that might ultimately compete for taxes and loyalty with their own citizens. Which explains why it remains complicated for the EU to make more decisive steps towards the networking and relational media approach that is required to use the soft power inherent in its brand.

Interestingly, the EU and USA not only confront each other in the Ryder Cup, as Mr Annerberg claims, but also as foreign policy actors with often conflicting agendas and sharply contrasting foreign policy styles. This makes the development of 'Brand USA' a particularly telling case study.

Brand USA

Michael Nelson has argued that it was not due to its military superiority that the West won the Cold War but, rather, due to 'the subversive effects on its population of Western media such as Hollywood, Voice of America and MTV' (Nelson 1997; see also Bernhard 1999; Osgood 2002). Buzan and Segal equally claim that '[b]ecause of the attitudes, morals, lifestyles, and cultural values it conveys, the prime-time soft-porn television programme *Baywatch* is much more subversive than CNN to authoritarian countries' (Buzan and Segal 1996: 10). This suggests that the USA has used (and occasionally abused) the soft power embedded in its popular culture for widespread political and economic goals.

America's media and cultural power during the Cold War has been labelled Coca-Colonization, the Marilyn Monroe doctrine, or Rock 'n' Rollback. But, of course, *Baywatch* did not end the Cold War, although it did give the USA a false sense of superiority and security based on its self-image of a confident and superior society. Due to its Cold War victory, for a decade the USA neglected place branding in the belief that its own societal model was no longer seriously challenged by an ideological competitor. The events of 9/11 have been a rude awakening that this societal model remains vulnerable, and that continued efforts are required to neutralize critics and sway sceptics. Place branding and public diplomacy are now seen as the keys to make up for this decade of complacency by reinvigorating America's unique and under-utilized soft power.

In America's new quest for sympathy and support across the globe, media, PR and marketing specialists are no longer a sideshow to traditional government-to-government diplomacy. Brand thinking and brand asset management now dominate American life, also affecting the nature and dynamics of US politics. Former US Secretary of State Colin Powell famously defined American diplomacy: 'We're selling a product. That product we are selling is democracy.'[6] A clearer illustration of a brand-dominated US diplomacy is hardly imaginable.

American place branding is a complex phenomenon aimed at conveying US commitments, goals and intentions to the world by a wide variety of means and channels. This can be illustrated by the social construction of the USA as a political/strategic brand.[7] The USA often uses the soft power offered by its cultural hegemony. The US brand radiates cultural superiority, political power and military dominance. In many ways, Mickey Mouse, Madonna and Brad Pitt are on-screen role models for an America that not only overpowers the hearts and minds of people around the world, but also one that sets the global political and military agenda.

Richard Haass, former US State Department's director for policy and planning, has argued that his country should assume 'the role of international sheriff, one who forges coalitions by posses of states and others for specific tasks.'(Haass 1997: 6). The moral basis of US sheriffhood is not merely abstract values (such as individual liberty and democracy), but mainly the packaging and visual imagining of these values in Hollywood epics such as *Pearl Harbor* and *Saving Private Ryan*. It is frequently argued that hard and soft power are juxtaposed, as if hard-nosedness detracts from attractiveness. Indeed, soft power can be defined as the ability to achieve the policy outcomes one wants by attraction and persuasion, rather than by force and coercion (Nye 2004). Hard and soft power, however, go hand-in-hand, since America's popular culture 'writes' and imagines the USA as a superpower. In a way, the US practice of global intervention is enabled by America's superpower-brand. As Cynthia Weber has argued, 'the form of a justification in effect participates in the constitution of both the state as a sovereign identity and the interpretive community to which the state's justifications are directed' (Weber 1995: 5).

Little surprise, therefore, that much of global anti-Americanism feeds on the image of the USA as a trigger-happy capitalist crusader. The trend of mounting anti-Americanism within Europe, Asia and other parts of the world is an element of that same process.[8] Opinion polls conducted by the German Marshall Fund and the Pew Charitable Trusts[9] indicate that America's image has declined precipitously in most European countries due to Washington's foreign policy conduct after 9/11. For example, the majority of the population of Germany (83 per cent), France (85 per cent), and Spain (81 per cent) disapproves of US foreign policy – only in countries such as The Netherlands (60 per cent) and Poland (36 per cent) is popular displeasure and distrust less pronounced. And, as the Pew Report (2004) points out, 'the bottom has fallen out of support for the U.S. in the Muslim world. Negative views of the U.S. in the Muslim world – which had been largely confined to the Middle East – are now echoed by Muslim populations in Indonesia and Nigeria ... [F]avorable ratings for the U.S. have fallen from 61 per cent to 15 per cent in Indonesia and from 71 per cent to 38 per cent among Muslims in Nigeria.'[10]

Place branding and public diplomacy are widely seen as an essential tool to win over the hearts and minds of foreign audiences, and convince them that their values, goals and desires are similar to those of the USA. Following 9/11, the Bush administration therefore initiated a flurry of initiatives to rebrand the USA from a 'global bully' to a 'compassionate hegemon'. In an effort to touch ordinary citizens of Muslim countries (and especially the so-called Arab street), place branding and public diplomacy are considered crucial to exercise America's ample soft power assets. The argument is that 'millions of ordinary people ... have greatly distorted, but carefully cultivated images of [the USA] – images so negative, so weird, so hostile that a young generation of terrorists is being created' (Beers 2003). US policy towards the Muslim world is based on the assumption that these negative ideas should be neutralized and, in the end, changed, by a focused effort of branding and public diplomacy. This approach has quickly become a central plank of America's 'war on terror.' Washington now realizes that you cannot kill ideas with bombs, however precision-guided they might be.

But, as America's low ranking in global opinion polls testifies, existing branding and diplomatic efforts are failing miserably. The most important mistake has been that 'getting the American message out' is too limited a goal to set the 'Brand USA' in today's marketplace of ideas. The assumption has been that America's image problems are either due to envy of US power and prosperity, or simply a basic misinterpretation of America's foreign policy goals. Washington's post-9/11 public diplomacy initiatives reflect this approach. These efforts included setting up 'American Corners' (with libraries and information) across Muslim-majority countries, the production of documentary material, and the launching of Persian- and Arab-language radio stations (such as *Radio Farda* and *Radio Sawa*), and an Arab-language satellite TV station (*Al-Hurra*) that seeks to compete with the popular, but rather anti-American, *Al-Jazeera*. Most proposals to adjust the course of US place branding and public diplomacy aim at making the

American machinery to communicate with the Arab and Muslim world more effective.[11] For example, an Arab Youth Initiative was started in 2004, together with a so-called Partnership for Learning (P4L) encompassing a US high school exchange programme with the Arab and Muslim world. Policy suggestions have further included strengthening the coordination of public diplomacy with the Executive Branch and stronger Presidential leadership, recognizing that a 'one-size-fits-all' approach is bound to fail (since the public in Egypt, Indonesia and Senegal obviously differ markedly), and increasing the active support of Arab and Muslim communities in a real dialogue with the USA (and the West in general).

Branding and politics: Media image and political reality

The key problem with this approach, however, is that it does not take fully into account a simple, basic rule of marketing: 'It's not what you *say*, but what others *hear*, that is important!' Whereas US policy-makers say 'freedom, justice and opportunity', the general Arab population seems to hear 'domination, chaos and cynicism.' When Washington says 'liberation', a majority of Arabs and Europeans see 'occupation'. Obviously, the proof of the pudding is in the eating and, for many Arabs, US foreign policy just does not taste good. The problem is that Arabs and Muslims will not attach credibility to US place branding and public diplomacy efforts as long as American policies in the Middle East and beyond remain unchanged. Especially as long as US support to autocratic Arab regimes and Israel continues unabated, Washington's rhetoric about freedom and democracy carries little conviction.

These lessons come at a high price. Already in 1999 Yayha Kamalipour had argued that 'more than any other factor, political relations determines what citizens of other nations see, read, or hear in their domestic media about the United States and vice versa. In other words, the quality of political relations between two countries is a critical factor in the image that they portray of each other in their mass media' (Kamalipour 1999: 35). Regardless of its attitude to branding, Washington's foreign policy seems to follow Machiavelli's dictum that it is far better to be feared than to be loved, and better to compel than to attract. But how valid is the claim that the (successful) use of military (hard) power generates the requisite (soft) power of legitimacy?

Looking at today's Iraq and the dismal standing of the USA in public opinion polls across the Middle East, the opposite argument seems more likely – namely, that ostentatious (hard) powerplay simply eclipses low-profile public diplomacy. For the USA, it has proven difficult to brand itself as a force for good and democracy, with stories about torture and human rights abuses in Abu Graib and Guantánamo hitting the headlines of newspapers all over the world. Global media have turned the images of torture and humiliation into icons of war, resonating in people's minds and undermining US government rhetoric about 'spreading democracy'.[12] Marketing experience learns that it is more important to *show*, than to *tell*. For US branding, this implies that America's performance on the global stage will speak louder than any smooth words it might voice simultaneously. Only one conclusion can therefore be drawn; namely that (as Simon Anholt has argued): 'You can't smash them with your left hand and caress them with your right. It you're going to war you should suspend diplomacy because if you're attacking a nation that's all there is to it' (Lewis 2003: 28.).

Conclusion: Globalization and the necessity of difference

Self-conscious place brands realize that – as with Coke and Pepsi – most of them offer the same product: territory, infrastructure, educated people and an almost identical system of governance. Territorial actors compete with each other for investment, tourism and political power, often on a global scale. The USA, the EU and Amnesty International all vie for the same business, blissfully disregarding their unequal legal position and political weight. Globalization and the harmonizing effects of European integration put further pressure on territorial entities to develop, manage and leverage their brand equity. In order to stand out from the crowd, and capture significant mind share and market share, place branding has become essential. At the centre of this challenge lies the role of the media in constructing and disseminating successful place branding on a global scale.

The two short case studies on the EU and USA's recent experiences with place branding indicate that it proves difficult for state actors to make the shift from a mass communication approach to a network communication approach. States remain embedded in the practice of an information-centred strategy that focuses on message content, thereby neglecting message exchange. They are restricted too much by hierarchical structures, which results in strategies that apply a command-and-control attitude relying heavily on an old-fashioned mass communication approach. But today's hypermedia environment increasingly requires a communication strategy based on connectivity, interactivity and cultural diversity.

Both the EU and the USA only gradually come to terms with the requirement of using the interactive features of the new technologies to get in touch with the 'hearts and minds' of 'their' audiences. This requires a new media policy, since publics are no longer passive recipients of information but, instead, active participants. It also implies that no master narrative can, or perhaps should, be devised from the onset. Both the EU and the USA no longer control their own messages. They are players in a network communication structure where the mass media (TV, in particular) are still the key power holders, but where networks are taking over as the new power brokers. Since place branding and public diplomacy are well placed to adjust to this new media landscape, states will gradually (have to) adjust to this new hypermedia environment. If they fail to do so, they have little chance to compete with more flexible and agile NGOs and smaller territorial actors such as cities and regions.

Notes

1. 'The Case for Brands', *The Economist*, 6 September 2001.
2. Apart from *Euronews*, France and Germany are sponsoring the dual-language channel ARTE, which specifically aims at avoiding that commercial interests will come to fully occupy Europe's cultural space. See Susan Emanuel, 'A Community of Culture? The European Television Channel', *History of European Ideas*, 21(2), (1995).
3. European Commission Green Paper, *Television Without Borders* (Brussels 1984).
4. Simon Anholt told the author (in July 2007) that the meeting did not take place, but that the rumour of the European Commission even *thinking* about hiring a branding expert was obviously sufficient to cause a stir.
5 Andrew Bounds, 'Brand Experts Study EU Identity Crisis', *Financial Times*, 1 May 2006.
6. 'Brand U.S.A.', (2001) *Foreign Policy*, 127: 19.
7. Special issue of *Adbusters* magazine, 39, (2002), dedicated to debunking 'Brand U.S.A.'.
8. The Pew Global Attitudes Project, *A Year After Iraq: A Nine-Country Survey* (Washington, DC: March 2004).

9. GMF Transatlantic Trends 2005, and the Pew Global Attitudes Project, *America's Image Slips, But Allies Share U.S. Concerns Over Iran, Hamas* (13 June 2006). Available at http://www.transatlantictrends.org/ and http://pew-global.org/reports/display.php?ReportID=252 (15 February 2007).
10. Pew Global Attitudes Project (2004), *A Year After Iraq.*
11. Testimony of Under Secretary for Public Diplomacy and Public Affairs Margaret Tutwiler to the Committee on Foreign Relations of the United States Senate (26 February 2004). Available at http://foreign.senate.gov/testimony/2004/TutwilerTestimony040226.pdf
12. Ulrich Raulff, 'Die 120 Tage von Bagdad', *Süddeutsche Zeitung*, 4 May 2004.

References

Anderson, B. (1983) *Imagined Communities* (London: Verso).
Anholt, S. (2002) ' "Foreword" to the special issue on nation branding', *Journal of Brand Management*, 9(4–5), April.
Arquilla, J. and Ronfeldt, D. (1999) 'What If There is a Revolution in Diplomatic Affairs?', *Virtual Diplomacy*, 25 February, United State Institute of Peace, Washington, DC).
Arquilla J. and Ronfeldt, D. (1999) *The Emergence of Noopolitik: Toward an American Information Strategy* (Santa Monica, CA: RAND).
Beers, C.L. (2003) 'American Public Diplomacy and Islam', Prepared Testimony Before the Committee on Foreign Relations of the United States Senate, 27 February.
Bernhard, N.E. (1999) *US Television News and Cold War Propaganda, 1947–1960* (Cambridge: Cambridge University Press).
Bounds, A. (2006) 'Brand Experts Study EU Identity Crisis', *Financial Times*, 1 May.
Buzan, B. and Segal. G. (1996) 'The Rise of Lite Powers: A Strategy for the Postmodern State', *World Policy Journal*, 13 (3), fall.
Castells, M. (1996) *The Rise of the Network Society* (Cambridge, MA: Blackwell).
Deibert, R. (1997) *Parchment, Printing and Hypermedia* (New York: Columbia University Press).
Economist, The (2001) 'The Case for Brands', 6 September.
Emanuel, S. (1995) 'A Community of Culture? The European Television Channel', *History of European Ideas*, 21(2).
European Commission Green Paper (1984) *Television Without Borders*, Brussels.
Foreign Policy (2001) 'Brand U.S.A.',127.
Haass, R.N. (1997) *The Reluctant Sheriff. The United States After the Cold War* (New York: Council on Foreign Relations Press).
Hale, J. (1993) 'The Renaissance Idea of Europe', in Soledad Garcia (ed.), *European Identity and the Search for Legitimacy* (London: Pinter).
Humphreys, P.J. (1996) *Mass Media and Media Policy in Western Europe* (Manchester: Manchester University Press).

Kamalipour, Y.R. (1999) 'U.S. Image and the Political Factor', in Y.R. Kamalipour (ed.), *Images of the U.S. around the World: A Multicultural Perspective* (Albany, NY: State University of New York Press).

Kunczik, M. (1997) *Images of Nations and International Public Relations* (Mahwah, NJ: Lawrence Erlbaum).

Laitin, D.D. (1997) 'The Cultural Identities of a European State', *Politics and Society*, 25 (3).

Lewis, E. (2003) 'Branding War and Peace', *Brand Strategy*, 167.

Meyer, M.H. and Zack, M.H. (1996) 'The Design and Development of Information Products', *Sloan Management Review*, 37(3), spring.

Nelson, M (1997) *Wars of the Black Heavens: The Battles of Western Broadcasting in the Cold War* (Syracuse, NY: Syracuse University Press.

Nye, J.S. Jr (2004) *Soft Power: The Means to Success in World Politics* (New York: Public Affairs.

Olins, W. (2002) 'Branding the Nation – The Historical Context', *The Journal of Brand Management*, 9(4–5), April.

Olins, W. 'DEbate: Deutschland – Europa'. Available at jyanet.com/cap/1999/0310fe1.htm

Osgood, K.A. (2002) 'Hearts and Minds: The Unconventional Cold War', *Journal of Cold War Studies*, 4(2), spring.

Packard, V. (1957) *The Hidden Persuaders* (New York: Mackay).

Pew Global Attitudes Project (2004) *A Year After Iraq: A Nine-Country Survey*, March, Washington, DC.

Pew Global Attitudes Project (2006) *America's Image Slips, But Allies Share U.S. Concerns Over Iran, Hamas*, 13 June, Washington, DC.

Rafaeli, S. (1988) 'Interactivity: From New Media to Communication', in R.Hawkins et al. (eds) *Advancing Communication Science: Merging Mass and Interpersonal Process* (Newbury Park, CA: Sage).

Raulff, U. (2004) 'Die 120 Tage von Bagdad', *Süddeutsche Zeitung*, 4 May.

Sain, P. (2006) 'In Search of a European Brand', *EuropaWorld*, 4 May.

Schlesinger, P. (1993) 'Wishful Thinking: Cultural Politics, Media, and Collective Identities in Europe', *Journal of Communication*, 43(2), spring.

Tutwiler, Margaret. Testimony of Under Secretary for Public Diplomacy and Public Affairs to the Committee on Foreign Relations of the United States Senate, 26 February 2004.

van Gelder, S. (2002) 'A View on the Future of Branding', Unpublished paper, April 2002.

van Ham, P. (2005) 'Branding European Power', *Place Branding and Public Diplomacy*, 1(2), March.

Weber, C. (1995) *Simulating Sovereignty. Intervention, the State and Symbolic Exchange* (Cambridge: Cambridge University Press).

Zaharna, R.S. (2007) 'The Soft Power Differential: Network Communication and Mass Communication in Public Diplomacy', *The Hauge Journal of Diplomacy*, 2(3), October.

8
Identity and Appeal in the Humanitarian Brand

Anne Vestergaard

Non-profit organizations belong to a sector where the diffusion of corporate norms and values has been very pronounced in recent years, bringing into play inherent tensions between commercial and non-commercial logics. This chapter examines humanitarian discourse as an example of a domain of social life that is branded and marketed as if it were a corporate product. It discusses the factors that brings this change about and, on the basis of analyses of two humanitarian TV spots, investigates the consequences in terms of the transformed organizational identities that emerge from their mediatization.

In the past few decades, the number and influence of non-governmental organizations (NGOs) has escalated manifestly. The global number of NGOs with a social agenda more than quadrupled between the mid-1970s and the mid-1990s (Keck and Sikkink 1998). In the UK, for example, 185,000 charities were registered in 1999 (Sargeant 1999), the number continuing to rise by as much as 5000 a year. In the USA, non-profit expenditures grew 77 per cent faster than the American economy as a whole between 1977 and 1999 (Foroohar 2005). Globalization, the end of the Cold War and the emergence of new communication technologies are commonly considered to have a tremendous impact on the growing importance of NGOs (della Porta et al. 1999; Risse et al. 1999; Warketin 2001). Seeking to influence the direction of international public policy, NGOs and humanitarian organizations play an increasingly important role in monitoring global governance, and bringing principles and values to the attention of policy-makers (Held and McGrew 2002; Keane 2003). By holding both private and public sectors accountable, these organizations 'are an important part of an explanation for the changes in world politics' (Keck and Sikkink 1998: 2). Growing competition in the global market place, most probably, has an equal role to play in a parallel development of the for-profit sector. Not only has the non-profit sector become a billion-dollar business in what Oxfam International executive director, Jeremy Hobbs, calls the 'moral economy'. In recent years, social responsibility is becoming an increasingly important element in the marketing strategies of large business corporations as a means for singling out their products and services in an increasingly competitive global market.

As the number of NGOs grows, their conditions of existence change and their managerial practices are pushed in new directions. Modern NGOs are, to a lesser extent, activist, non-hierarchical grassroots structures, but increasingly engage staff with subject-specific expertise (law, management, journalism, marketing and so on), while the role of voluntary work decreases (Meyer and Tarrow 1988; Staggenborg 1997; Martens 2006). The mere number of NGOs that must compete for public attention, donations and government subsidiaries brings about new demands for their ability to promote themselves. At the same time, neo-liberal political ideals have put pressure on the public sector and, as a consequence, many non-profit organizations have suffered from declining government support (Csaba 2005). Finally, due to numerous scandals in the non-profit sector in the 1990s, as perhaps most notoriously in Rwanda (Polman 2003), NGOs have faced growing demands for accountability and efficiency in their performance. The capacity of organizations to account for their *raison d'être* and performance is becoming ever more vital in attracting and retaining support, as well as meeting the expectations of various stakeholders.

NGOs and mediatization

These factors have lead to a blurring of the distinction between the traditional roles of the for-profit and non-profit sectors, and have pushed non-profit organizations more forcefully into the media field. The operation of NGOs is now fundamentally, and self-perpetually, tied to the media and their creation of visibility, transparency and legitimacy in relation to the general public, as well as specific stakeholders. One aspect of this attachment to the media is the increased attention to marketing and the introduction of branding into the sector.

> Charities with a strong recognizable brand attract more voluntary donations than those without.... Increasingly, charity brand status is being used to communicate meaning through a unique set of values or associations that define the charity not only in terms of what it does (its cause) but more importantly in terms of the values it represents. Transforming charity into brands allows donors to identify more precisely what the charity does and the values it represents. This in turn allows donors to identify and select those charities whose values most closely match their own. (Hankinson, 2001: 1)

Practitioners as well as academics view corporate branding as an indispensable tool for any corporation in a globalized market (for example, Aaker 1996; Aaker and Joachimsthaler 2000; Hatch and Schultz 2001; Balmer and Greyser 2006). Corporate branding should serve to enhance the esteem and loyalty of shareholders and to afford a means of differentiation from competitors, the need for differentiation bringing centre stage the emotions and values of an organization (Balmer and Gray 2003). Brands can be understood as logical structures that channel consumer perceptions, akin to metaphors or myths, and give meaning to products and services for consumers (Holt 2004; Kay 2006). In this sense, a brand is the distillation of a product, service or corporate identity into a symbolic representation, a discursive construct. This construct occupies a discursive space with multiple competing discourses (Fairclough 1992; Leitch and Richardson 2003) and brands might therefore have multiple meanings attached to them. Branding, then, is the strategic management of these discourses, and the unique selling proposition of an organization becomes not its product or service, but the cultural status associated with it. Proponents of NGO branding argue that branding is simply an opportunity to communicate more explicitly the organization's core values, mission and vision, differing in no substantial way from the traditional communicative practices of non-profits (for example, Grounds 2005). Indeed, some observers argue that the larger NGO brands are now becoming models exemplary for the commercial industry: 'NGOs have become the new sophisticated communicators and perceived instigators of change in the global market place ... NGOs are no longer perceived as small bands of activists but rather as new "super brands" surpassing the stature of major corporations, government bodies and even the media among consumers' (Wootliff and Deri 2001).

The value of introducing commercial strategies into the sector is far from uncontested. Branding of NGOs is ardently criticized for conflicting with basic ideals of the non-profit organization such as altruism, voluntarism and grass-roots activism. The spread of managerial principles and advancement of capitalist logic and consumerism is by many considered a threat to civil society and democracy (Csaba 2005). The re-articulation of humanitarianism in a discourse of advertising is seen as introducing a moral conflict by staging human misery alongside commodities in a field of desire, seduction and consumption, thrill, pastime and passivity. As formulated by Baudrillard: 'We are the consumers of the ever delightful spectacle of poverty and catastrophy, and of the moving spectacle of our own efforts to alleviate it' (Baudrillard 1994: 67).

Baudrillard's quote throws into relief another dimension of mediatization that decisively impacts on humanitarian discourse: the media's capacity to fictionalize or trivialize suffering, emptying out its moral content in favour of its spectacular performance. Indeed, humanitarian discourse has long been dependent on the media and their ability to bring the misfortune of people outside of our immediate social environment into our living rooms. Increasingly, however, the vastness of misfortune and suffering to which the media expose us is felt to have a domesticating and numbing effect, which might leave the spectator indifferent and cause what is commonly referred to as 'compassion fatigue' (Tester 2001). The majority of the relatively few attempts in the literature to define compassion fatigue as a sociological concept point to the inaccessibility of action as a prime factor in its development (for example, di Giovanni 1994; Moeller 1999; Tester 2001). Witnessing human misery lays a moral demand upon us, which we cannot satisfy through direct action when the misery is distant and mediated. In Zygmunt Bauman's words, the media give us artificial eyes and so 'to restore the lost moral balance, we would need "artificial hands" stretching as far as our artificial eyes are able to' (Bauman 2001: 42). Our moral integrity as witnesses depends, in this view, on the media's ability to transmit a perception that action is possible and that the misery we witness is not inalterable and inevitable (Silverstone 2006).

The character of media reports on suffering since the 1980s has been widely criticized for creating the impression that the suffering of the developing world is irremediable (for example, Kinnick et al. 1996; Ignatieff 1998). Market led journalistic practices are held responsible for creating simplistic and formulaic reports on suffering, that point to no causes or solutions, are ephemeral and compete for spectacularity. The relentless occurrence of new, more or less de-contextualized instances of suffering flickering through the media is thought to perpetuate the perception that, as distant witnesses, we can do nothing to alleviate suffering in far away places. Compassion fatigue and the public's perception of its social inefficacy compose a challenging dilemma for humanitarian organizations, which have previously used the depiction of suffering in the media both to create legitimacy for the organization and its cause and to mobilize support from the public. Numerous studies have shown that, far from passively absorbing the spectacles put before them, television viewers put to work important critical capabilities, enabling them to distance themselves from spectacles and make inferences about the intentions behind the production other than those manifestly presented in a programme (Liebes and Katz 1989). This critical relationship introduces suspicion – sometimes latent, at other times explicit – about the emotions, desires and intentions that accompany representations of suffering (Boltanski 1999).

In this way, the media confront humanitarian organizations with a two-pronged challenge with a perceived social inefficacy in their audiences on the one hand, and high degrees of media literacy on the other hand. These are challenges linked specifically to these organizations' presence in a highly competitive media landscape. They force humanitarian organizations to fashion new strategies by which to use the media in a morally compelling manner.

Analyzing public humanitarian discourse

The nature of humanitarian organizations' branding strategies might have crucial implications for the construction of humanitarianism and – probably, more generally – morality in the public sphere. In *The Spectatorship of Suffering*, Chouliaraki (2006) provides an analytical framework for investigating the construction and legitimation of ethical norms by the media, concerned in particular with the way the semiotic resources of media reports on distant suffering shape the public's relations and dispositions in relation to distant sufferers. This 'Analytics of Mediation' is a framework for studying television as a mechanism of representation that construes human suffering within specific semantic fields where emotions and dispositions for action are made possible for the spectator. It takes its point of departure in the ethical norms embedded in reports on suffering, and seeks to problematize the meaning-making procedures through which these norms acquire systematicity and legitimacy in and through television.

> The assumption behind the 'analytics of mediation' is that choices over how suffering is portrayed, where, when and with whom the suffering is shown to occur always entail specific ethical dispositions, independently of our own evaluative judgment on these dispositions as undesirable or desirable. The value of the 'analytics of mediation', in this respect, lies in its capacity to re-describe the semiotic constitution of suffering and, in so doing, to explicate the moral implications and political agendas that inform this constitution. (Chouliaraki 2005: 148)

It is a crucial aspect of Chouliaraki's Analytics of Mediation that it encompasses both the semiotics of the text, by looking into the multi-modality of media texts, and the power relations that constitute its social context, by looking at the constructions of the scene of suffering and the connectivities between sufferer and spectator in the texts. This dual focus implies that we cannot study the relations between the social entities, implicitly or explicitly involved in the text, unless we pay attention to the multimodality of mediation, which accommodates consideration of the impact of technological factors on media semiosis. In the analyses below, I have adapted this integrated perspective on mediated suffering, on the one hand, and the conception of media semiosis, on the other, in order to frame the analysis of two branding spots from the Danish sections of Amnesty International and the Red Cross.

The Red Cross (RC) and Amnesty International (AI) have what are arguably the strongest international humanitarian brands. The International RC has been found to be the best known international humanitarian organization in all regions of the world, known by 75 per cent of the population, 99 per cent of which evaluate it positively (Gallup: Voice of the People 2005). Similarly, AI has been rated the most trusted brand in Europe (Edelman Public Relations 2003). While the RC is a state-subsidized, operational NGO, focused on providing humanitarian relief across national boundaries on the basis of a strict neutrality and impartiality clause, AI is an independent advocacy organization, which operates discursively, identifying persecutors and pressurizing state authorities through international, public disclosure. In this way, the two organizations operate under very different financial and communicative circumstances. Yet, the two organizations enjoy similar levels of public support. In Denmark, AI counted 74,000 members in 2007 and the RC 78,000 (or approximately 1.5 per cent of the population). In the following, we shall see that the examples show how in Denmark the two organizations, in spite of their differences, respond in very similar ways to the challenges described above. The two TV spots that are analyzed, both accommodate perceived social inefficacy and high degrees of media literacy in their audiences. They testify to the problems involved in these organizations' presence in a highly competitive media landscape, and to the conflicts between education and advertising discourses to which this gives rise.

Amnesty International, 2001

The spot from AI is composed of three tracks, a verbal, a visual and an auditory. There is no real-sound in the auditory, which is a simple rhythmic theme of bongo drums and guitar scales. The verbal content of the spot is presented visually in the form of six simple sentences displayed on-screen synchronously with the unfolding of six mutually unrelated visual scenes.

All visual scenes show leisurely activity. In the first scene, a group of young boys is competing in an amateur soccer match, one boy jumping triumphantly in the field. Three elderly men bathing in the ocean, in the second scene, have a laugh and a toast with their coffee mugs. The theme of joy and celebration is repeated in the reunion of a young man with his girlfriend who returns from travels in scene three, and hooligans dancing merrily in a fountain in scene four. Finally, in the fifth scene, two laughing children are chasing soap

Table 8.1   Breakdown of Amnesty International advertising theme

Verbal		Visual
Frame	**Theme**	**Visual scene**
We could have shown	*TORTURE*	Boys playing soccer
We could have shown	*HATRED*	Elderly men relaxing in the sea
We could have shown	*ISOLATION*	A traveller's arrival and reunion
We could have shown	*FEAR*	Soccer supporters celebrating
But instead of showing	*WHAT WE FIGHT AGAINST*	Children playing with soap bubbles
We show	*WHAT WE FIGHT FOR*	Newborn in mother's arms
Support the fight for human rights – www.amnesty.dk		

bubbles, while we see a mother holding her newborn baby in the sixth and last scene. These joyous and celebratory visual scenes create a mood of euphoria that seems almost triumphant. In spite of this mood, however, what we see is not a celebration of accomplishment. On the contrary, all of the images depict futile action, pastime.

The setting, as well as the white, middle-class actors in the spot, convey a sense that what is depicted is 'us' in the privileged West. Indeed, there are several cultural references specifically to Denmark, such as the red and white hooligans performing a Danish ritual of celebration when flippantly dancing in the fountain. The giddiness of such scenes creates the impression of celebration of the audiences' own national culture. In this way, the affective appeal of the spot seems to a great extent to rely on nostalgia over the recipients' culture and values.

The verbal content is displayed on screen, one sentence per scene, with the last word, the 'theme', staggered: displayed in enlarged font on a separate line, appearing with a short delay and lingering on after the frame of the sentence has vanished. The isolated, enlarged display of these themes suggests them as headings for each of the visual scenes – a suggestion which, in fact, accentuates the harsh contrast between the two (see Illustration 8.1). The verbal text concludes with '*instead of showing what we fight against, we show what we*

Illustration 8.1   we could have shown HATRED

fight for', followed by *'Support human rights'*, and so a correlation is created between the signification of the visual statements and the substance of human rights. What AI fights for, then, the ideals it wants to further and the values that are secured by human rights are those portrayed in the images. In this way, the spot portrays the substance of human rights as a notion of safety equated with carefree light-heartedness and a notion of freedom as leisure.

These ideals are contrasted with the contents of the verbal, which presents what Amnesty 'fight against'. The four themes – *torture, hatred, isolation* and *fear* – are connected with different degrees of specificity to the agenda of the organization. While both *torture* and *isolation* might be taken as concrete references to AI's agenda as a means of exertion of power that can be advocated and legislated against, the word *isolation* – and, to some extent also, *torture* – occupies an ambiguous position between such semantics of activity and of emotional states. The last two themes, *hatred* and *fear*, clearly belong to an emotional semantic and are connected with the agenda of AI only to the extent that they are emotions that might result from or induce the exertions of power denoted by the other two themes. While *torture* and *isolation* might be defended as necessary instruments in the exercise of jurisdictional authority, *hatred* and *fear* are unequivocally negative. Making these expressions adjunctive to the expressions *fear* and *hatred* might, to some extent, emphasize the emotional aspects of the meaning of *torture* and *isolation*. In so doing, this might dissociate the sum statement from the political realm while inscribing it into a private, emotional discourse, which is easy to relate to and hard to dismiss.

Following the logic of advertising, the spot resorts to recognizability and identification, achieving its force and sense of urgency by an affective appeal to a euphoric nostalgia over the audience's own cultural ideals. At the same time, however, the spot quite explicitly addresses its own reflections as to how to appeal to its audience. Discussing what to 'show', it places acts of visual representation centre stage in the genre of humanitarian appeal and, in this way, emphasizes the act of mediation that AI takes upon itself to perform between distant suffering and Western publics. The repeated reference to what is *not* shown stresses the calculated nature of the representation, and so points to its rationale without actually substantiating it. Presupposing the reasons not to show suffering not only assigns the audience with knowledge of these reasons, but also to some extent attributes to them aversion toward visual representations of atrocities. In this way, a presupposed compassion fatigue discourse lies at the core of the spot. The suffering, courtesy to the audience, is precluded to silent, verbal statements displayed on the screen, where it becomes like a whisper behind the perceptually more powerful visual representation.

Danish Red Cross, 2005

The second TV spot was part of a campaign associated with a branding partnership formed between the Danish RC and the mineral water Aqua d'Or'. A small part of the purchase price of a bottle of water is donated to the RC campaign for clean drinking water in Africa, while Aqua d'Or gains the right to use the RC logo for branding purposes. The spot is 30 seconds long and visually minimalist, displaying two young actors in a white space, accompanied by an auditory track consisting of the gentle trickling of water, a simple piano tune and a hushed, female voiceover.

The imagery is taken entirely out of the realm of realism. What we see resembles a magazine fashion advertisement coming to life in a sort of *tableau vivant*. The spot involves two actors, a young male and a young female, both of them well-known Danish supermodels, in white cotton underwear. The theme of the spot is explicitly erotic, displaying a series of erotic positions with only one party visualized in full at a time, while the two only appear simultaneously in small shots. In the first screen, we see the girl in a posture of passionate absorption against

Red Croos spot: 00:22   Red Cross spot: 00:23

Illustration 8.2   Red Cross advertisement

Illustration 8.3   Red Cross advertisement

a wall, she fades away as the male party appears fulfilling his role in the display, and this pattern is repeated throughout the spot.

The synecdochal strategy of never showing the erotic scene in its entirety renders the display more symbolically erotic than perceptually so. In fact, a discourse of purity can be argued to expand the semiotic modes – from the serenity of the trickling water in the audio, the white and cleansed space, to the perfection and discipline of the human bodies. Rather than portraying the life-sustaining qualities of water, which make it relevant to the RC, the spot draws on its cleansing qualities to portray an ideal of beauty and purity that makes it attractive as a life-style object.

> Everybody knows sex sells. That's why Louise and Christian have dropped their clothes. Maybe it's a cheap trick, but, you know what?...if it can help more than a billion people who don't have

clean drinking water, then that's ok by us. You can help too. Just by drinking more water. Buy Aqua d'Or and support Red Cross.

The voiceover is read in the hushed, breathy voice of Danish Hollywood actress Connie Nielsen, using a language belonging to a young, casual and familiar register. Through its linguistic style, the spot not only addresses a young audience, but also enlists with this segment itself. The voice that the organization is provided with is far from a voice of power, of authority or reprimand. On the contrary, it is a voice that shows full solidarity with its youthful audience. The voice does not commit to any involvement as to the visual contents, but commits only to accepting it. The only agents in the verbal are the models, while there is no intentionality involved for anyone else, thus dissociating the RC from this commodification of its cause, while at the same time allowing the RC to benefit from applying this type of aesthetics. While a certain cynicism about the state of the public's sense of responsibility for the well-being of far-away others seems to be at play, along with a rhetoric of 'the end justifies the means', which one would have thought foreign to humanitarian ideals, this occurs without irony. Commercial strategies are not taunted by the spot, neither is the audience taunted with the decadence that is ascribed to it by the visual. The text presents its own persuasive strategy as a means to an end and, in so doing, the text suggests a contrast between the motivations it attributes to its audience with respect to why they might support the cause and its own motivation. It achieves this contrast without being condescending or moralizing, in part because of its clear, linguistically coded, loyalty with its audience. At the same time, while the visual appeals to desire and consumption, as does any advertisement, and thus constructs an addressee who will respond as intended only if offered a lifestyle object for consumption, the verbal text does accommodate a different kind of recipient. In *'you can help too'*, are the contours of a donor, who does feel a humanitarian call to help people in need and will respond according to the intentions of the addresser by virtue of this call.

Similarly to what we saw in the Amnesty spot, the verbal and the visual present separate, contrastive discourses. The visual presents an advertising discourse on purity, whereas the verbal – this time, literally in a whisper – presents the humanitarian cause behind the spot. The representation of the humanitarian cause, and the suffering that

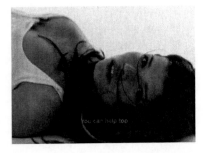

Illustration 8.4   Red Cross advertisement

underlies it, is limited to the subordinate clause *if it can help more than a billion people who don't have clean drinking water* presenting the problem the RC targets, separated from its context, sources and consequences. Although in this sense, the cause is backgrounded, the magnitude of the problem is represented numerically, providing a powerful impact that is, in fact, intensified by its understatement. Not only does this way of representing suffering steer clear of a moralizing approach to the recipient, the powerful understatement also serves to defuse any reverse moralization with respect to the commerciality of the persuasive strategy on the part of the RC. The result is at once provoking and disarming.

The RC spot is an extreme example of the paradox that emerges at the intersection between commercial and altruistic interests. By virtue of entering into a branding partnership with an organization with a product to sell, the traditional humanitarian action is substituted by the purchase of a product and, thus, the RC volunteers their cause to be, quite literally, commodified. What makes the paradox extreme is that this commodity is water, marketed as a luxury product, while it is, at the same time, the vital basic need that the RC aims to provide for the billions of people whose lives are threatened from the lack of it.

Appealing identity or humanitarian appeal?

Competition for visibility, and demands for professionalism and efficiency drive humanitarian organizations into a media landscape that is characterized with scepticism of representation, high media literacy and some degree of compassion fatigue. Not only must the humanitarian organization find new ways of mobilizing the public;

in addition, market forces compel the organization to rebrand itself to create a new kind of legitimacy that is not compassion based. This is the dilemma that humanitarian organizations are faced with today. Although neither of the two spots presented here refers directly to this dilemma, they – along with many, if not most, other such advertisements today – are saturated with it. The spots both employ an advertising aesthetic, and their persuasive force is not compassion or justice based. In the two cases discussed here, the affectual potential draws on nostalgia and desire, while using properties of the audience's own culture to appeal to values of light-heartedness, in the case of AI, and purity, in the case of the RC. In neither of these cases is it by any means obvious that these values correspond to the values that shape the identity of the organization. Branding is encouraged in the non-profit sector as an opportunity for the organization to be reflexive about its values and communicate these more explicitly. However, while AI defines themselves with expressions such as 'international solidarity', 'justice', 'outrage' and 'critical dialogue', and the defining principles of the Danish Red Cross are 'humanity', 'impartiality' and 'neutrality', neither of these sets of values seem to be reflected in the spots discussed in this chapter. To the extent that these values might still play a role in understanding the spot, this is based on existing brand knowledge.

In response to compassion fatigue, the new branding strategies of these organizations, somewhat paradoxically, involve the suppression of the humanitarian causes they serve. The beneficiary of the appeal is excluded from representation and to the extent that suffering, which is the *raison d'être* for these organizations, is present in the spots, it is so in the form of a whisper – by means of silent words in the AI spot and a hushed subordinate clause in the voice over of the RC. Both spots are characterized by a contrast between the contents of the verbal and the visual. The spots point to their makers' reflections over what to represent visually and, while they lay emphasis on the fact that they are not representing suffering, misfortune and injustice, they provide no rationale for this choice. Rather than making themselves subject to the 'scepticism of representation', as Luc Boltanski calls it (Boltanski 1999; Vestergaard 2006), the spots use a montage technique, where the dissonance between two explicit discourses forces the recipient himself to construct a meaningful relation between them. Out of this sense-making, a new discourse is constructed. This new discourse belongs to the recipient only, and so the creator of the message cannot be held accountable for it. In the spots discussed in this chapter – and these are by no means unique but are, rather, examples of a new genre of humanitarian appeal – there is a discourse of reasons to act relegated to this third internal representation, where the credibility of the organization is not at stake. This might be a discourse of compassion or solidarity but, crucially, the reasons to act are not provided or controlled by the organization. The spots recognize their young audiences' media literacy and knowledge of the repertoire of persuasive devices at the media's disposal. In order to maintain credibility, while using strategies that traditionally belong to the commercial sector, the non-profit organizations point to the fact that this is, indeed, what they do, thus including the audience, not as objects or victims of persuasion, but as colluders and complicits.

The spots raise two essential questions about humanitarianism as rearticulated in an advertising discourse. First, is it possible to make an advertisement appealing on the basis of one set of values, while at the same time providing reasons for action based on another set of values? If, for instance, the AI spot is appealing because its produces nostalgic feelings about the audience's culture, is it possible for it to provide a reason for action that lies beyond this nostalgia, or is the spot actually inviting us to protect human rights in order to protect or promote this culture? By not offering the public reasons to act that correspond to the organization's own, humanitarian organizations might run the risk of being appealing at the cost of the humanitarian appeal.

Second, is there an inherent contradiction between the logic of recognition (central to advertising) and the logic of education or awareness-raising (central to the identity of most, if not all, humanitarian organizations)? While the social change, which is the ultimate goal of such an organization, might be aided by donations that allow the organization to go about its business, the arousal and maintenance of public social awareness is, after all, its fundamental prerequisite. In this way, despite promises of making visible and explicit the identity of an organization, mediatization might, in fact, obligate the brand to such forceful consumer demands that a deep conflict of identity is produced that might ultimately lead to the complete transformation of the identity of the organization.

Note

Grateful thanks are extended to Amnesty International's Danish section for permission to reproduce the illustrations in Chapter 8. They first appeared in the TV-spot 'Se hvad du kan goere'.

References

Aaker, D. (1996) *Building Strong Brands* (New York, NY: Free Press).

Aaker, D.A. and Joachimsthaler, E. (2000) *Brand Leadership* (New York, NY: Free Press).

Balmer J.M.T. and Gray, E.R. (2003) 'Corporate Brands: What are They? What of Them?', *European Journal of Marketing*, 37(7/8).

Balmer, J.M.T. and Greyser, S.A. (2006) 'Corporate Marketing: Integrating Corporate Identity, Corporate Branding, Corporate Communications, Corporate Image and Corporate Reputation', *European Journal of Marketing*, 40(7/8).

Baudrillard, J. (1994) *The Illusion of the End* (Cambridge: Polity Press).

Bauman, Z. (2001) *Community – Seeking Safety in an Insecure World* (Cambridge: Polity Press).

Boltanski, L. (1999) *Distant Suffering: Morality, Media and Politics* (Cambridge: Cambridge University Press).

Chouliaraki, L. (2005) 'Spectacular Ethics', *Journal of Language and Politics*, 3(2).

Chouliaraki, L. (2006) *The Spectatorship of Suffering* (London: Sage).

Csaba, F. (ed.) (2005) *The Limits of Corporate Branding: The Application of Branding to Non-Profit Organisations and Places* (Copenhagen: CBS Press).

de Chernatony, L. (2001) *From Brand Vision to Brand Evaluation: Strategically Building and Sustaining Brands* (Oxford: Butterworth Heinemann).

di Giovanni, J. (1994) 'Tired Moving of the Pictures: Bosnia and Rwanda', *Sunday Times*, 14 August: 10/8.

Edelman Public Relations (2003) www.edelman.com.

Fairclough, N. (1992) *Discourse and Social Change* (Cambridge: Polity Press).

Foroohar, R. (2005) 'The $1.6 Trillion Non-Profit Sector Behaves (or Misbehaves) More and More Like Big Business', *Newsweek*: 37–41.

Gallup International/World Economic Forum (2005) Voice of the People Survy. Geneva: World Economic Forum.

Grounds, J. (2005) 'Editorial: "Special Issue on Charity Branding"', *International Journal of Nonprofit and Voluntary Sector Marketing*, 10: 65–7.

Hankinson, P. (2001) *Better Branding Leads to More Charitable Giving* (Swindon: ESRC).

Hatch, M. and Schultz, M. (2001) 'Are The Strategic Stars Aligned For Your Corporate Brand?', *Harvard Business Review*, 79(2).

Held, D. and McGrew, A. (eds) (2002) *Governing Globalization* (Cambridge: Polity Press).

Holt, D.B. (2004) *How Brands Become Icons: The Principles of Cultural Branding* (Boston, MA: Harvard Business School Press).

Ignatieff, M. (1998) *The Warrior's Honor: Ethnic War and the Modern Conscience* (London: Chatto & Windus).

Kay, M.J. (2006) 'Strong Brands and Corporate Brands', *European Journal of Marketing*, 40(7/8).

Keane, J. (2003) *Global Civil Society?* (Cambridge: Cambridge University Press).

Keck, M.E. and Sikkink, K. (1998) *Activists beyond Borders* (Cornell: Cornell University Press).

Kinnick, K.N., Krugman, D.M. and Cameron, G.T. (1996) 'Compassion Fatigue: Communication and Burnout toward Social Problems.' *Journalism and Mass Communications Quarterly*, 73.

Leitch, S. and Richardson, N. (2003) 'Corporate Branding in the New Economy', *European Journal of Marketing*, 37(7/8).

Liebes, T. and Katz, E. (1989) 'On the Critical Abilities of Television Viewers', in *Remote Control: Television, Audience and Cultural Power*, E. Seiter et al. (eds) (London: Routledge).

Martens, K. (2006) 'Professionalised Representation of Human Rights NGOs to the United Nations', *International Journal of Human Rights*, 10(1): 19–30.

Meyer, D. and Tarrow, S. (1988) 'A Movement Society. Contentious Politics for a New Century', in D. Meyer and S. Tarrow (eds), *The Social Movement Society* (Lanham, MD: Rowman & Littlefield).

Moeller, S.D. (1999) *Compassion Fatigue: How the Media Sell Disease, Famine, War and Death* (New York: Routledge).

Polman, L. (2003) *We Did Nothing: Why The Truth Doesn't Always Come Out When The UN Goes In* (London: Viking).

Porta, D. della, Kriesi, H. and Rucht, D. (eds) (1999) *Social Movements in a Globalising World* (Chippenham: St Martin's).

Risse, T., Ropp, S. and Sikkink, K. (1999) *The Power of Human Rights. International Norms and Domestic Change* (Cambridge: Cambridge University Press).

Sargeant, A. (1999) *Marketing Management for Nonprofit Organisations* (Oxford: Oxford University Press).

Silverstone, R. (2006) *Media and Morality on the Rise of the Mediapolis* (Cambridge: Polity Press).

Staggenborg, S. (1997) 'The Consequences of Professionalization and Formalization in the Pro-Choice Movement', in A. Snow and D. McAdam (eds), *Social Movements: Reading their Emergence, Mobilization, and Dynamics* (Los Angeles, CA: Roxbury).

Tester, K. (2001) *Compassion, Morality and the Media* (Philadelphia: Open University Press).

Vestergaard, A. (2006) 'Humanitarian Branding and the Media. The Case of Amnesty International', *Journal of Language and Politics*, 7(3).

Warketin, C. (2001) *Reshaping World Politics. NGOs, the Internet and Global Civil Society* (Lanham, MD: Rowman & Littlefield).

Wootliff, J. and Deri, C. (2001) 'NGOs: The New Super Brands', *Corporate Reputation Review*, 4(2), 1 July: 157–64.

9
The Construction of Businesswomen in the Media: Between Evil and Frailty

Barbara Czarniawska

Is there something special about the connection between business and the media? One such thing is the central place business acquired in the mass media, at least in Sweden, in recent decades. Due to pension reforms, most Swedish citizens became interested in the financial markets. Together with the traditional attention paid to labor relations in Sweden, this has called for special attention to business in the media: this on the local and concrete level. In the global economy, the processes of imitation run in all directions, but especially from the centre to the periphery. This chapter illustrates this process on the example of the ways the media described the cases of a Swedish woman banker and a US woman banker located in London and working for a German bank. The case is analyzed along the lines suggested by the so-called 'circuit model of culture', presented in the next section. The chapter ends with speculation concerning future ways of describing businesswomen in the media.

The circuit model of culture

Simplifying somewhat, one could say that there are two common models of how the mass media function in contemporary culture, both with an ideological subtext. According to the critical model, mass media manipulate the public and are, themselves, manipulated by the capitalists, the political elite, or both. According to the eulogistic – that is, a laudatory model – mass media represent reality as it is, but also include educational and inspirational elements, even those representational in the sense of representing the most recent achievements in arts and sciences. In this chapter, I propose to go beyond these two and analyze examples of the functioning of the media in relation to business and industry in accordance with a circuit model of culture, suggested by Richard Johnson (1986–7).

Johnson belongs to the critical school of cultural studies, yet his model is a result of the observation that simplifications produced by critical theorists (and the corresponding ones by eulogists) obfuscate rather than help to explore central processes in contemporary culture – namely, the production, circulation and consumption of cultural goods – and especially popular culture, where mass media belong. The eulogist camp continues to propagate the eighteenth-century idea of science and its popularizers, the media, as 'the view from nowhere' (Nagel 1986). The critical camp sees the 'masses' as double dupes, as Latour (1993) expressed it: on the one hand, blinded by their false consciousness, they do not understand the strength of external forces that determine their fate; on the other, they do nothing to oppose those forces.

Johnson remains faithful to the tradition he comes from by retaining the vague concept of 'the capitalist conditions of production' but, as these are in fact the conditions ubiquitous in contemporary economies, I consider the concept superfluous. In what follows, I

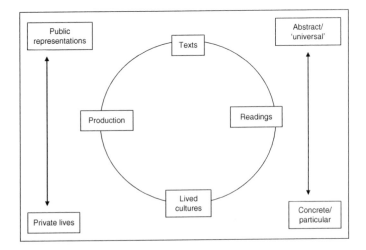

Figure 9.1   Circuit model of culture
Source: Adapted from Johnson, 1986–7: 47.

present the variation of Johnson's model that inspired the present text, and then develop my own interpretation of it.

Carl Rhodes and I (Czarniawska and Rhodes 2006) extended Johnson's model in the following ways. First, in the version given in Figure 9.1, the model applies better to the so-called high culture than mass culture, where media belongs. Centrifugal movements characterize the latter, with the circuit becoming larger and larger at each turn. Popular culture, and especially media, reaches many people – including the producers of the next wave of popular culture – across genres and cultures.

Second, it is important to point out that – at least, according to the eulogists – mass media furnish descriptions of reality, and enlightening comments on those realities, thus transmitting values and ideals. Indeed, the media do all this, but even more; they teach practices and provide the means through which practices might be understood: *the interpretative templates.*[1] Adding this concept enriches the meaning of the circuit model. Not only does production become consumption (reading) but also *expression* (of common feelings and thoughts) becomes *control*, as popular culture selects and reinforces certain wishes and anxieties of its audience (Traube 1992: 99); then, control provokes further expression, signalling both submission and resistance. My daily newspaper informs me about scandals happening, allegedly, at my own school; I run to the office to investigate the issue and to mobilize the opposition. It also might tell me what other schools are doing, so that my colleagues and I might consider imitating it. It constructs and demolishes our public image; it gives us ideas, ideals and counter-ideals. Action becomes represented and representation provokes further action.

Third, the terms in the model need some unpacking. The *production* – in the case of mass media – has its technologies, in the literal and metaphorical meaning. Dramatization, simplification and personification are the main technologies of creating a political drama in the media, as shown by Murray Edelman (1988). *Texts*, as with all other cultural forms, are subject to fashion, invention and imitation. *Readings* are not determined in advance but also are not free: there is an institutionalization of readers' responses (Czarniawska 1997), which means that each period of time and each place has its dominant and marginal readings, the latter including 'novel readings' (DeVault 1990), which might or might not become dominant in the next period. No one can manipulate other people's responses, but everyone tries: after all, persuasion is a synonym for verbal manipulation. *Lived cultures* are deceptive in their stability: much as societies reproduce themselves, identities might change by a sheer accident in the act of reproduction. Realities are re-made everyday, with subtle differences that, in time, might bring changes that not even revolutions can obtain.

Business and media are parts of the circuit of culture but, even if they are but a part, I am unable to analyze their role completely. In what follows, I will narrow the model to two applications. One considers a circuit of genre construction, where one genre influences another and then is influenced, in turn. The second example illustrates the circuit of production and reading across cultures. Both examples concern the media's representation of women working with finance.

Circuit 1: From facts to fiction to facts

The facts of the matter

> STOCKHOLM (TT)
> **February 1999**
> **Stockbroker cheated Nordbank.**
>
> A stockbroker at Merita-Nordbank is suspected of having swindled the bank out of millions – through illegal deals. The deals caused the bank a loss close to 300 million kronor. The stockbroker was arrested on Monday, suspected of serious breach of trust and serious malversation...The illegal deals continued for several months.[2]

The stockbroker made so-called blanking deals; that is, deals with borrowed shares (similar to Nicholas Leeson, the Englishman who caused the bankruptcy of Barings Bank in 1995). The next day, the readers learned that the stockbroker was a woman. *Dagens Industri* published a long article explaining what had happened in financial terms, and concluded with the following: 'For this stockbroker, as for all others who ended up in a dangerous spiral, it is a catastrophe. She is right now alone against the whole world and risks a prison sentence' (*DI* 3 February 1999).

Alone against the whole world? The District Court had concluded that the stockbroker acted incorrectly, but that the fault was that of the bank: they did not train and monitor her properly. The Court was also very critical of the prosecutor's and the Finance Inspector's way of presenting the case. The prosecutor's office turned to the Appeals Court, and the trial took place four years later.

It is my contention that, at that time in 1999, there were no interpretative templates easily available, thus the portentous but rather empty formulations of the *DI* article. The case of Nicholas Leeson was closest at hand, but there were several problems with constructing such an analogy. To begin with, Leeson was not a woman. Linda McDowell, who studied women at the City of London, quoted a journalist who, at the time of the Leeson affair, expressed a strong conviction that 'there could never be a female Nick Leeson', not merely because there are so few women dealers and stockbrokers, but also 'because of their characters' (Czarniawska 1997: 174).

Gender was not the only difference. If the movie *Rogue Trader*[3] can be treated as representing the interpretative template of the time, its major elements were, first and foremost, a class clash between the elders of Barings Bank and the working class Leeson. While he did not understand the implicit moral code of the profession, they mistook his gambling tendencies for the youthful endeavour to change traditional customs. Thus the lethal mixture: two classes, two generations, changing times in finance, and the (eternal) gambling proclivities of some men. While this interpretative scheme is quite convincing, it was hardly applicable to the Swedish woman's case.

The fiction intervenes

In 2001, two years after the first case against the Swedish stockbroker and two years before her final trial, Swedish writer David Lagercrantz published a detective novel called *Star Fall*. The novel begins with a stock market crash. This news is accompanied by a disquieting rumour that two people have been murdered in Stockholm: General Bank's analyst Elin Friman, and a famous inventor whose IT company has just gone public. It seems that the murders were committed only hours after the rates started to fall on the New York Stock Exchange (NYSE).

It cannot be either proved or disproved that the case of a female swindler inspired Lagercrantz to create one of his main characters (authors are not obliged to report, or even know, the sources of their inspiration). There is no doubt, however, that Lagercrantz's choice of the setting and the topic was influenced by the fact that the events related to stock markets became relevant to the Swedish public as never before (Ohlsson 2007).

In what follows I will concentrate on the construction of the persona of Elin, who turns out to be not only a victim, but also a criminal.[4]

Her male colleagues saw Elin primarily as a sex object: '...her smile, at the same time uncertain and cool, which sometimes seems to be an erotic promise an impression that she carefully cultivated. She made him talk, made him elaborate long theories on economy, the company, love, human longing. Her presence intoxicated him' (Lagercrantz 2001: 11).

Her 'willingness to serve' (*ibid.*) concerned not only men but also the organizations they represented. She was an ideal employee of the General Bank, completely immersed in its culture:

> He encouraged ambition and responsiveness to General Bank's corporate culture, but Elin went too far. The bank absorbed her totally, so that sometimes she seemed to lack a core. She could be anything: a mountain climber, a poet, an evening press reporter, a university lecturer but also a hippie. (Lagercrantz 2001: 11)

One of the men neglected by Elin and therefore, one could surmise, more prone to a detached analysis of her case, thought that this lack of an individual identity could have been produced by a collision between her natural talents and her working class background:

> What he sees as a weak self can have resulted from her youth and uncertainty. She is twenty-seven, her father is an unemployed bus driver who drinks...so she probably wanted to escape from it all, find another world, whatever the cost. She has an analytical talent. She immediately grasps the most complex situations and she remembers numbers – especially quotations – in a way that almost frightens him. (Lagercrantz 2001: 12)

The readers of Oliver Sachs will recognize these traits as patho- logical: the extraordinary capacity of mechanical memory, usually accompanied by a complete inability to function in social life. She was also a chess master, a typical indication of a villain in Bond-style movies.

Lacking her own identity, she assumed that of the man she was enchanted with at the moment. In love with sensitive leftist Daniel, she was against the world's injustice. When Daniel quit his job, she fixed her adoring gaze on the bank's Managing Director. Eventually, it turned out that she was faithful to one man and one ideology, in a way that verged on fanaticism, her colleagues decided afterwards. In its name, she cheated and exploited, but always for a higher cause. A veiled Marxist, she condemned capitalism in general and her bank in particular, but saw no problem in manipulating the shareholders.

The description of Elin can be contrasted with other feminine personae in the novel. There is a woman psychiatrist, who is a clearly positive female character, but then she has a suitable job for a woman: she tries to understand people and their problems. There are two other women who work with finance, but their presentations are brief. One is a top manager at Nordea, another bank, and will become the Financial Deputy at General Bank at the end of the novel. She speaks to the public about shares in a 'folksy' way, an allusion to the 'domestication' of the world of finance typical of the Swedish mass media in the 1990s and 2000s (Ohlsson 2007). The other woman analyst at General Bank is presented only as 'tough and cool. Elin did not threaten the male self-esteem in the same way' (Lagercrantz 2001: 58).

The detective story genre has its rules, and a dramatization of events and a demonization of (some) characters belong to the most typical. Nevertheless, the character of Elin deserves attention, as it offers both the received image of today's finances (inside and outside financial circles) and of people in financial services. Extremely high intelligence (rather than formal education) is both assumed and claimed by stockbrokers and analysts. Elin is even more intelligent than most, thus reinforcing the conviction that, for the same job, women need to be twice as good as men. Her sexual intrigues also correspond to the image of a 'work hard, play hard', no-family world; but, while men are presented as ensnared in her sexual intrigues, Elin is presented as the one who initiates them. Last but not least, lack of moral guidance is a trait supposedly prominent in financial dealings, but while young men seem to be amoral, Elin is immoral, actively contributing to evil. Lest this characterization create an image of a Superwoman, it needs to be added that Elin performs all her evil deeds instructed by a man, the true mastermind behind the plot. Female after all: a will-less tool in the hands of a purposeful man.

While there is no doubt about the fictitiousness of Elin's character, the message (perhaps unintended) is clear: the world of finances is no place for women. Those who made it there are 'unnatural' – twice everything else the men are, especially the vice, and not even aware of it. While the novel contains many thoughtful men, acutely aware of traps and dangers connected to this world, women, it seems, can only be the victims and the villains in it.

Back to the facts

The Swedish stockbroker was to appear in the Appeals Court on 14–15 January 2003. Ten days before the trial, the weekend supplement to *Göteborgs-Posten*[5] published a portrait of the stockbroker, giving her the fictitious name 'Lisa' (Swedish law prohibits publishing the proper names of people standing trial). The title ran: 'Here vanished 269 million', and under this, in the mock soap opera style, it said:

> A young woman who just became a mother. A quarter of a billion that got speculated away. An angry prosecutor, seeking revenge. A clumsy bank. On Wednesday a new installment of the drama 'Nordbank v. the stockbroker' in Svea Appeals Court. Two Days met the now 35-year-old Lisa from Kullavik, south of Gothenburg. A super-intelligent lass – who went astray.

This was followed by a drawing of a childish-looking girl in glasses sitting in front of a computer, quotation list to her left, two men in the background, and a colour drawing of a sailboat in a blue bay to the right. The caption said: 'TALENT. Lisa was not only a star stockbroker. She has participated in the European Sailing Championship. And she talked three foreign languages fluently. When she spoke on the telephone, she often used French, so that her boss and her colleagues wouldn't understand' (the deals were done by Lisa with the help of a woman friend at Credit Lyonnais in France).

Under the headline 'Clever in Most Things', the article gave the following description of Lisa:

> Who is this 31-year-old woman...? She who speculated away 269 million – and her future.

And what a future it was. She finished the natural sciences high school with the highest grades. Her performance was equally outstanding at the Stockholm School of Economics [Elin's alma mater], where she was also active in the students' union. She studied in Germany and France; she worked in Hamburg, London, and Paris. She wrote her thesis on share-index swapping using Credit Lyonnaise as her case.

Lisa speaks fluent English, French, and German and can converse in Italian. She plays piano, guitar, and clarinet. She has had training at Sotheby's in London and did research on impressionism and modern art. As a junior she participated in sailing championships but also skied, played tennis, squash, and golf, and she danced and practised gymnastics.

A real 'A' child in other words. And yet it all went wrong. Not that she is in a bad spot. She recently married a man from West Sweden, who is the managing director of a small food company within a big corporation. He has moved from Masthugget in Gothenburg and she from Östermalm in Stockholm to a town in Scania. They live in an English style terrace house bought for 2.4 million kronor. But Lisa is on sick leave for 'reactive depression' and gets about 10,700 a month after taxes. Last year in the bank she earned about 1.5 million in salary and bonuses. (*Två Dagar, GP*, 4 January 2003)

The article was very long. It told the readers that Nordbank employed Lisa in 1996 as a stockbroker dealing with institutional investments. She quickly showed her talents and soon she was at the top of the earning list in her bank. In 1998, she earned 22.9 million for the bank, four times the targeted amount. Interrogated by the police, her colleagues recited a long list of her merits as a stockbroker: capable, ambitious, inspired, incredibly intelligent, great social competence, talented, good sense of the market, a star trader. Their opinions of her person were not worse: humble, never bossy, nice, helpful, easy to get on with, pleasant, kind, decent, happy, eager to please.

But there was also another side to her, according to them (the formulation is almost identical to that used to describe Elin in the novel). She was competitive and always wanted to be best. When she failed, she could cry over the loss of a couple of thousands, especially at the beginning of her career. Her colleague at Credit Lyonnais, who was also taken to court (she did not have the right to approve the deal that she did), and who shared a flat with Lisa in London, said:

> She dramatized a lot and exaggerated. It always sounded worse than it was...She took on herself all the world's problems as if they were her fault. A peculiar personality trait. (*GP* 4 January 2003)

According to Lisa herself, she did nothing wrong. Her clients and her bosses bluffed, cheated and erred, while she followed their instructions. According to her father, she has been made a scapegoat by the incompetent people at the bank. The prosecutor had another explanation:

> This, in his opinion, extraordinarily intelligent woman was understimulated in her job: therefore one can guess that she was hit by a gambling obsession. People in this profession have a certain tendency to suffer from gambling obsession. (*GP* 4 January 2003)

The Appeals Court decided in March 2003 that convincing evidence was presented showing that she was guilty as accused. The Court was of the opinion that fines were not enough, and ordered a psychiatric investigation to determine whether or not the woman could endure a prison sentence. The result of the investigation was negative and, in May, the woman was sentenced to psychiatric custody. The family considered appealing to the Supreme Court. The final comment from the prosecutor was reported thus:

> He perceives the case's tragic aspects and hopes that the woman, now on sick leave, will find a new place in society: this is an intelligent person with great qualities. But she will hardly find an appropriate job in this particular sector. (*GP* 29 March 2003)

Four foreign languages, three instruments, seven sports, and an art connoisseur. One can wonder what it all has to do with work with finance and with honesty or dishonesty in the job. I would claim that these traits were required by an interpretative template used, as the readers will see also in the next case. Such a template can be found in the most distilled (and therefore exaggerated) version in fiction, but is then used in an adjusted form in the media.

Extraordinary intelligence and psychological instability were the two traits that connect Lisa and Elin. Working class background and the urge to advance in the world connect Elin to Leeson, whose case no doubt has an impact on Lagercrantz's shaping of his characters. With the exception of the class background, Lisa's case is close to Nicholas Leeson's (the same type of misdemeanour, alleged gambling tendencies). However, nobody analyzed Leeson's personality in such detail – the descriptions mostly concerned his behaviour, with some comments on his *not* high intellectual powers (McDowell 1997: 172–3). It seems that, in a popular rendition, the combination of high intelligence (unusual) and instability (usual) in women is explosive.

As in the genre of detective stories, the genre of journalistic accounts has its specificity. The business spectacle seems, however, to be constructed along the same lines as political spectacle (Edelman 1988): dramatization, simplification and personification (more precisely, psychologization). Interpretive templates are built with the help of strong plots (Czarniawska and Rhodes 2006). In this case, the plot seems to be: the women who enter finance are unusual, and end badly. The interpretive template thus suggests that this 'particular sector' might not have 'appropriate jobs' for women.

Circuit 2: Among the media

The next part of the chapter contrasts the two ways of reporting on women and finance in the UK and Germany, suggesting that, in time, German media started imitating the UK media, using the interpretive template as characterized above.[6] The case in question concerned Robin Saunders, a US citizen who moved to London in 1992 with Citibank. She then moved to Chemical Bank, then to Deutsche Bank (DB), and, together with her team from DB, to Westdeutsche Landesbank (WestLB) in July 1998. She became the focus of media interest in June 2003. I begin with a short calendar of events in order to give the background of the case.

Calendar of events

1998
Saunders arranged a loan of US$1.4 billion to Bernie Ecclestone, owner of Formula One.

2000

In March, WestLB decided to support Phillip Green, a retailer and the owner of a chain of department stores, Bhs, with the sum of £200 million.

2001

In January, WestLB granted a £750 million loan to Boxclever, Green's video rentals.

In October, WestLB decided to finance the acquisition of Whyte and Mackay whisky producers by Jim Beam (£200 million).

2002

Pubmaster, 40 per cent owned by WestLB, bought 1200 shares of Pub from Nomura for £523 million.

WestLB offered £420 million for the renovation of Wembley Stadium.

2003

In March, private equity group Cinven acquired the British cinema chain Odeon for £431 million.

In May, WestLB was forced to accept losses caused by Boxclever reaching €1,67 billion.

In June, WestLB retreated from backing a takeover of Anglian Water's parent company AWG by the Buyout-Team Bream Investments. (Reuters 23 June 2003)

Here is the calendar of 'the hot days in June', which attracted attention of both UK and German press to WestLB and Robin Saunders:

23 June
Telegraph:
WestLB shareholders meet today to consider the future of Robin Saunders' principal finance unit, report of German banking regulator available.

24 June
BBC:
WestLB CEO Juergen Sengera has quit following shareholder meeting yesterday. BaFin, the German regulator, described lax risk control at Robin Saunders' principal finance unit, which lost £354 million on Boxclever.

26 June
Times:
WestLB Crime Probe. German Banking regulator BaFin has handed to criminal prosecutors its dossier on WestLB's London finance unit.

04 August
Independent:
Boxclever German bank regulator tells WestLB to increase provisions by 140 million to £490 million, covering its total exposure to the deal.

07 August
Telegraph:
WestLB German bank writes off remaining £200 million of loan to Boxclever, under pressure from German bank regulator BaFin.
(*Legal Day-News*, 22–28 June 2003, 1–8 August 2003)

Robin Saunders resigned from the supervisory board of Boxclever, but this was (officially) motivated by the fact that her directorate was connected to the loan that had been solved earlier than planned. Let me now show how the two presses wrote about Saunders before, during and after the events reported above.

Before

In March 2000, *Property Week* presented Robin Saunders and her group of asset securitization[7] at Westdeutsche Landesbank under the title 'WestLB Iron Lady invades UK real estate market'. A connection between Saunders and Thatcher was thus established, Saunders' blonde hair and US origins were mentioned, together with her propensity to work in a team.

In June 2002, the *Daily Mail* reported on 'city high-flyer's £400,000 birthday bash' in a historical palace in Florence. Saunders celebrated her birthday, her 10th wedding anniversary to a German colleague, and the baptism of her twins: 180 guests attended, among them Phillip Green and Bernie Ecclestone. This party would be remembered the following year.

In September 2002, *The Guardian* ran an interview with Saunders, under the title 'Beating the boys at their own game'. 'Clad in black', she had just masterminded the £426 million loan for Wembley. 'Saunders is a rare example of a woman who has made it to the top in the City. It has made the formerly trained dancer very rich. ... The failures do not faze her. ... The mother of two-year-old twin daughters, she is regarded as a shining example of how to thrive in the macho culture of the City.' More about being a team player, hard worker and a lavish birthday party organizer.

In February 2003, Saunders was preparing a £900m bid for Anglian Water's parent company, AWG, and she appeared as a 'Business Profile' in the *Telegraph*. I will spare the readers constant puns on her first name, and quote some of the descriptions given:

> I am expecting someone athletic with perfect hair, make-up and a big Yank voice to match. Instead, a tiny, pretty and slightly dishevelled girl slips into the room ... Saunders, a trained dancer, is not just any old investment banker. ... In her mind, the creativity she brings to finance is not far removed from the painting, dancing, piano playing and sewing she adored as a child ... And she still finds time to 'religiously' attend hip-hop dance classes. ... The rest of her spare time is spent with her daughters or sitting on the Serpentine Gallery council – a hectic lifestyle not helped by the fact that she doesn't drive and is reliant on 'my husband or minicabs' to get about. (*Telegraph* 16 February)

The combination of financial talents with artistic proclivities seems to be a stable ingredient in the interpretative template applied to women in finance (for more examples, see Czarniawska 2008). It is possible that the Swedish press borrowed it from the UK media as well. It might be a way of stressing the femininity of the woman in question (in older times, she would be said to be very good at embroidery).

On 16 February 2003, *The Observer* pictured Robin Saunders (who, all of a sudden, was driving) against the background of 450 paratroopers surrounding Heathrow on that day:

> Of course, not everyone believes that Saunders is all that she is cracked up to be, but in many instances, the critics are jealous rivals or male competitors, envious of her success, or, too often, resentful that a woman has made it in the notoriously male-orientated

Square Mile. ... There are, of course, women in powerful positions in the world of finance, but they are few and far between. ... The big investment banks such as JP Morgan, Goldman Sachs and Morgan Stanley are led by prosperous, middle-aged men who eat lunch, drink and play golf with other prosperous, middle-aged men. ... Last year, Saunders sought to set up a breakaway business, but with backing from WestLB. ... West LB turned down Saunders' request for independence, but she is understood to have received a fresh commitment on funding, as well as being allowed greater autonomy.

What they said: 'She knows how to schmooze – a real charmer, but quite cunning with it'.

At that time, the German press simply did not write about Saunders.[8] The first reports appeared close to June 2003, and they were mostly quoting the British press:

14 May
Financial Times Deutschland:
A London financial paper referred to her as a 'Tigress with £3 billion on her back' ... In the United Kingdom people like her are said to have the 'Midas touch' – whatever they touch turns into gold.

16 May
Die Welt:
Successful, attractive, rich – if one believes the British press, then Robin Saunders is 'the glamour girl' of London's financial district, the city's answer to Claudia Schiffer.

The distancing is obvious: 'in the UK people like her are said to have', 'if one believes the British press'.

During

On 17 May, WestLB reported a pre-tax loss of €1.67 billion instead of a planned €1 billion – due, among other things, to £354 million of 'bad debt' at Boxclever. The bank launched an investigation into its UK unit, while Saunders' boss, Jürgen Sengera, 'sparked speculation about Ms Saunders' future by apparently dodging an opportunity to publicly back her' (*BBC News*).

25 May
The Sunday Telegraph:
The German bank is considering legal action against the *Financial Times* after it raised questions about conflict of interest in the personal investments of Robin Saunders, head of the bank's principal finance unit.

The Sunday Times:
Robin Saunders, head of the bank's principal finance unit, has told friends she still has the support of the bank and plans to ride out the storm surrounding her stakes in companies where she was a dealmaker. Her unit told the Takeover Panel on Friday that it is still pursuing a £1 billion takeover of water group AWG.

3 June
Business Week:
Stormy Days for a Rainmaker... Saunders quickly rose on Wall Street, then in London. Her flamboyant style and energetic personality have long irritated some of the more sober bankers who hold sway at WestLB. But as long as she was making big profits, they were in no position to try to criticize her. Now their chance has come. It may only be a matter of time before Saunders and the bank part ways.

12 June
Telegraph:
Troubled German bank WestLB has called in Citigroup to advise on a possible sale of its controversial London-based principal finance unit run by high-profile dealmaker Robin Saunders. It is understood that Mrs. Saunders is certain to table a bid... The move came as the bank pulled the plug on Mrs. Saunders' plan to back a takeover of water company AWG by Bream Investments. The decision, made by WestLB's board, followed a meeting between Mrs. Saunders and Johannes Ringel, the director responsible for principal finance. Mrs. Saunders was not invited to present her conclusions to the board, and did not speak to chief executive Jürgen Sengera.

The German regulators delivered their report on 20 June: on 23 June, Jürgen Sengera quit his job. Saunders' future was yet to be decided but, said *BBC News*, ' the 40-year-old American's buccaneering style has brought her into conflict with WestLB's shareholders in Germany, who were unhappy about the level of risk to which the bank is exposed'. The coverage of the British media seemed to suggest that Saunders' days were numbered, due to the negative reaction of the (conservative) German bankers and shareholders to Saunders' 'American style'. It was her foreignness (to both Germany and the UK) that seemed to explain her displacement, rather than her gender.

24 June
Times:
Efforts by some at WestLB to blacken the reputation of Robin Saunders seem to have backfired. The bank's principal finance division might not be without blemish, but WestLB's problems do not rest entirely with one fraulein.

It is worth observing that the press, while edging against Saunders, locates the source of problems in Germany.

14 September
The Observer:
WestLB, the German bank, is to axe its London-based principal finance unit headed by controversial financier Robin Saunders... Saunders has been stopped from undertaking any new deals, and WestLB has banned the practice that allowed her and colleagues to take individual equity stakes in firms the bank provided with funds.

Such is the short way from 'a shining example' to 'a controversial financier', an epithet that will be used constantly from now on.

On 24 September 2003 it was announced that Saunders would step down from the board of the retail chain Bhs.

25 September
The Guardian:
Although Ms Saunders has tried to distance herself from the Boxclever deal, the City continues to associate her with the operation. .... Even so, she is thought to have been involved in the current round of negotiations over attempts to refinance the business that WestLB had already refinanced a year ago. ...

The City continues to speculate about Ms Saunders' long-term future at WestLB because the German bank has prevented her from concluding any more deals. ... She has, however, survived the regulatory inquiry by BaFin, unlike WestLB's former chief executive, Jürgen Sengera, who left in June.

The German press originally wrote about Saunders differently. Mostly, it did not write about Saunders: it wrote about WestLB and its losses. *Financial Times Deutschland* wrote about BaFin's investigation on 16 June, but the main focus was on Sengera. *Manager-Magazin* wrote on 18 June that 'Robin Saunders warms up', but then tried to explain in detail what she said and did. *Süddeutsche Zeitung* wrote about 'Crisis meeting concerning the huge losses of the WestLB' on 23 June, but mentioned Saunders only in one sentence, where there was a speculation that both she and Johannes Ringel (who actually later replaced Sengera) would be 'on their way out'. The same newspaper wrote about Saunders on 24 June, but it attempted to explain to the readers what had happened, and the only touch of metaphor was in the title: 'Blinded by the glamour of the brilliant saleswoman'; *National Journal* from 26 June quoted the German press only, and wrote about Sengera ('Manager-remuneration under globalism'). *Süddeutsche Zeitung* wrote on 28 June about the losses of WestLB; Saunders' role was mentioned in the last paragraph; no metaphors or similes, just 'investment banker Saunders'. *Financial Times Deutschland* from 17 July reported deals made by the new CEO of WestLB, Johannes Ringel; in seven paragraph-long articles, one is about Saunders, and it says, 'Robin Saunders will stay'. *Frankfurter Allgemeine Zeitung* from 10 August reported the state of the Whyte and Mackay deal, and said only that Saunders and her colleagues were now explicitly forbidden to buy shares in companies they helped to finance.

But those who did write about Saunders quoted the UK press again, including the tabloids:

22 June
Welt am Sonntag:
CEO Jürgen Sengera cleans up. Star banker Robin Saunders has to go. The London subsidiary will be sold. The Financial Control confers a brusque reproof. According to the front-page of the *Sun* she was considered 'the city's answer to Claudia Schiffer', and the 'most beautiful dealmaker of the money world'.

23 June
Frankfurter Rundschau:
Falling Bird of Paradise. As a Result of the Blunders of his Venturesome Star Banker Saunders WestLB Boss Sengera has to Quit.

This turmoil [another bank's problem] is only a tempest in a teacup compared to the upheaval that a bird of paradise residing on the banks of the Thames has caused in the Rhine metropolis. It answers to the name Robin Saunders, is blonde and 40 years old. In spite of her methods, unconventional at times, the native US American was considered the star among the bankers in the service of WestLB until she squandered millions of pounds and thereby brought things to a deep crisis at the fifth largest German bank, also causing a lot of trouble for the North Rhine Westphalian government. As 'the City's answer to Claudia Schiffer' the English newspapers had once celebrated her after she had landed a few spectacular coups... The woman is without doubt as clever as she is tough.

25 June 25
Die Welt:
Femme fatale: Robin Saunders and the Business Dealings of the WestLB.

After her mentor Jürgen Sengera had to vacate his position as CEO at the Westdeutsche Landesbank (WestLB), the time has now also come for Robin Saunders, the London star banker, to say goodbye. ... For years journalists have written about the 'Claudia Schiffer of the city'. That they also wrote about the personal life of the reputed 'glamour girl' goes without saying in the British press.

I will not continue to bore the readers with the endless 'Claudia Schiffer' quotes, although it is curious why the City was looking for an answer to Claudia Schiffer. Had she asked a question?

After

The subsequent events seem to indicate that the WestLB has forgiven Saunders, but the UK press has not. On 24 September 2004, *This is London* (a site collaborating with the *Evening Standard*) hosted an article called 'Boxclever blow for Saunders':

Large divisions of Boxclever, the television rental company at the heart of the German bank WestLB's financial crisis, were plunged into administration today in a further blow to the reputation of former City wunderkind Robin Saunders... Saunders, currently

facing allegations about her private life, was part of today's decision...Robin Saunders' meteoric rise to fame and fortune has
spread far beyond the fusty confines of the City – culminating
this week with salacious details of her out-of-work friendship with
celebrity chef Marco Pierre White.

The *Telegraph* has written with real – or mock – sympathy (the title
is 'Poor Robin', which indicates heavy irony) on 28 September:

> How much more can go wrong? Saunders has been splashed all
> over the tabloids as they dig for dirt on her friendship with Marco
> Pierre White; she is leaving the Bhs board; and parts of Boxclever,
> which she helped to create, have collapsed...
>
> 'There is nothing in it', says a friend of White. Saunders also
> vehemently denies the speculation. 'We are not going to dignify
> this ludicrous tittle-tattle with a quote', says her spokesman.
>
> According to [one of her allies], Saunders is the victim of institu-
> tional media sexism. 'The financial press is appallingly sexist. *The
> Independent*, the *Guardian*, the *Financial Times*, they have all been
> revolting. They have written about her in a way they would never
> have written about a man.'

The Telegraph, as had the German press, was just quoting the
tabloids. It repeated all the misfortunes that had happened to her,
although they were old by now – presumably, to present all the facts.
Thus, it contributed to the campaign but washed its hands clean by
quoting 'an ally' towards the end. The very end, however, seems to
express a *Schadenfreude*: 'However, this North Carolinian is used to
getting back up on the horse. At the moment, it does not look as the
ride is going to get much smoother.'

This, however, is the latest news I found:

22 December 2005
The Times:
Saunders launches £1bn fund
By Jenny Davey
ROBIN SAUNDERS, the former WestLB financier, has teamed up
with Paul Bloomfield, the veteran property dealmaker, to launch a
£1 billion European property fund, *The Times* has learnt...

Ms Saunders and Mr Bloomfield are working in partnership with Birch Capital, an investment company run by Benoit de Biolley, the former banker for Deutsche Bank and Morgan Stanley ...

Ms Saunders said that the fund, which will target property across continental Europe and Britain, would be complementary to the activities of Clearbrook, which she set up after leaving WestLB in 2003.

Not even one allusion to her private life or her looks. Could the reason simply be that a woman has written the article, or might one hope that the UK reporting on women in finance has improved?

Not so the German. It seems that, via continuous quotes from the British press, the German press 'normalized' the way of writing about women in finances, which is different from the (sombre) way men are described. At one of the first public presentations of my analysis, there was a woman in the audience who, while working on her dissertation, was also employed by one of the German banks. She told me that, before the WestLB 'affair', the bank informed its employees only of the German press coverage of the world of finance. In the 'hot months' of 2003, the British media were quoted for the first time: after all, although the banker in question was in London, the bank was German. When this story began to turn stale, however, reporting from the British media continued.

Spiegel Online from 5 November 2004 presented 'A crown princess in the golden palace', Sallie Krawcheck from Wall Street, and wondered whether she was 'a popess or a pit bull'. The graft seems to have taken.

In the same pessimistic reading, the main difference between German and British reporting is that the German press wrote initially about women in finances as they wrote about men in finances, while the British press wrote about them as they write about women in general. There remains hope, however, in the possibility of an open discussion of problems experienced by women in male careers, present in at least some German coverage.

Interpretative templates

As could be seen in those two cases, the media are both producers and consumers of interpretive templates in the culture circuits that run across genres and countries. As the phenomenon has a circular character, fiction writers do the same thing: they borrow from the media and from other fiction writers. Production leads to consumption, and consumption manufactures material for the next production cycle. Lived culture is constantly renewed, but it also builds sediments, which sometimes can be brought to life again when production reaches for traditional elements (such as the Bible, Greek tragedies and so on) and translates them into the contemporary context. The forms of texts change constantly, but certain forms become institutionalized into genres and are taken for granted for long periods of time. There can be genre revolutions, but genres also change in the very act of reproduction, which is never only a mechanical copying. Responses change, too; as fashions fade out, audiences are no longer interested in what they liked before.

The cases above throw some light on the process of construction of new interpretative templates ('technologies' used both in production and in consumption; that is, reading). New events are, at the outset, interpreted according to old templates, which is especially visible in the media: there is no time to produce a new template when the news has to be announced. In this case, a template for interpreting a financial crime by a man had long existed, but it was also refreshed by the quite recent event of Nicholas Leeson's offence. A woman stockbroker, and a Swedish woman stockbroker, required a new – or, at least, adapted – template. How can a new template be made? Invention is always simply a new combination of old elements, as creativity theorists demonstrated long ago. The result can be startlingly different, or just a rehash of old stereotypes. In this case, a part of an old template (based on the characters of a working-class climber and a gambler) has been added to a part of another old template (the plot stating that women who leave home and enter the city are unusual and punished for their acts). The media, in turn, have had to tailor the abstract/universal template to fit a concrete case: the result was a superhuman woman (unnaturally beautiful, intelligent and artistically gifted), which explained her entry into the foreign domain (the financial world), which could not but end badly (the fallen woman, in one or another sense of the word). Perhaps, in this case, Rosabeth Kanter's (1977) 'token' argument might become true: with the entry of more women into finance, the interpretative template might change, or else the event would not deserve media attention, which would be just as well.

As to the question put at the outset, whether there was something special about the connection between business and the media, it does not seem so. The circuit model depicts abstractly – but, in my reading, correctly – the mechanisms of cultural production and consumption in the 2000s. But the central place business acquired (or perhaps re-acquired) in the mass media leads to the increased production and renovation of various types of interpretative templates. One can only hope that new interpretive templates for describing careers of businesswomen will emerge. However, such innovation must fit the general trend; that is, the shape of the circuit of mass media production and consumption. As this trend seems to be tabloidization (Baker 2007), the future of businesswomen – and, perhaps, men as well – in the media does not look very bright.

Independently of how business, the media, and the connection between them develop in practice, it could be that the circuit model of culture might be of use in the analysis of such developments. Its attraction lies in the symmetry imposed by its circularity. It does not make sense to criticize or to praise where the impact goes in both directions. Rather, it can be remembered that circuits can become virtuous or vicious circles, and that a change of any element might change the character of the whole. This old wisdom of systems theory might yet become of practical utility. At present, the tabloidization is put at the doors of the greedy owners. According to the circuit model, anybody – the journalists and the readers – can change it if they act collectively, which does not necessarily mean in an organized or planned way. There exist interpretative templates for this kind of action, too.

Notes

1. This notion may resemble Schütz's (1973) 'interpretational schemes', but the latter are understood as referential schemes, what Goffman (1974) would later call 'frames'. Interpretative templates are like templates on our computers: a master or pattern from which other similar things (in this case, interpretations) can be made.
2. All Swedish texts are rendered here in my translation.
3. Granada Films, 1998, director James Dearden, Leeson played by Ewan McGregor.
4. For a more detailed analysis of fictive representations of women in finance, see Czarniawska 2005.
5. The third daily in Sweden in terms of distribution numbers.

6. For an analysis of German and British ways of reporting in the light of Greek tragedies, see Czarniawska 2008.
7. Releases liquidity of non-core assets to generate new business or reduce borrowing as an alternative to raising equity (which dilutes earnings) or more expensive bank borrowing.
8. I am grateful to Andreas Diedrich for his help with translation of German press reports.

References

Baker, R. (2007) 'Goodbye to newspapers?', *New York Review of Books*, 54(13), 16 August.

Czarniawska, B. (1997) *Narrating the Organization: Dramas of Institutional Identity* (Chicago, IL: University of Chicago Press).

Czarniawska, B. (2005) 'Women in Financial Services: Fiction and More Fiction', in: K. Knorr Cetina and A. Preda (eds), *The Sociology of Financial Markets* (Oxford: Oxford University Press): 121–37.

Czarniawska, B. (2008) 'Femmes Fatales in Finance, or Women and the City', *Organisation*, 15(2): 165–86.

Czarniawska, B. and Rhodes, C. (2006) 'Strong Plots: Popular Culture and Management Practice and Theory', in P. Gagliardi and B. Czarniawska (eds), *Management Education and Humanities* (Cheltenham: Edward Elgar): 195–218.

DeVault, M.L. (1990) 'Novel Readings: The Social Organisation of Interpretation', *American Journal of Sociology*, 95(4): 887–921.

Edelman, M. (1988) *Constructing the Political Spectacle* (Chicago: University of Chicago Press).

Goffman, E. (1974) *Frame Analysis. An Essay on the Organisation of Experience* (New York: Harper & Row).

Johnson, Richard (1986–7) 'What is Cultural Studies Anyway?', *Social Text*, 16: 38–80.

Kanter, R.M. (1977) *Men and Women in the Corporation* (New York: Basic Books).

Lagercrantz, D. (2001) *Stjärnfall* (Stockholm: Piratförlaget).

Latour, B. (1993) *We Have Never Been Modern* (Cambridge, MA: Harvard University Press).

McDowell, L. (1997) *Capital Culture: Gender at Work in the City* (Oxford: Blackwell).

Nagel, T. (1986) *The View from Nowhere* (Oxford: Oxford University Press).

Ohlsson, C. (2007) *Folkets fonder. En studie av pensionssparandets språk och textbruk* (Gothenburg: Institutet för svenska språket, Göteborg University).

Renemark, D. (2007) *Varför finns det så få kvinnor i finanser? En studie av en vardag i finanssektor* (Gothenburg: BAS).

Schütz, A. (1973) [1955] 'Symbol, Reality and Society', in *Collected papers I, The Problem of Social Reality* (The Hague: Martinus Nijhoff): 347–56.

Traube, E.G. (1992) *Dreaming Identities: Class, Gender and Generation in 1980s Hollywood Movies* (Boulder, CO: Westview Press).

Index